APM

Body of Knowledge

APM Body of Knowledge

Fifth edition

Association for Project Management

Association for Project Management
Ibis House, Regent Park
Summerleys Road, Princes Risborough
Buckinghamshire
HP27 9LE

© Association for Project Management 2006

Fifth edition 2006
Reprinted 2006, 2007 (twice), 2008 (three times)
Fourth edition 2000
Third edition 1996
Second edition 1994
First edition 1992

The Association would like to thank the many contributors to this work for waiving
their moral rights to any or part of the complete work and for their continued support
of the charitable aims of the Association.

Users are responsible for the correct application of the information in this publication.
Concordance with the **APM Body of Knowledge** does not in itself confer any
immunity from legal obligations.

British Library Cataloguing in Publication Data is available.

ISBN–13:978-1-903494-13-4
ISBN–1-903494-13-3
(CD-ROM–1-903494-25-7)

Typeset in 10/12pt Palatino by Genesis Typesetting, Rochester, Kent
Publishing Manager: Ingmar Folkmans
Printed and bound by Hobbs the Printers Ltd, Totton, Hampshire
Cover design by Fountainhead, Middlesex

Contents

List of figures		vii
Preface		ix
Acknowledgements		xi
Introduction		xiii
Section 1	**Project management in context**	1
1.1	Project management	2
1.2	Programme management	6
1.3	Portfolio management	8
1.4	Project context	10
1.5	Project sponsorship	12
1.6	Project office	14
Section 2	**Planning the strategy**	17
2.1	Project success and benefits management	18
2.2	Stakeholder management	20
2.3	Value management	22
2.4	Project management plan	24
2.5	Project risk management	26
2.6	Project quality management	28
2.7	Health, safety and environmental management	30
Section 3	**Executing the strategy**	33
3.1	Scope management	34
3.2	Scheduling	36
3.3	Resource management	38
3.4	Budgeting and cost management	40
3.5	Change control	42
3.6	Earned value management	44
3.7	Information management and reporting	46
3.8	Issue management	48
Section 4	**Techniques**	51
4.1	Requirements management	52
4.2	Development	54
4.3	Estimating	56
4.4	Technology management	58
4.5	Value engineering	60

Contents

	4.6	Modelling and testing	62
	4.7	Configuration management	64

Section 5 Business and commercial — 67
	5.1	Business case	68
	5.2	Marketing and sales	70
	5.3	Project financing and funding	72
	5.4	Procurement	74
	5.5	Legal awareness	76

Section 6 Organisation and governance — 79
	6.1	Project life cycles	80
	6.2	Concept	82
	6.3	Definition	84
	6.4	Implementation	86
	6.5	Handover and closeout	88
	6.6	Project reviews	90
	6.7	Organisation structure	92
	6.8	Organisational roles	94
	6.9	Methods and procedures	96
	6.10	Governance of project management	98

Section 7 People and the profession — 101
	7.1	Communication	102
	7.2	Teamwork	104
	7.3	Leadership	106
	7.4	Conflict management	108
	7.5	Negotiation	110
	7.6	Human resource management	112
	7.7	Behavioural characteristics	114
	7.8	Learning and development	116
	7.9	Professionalism and ethics	118

Comparison with the 4th Edition of the
APM Body of knowledge — 121

Glossary of project management terms — 125

Project management acronyms — 165

Index — 171

Figures

1.1	The project management process	3
1.2	The relationship between project, programme and portfolio management	7
2.1	A stakeholder grid	21
2.2	The definition of value as per BS EN 12973:2000	22
2.3	The risk management process (Source: APM (2004) *Project Risk Analysis and Management Guide*, 2nd edition)	27
3.1	An example of a hierarchical structure	35
4.1	The value management process BS EN 12973:2000	60
5.1	The interaction between the organisation and the project procurement process	75
6.1	The project and extended life cycles	80
6.2	The organisational continuum	92
6.3	Governance of project management	98

Preface

Welcome to the world of project management knowledge. Whether you have picked this up for the first time or you are a knowing reader, you are now engaged with the well-established *Association for Project Management Body of Knowledge* , now in its fifth edition.

It is a clear, simple guide for the journey through the growing collection of worldly project management knowledge which will progressively be revealed and which can be accessed in layers.

This latest edition of the *APM Body of Knowledge* is an up-to-date representation of the topics in which practitioners, experts and academic scholars in the UK consider professionals in project management should be knowledgeable and competent. Essentially it defines the topics that comprise modern professional project management – it encapsulates the breadth of project management and demonstrates its depth. In itself the *APM Body of Knowledge* is not and does not pretend to be a self-contained textbook, neither is it a set of competencies for a project manager, nor an exam syllabus, nor a specific methodology.

In this fifth edition the authors and editors have retained many aspects from previous editions but we have also made changes. We have reviewed all the text and made it consistent in content and style. We have reviewed and updated the further reading – and recognise that this is a growing field. We have enhanced reader accessibility to the *APM Body of Knowledge* by improving the presentation of the book and by providing electronic formats.

We believe that these structural, content and presentation revisions will maintain the *APM Body of Knowledge* as a cornerstone of the project management community in the UK and further afield.

Thank you.

Tom Taylor, Chairman of APM

Acknowledgements

The production, processing and maintenance of a body of knowledge is a complex, time-consuming and intellectually stimulating collection of activities – a series of concurrent and sequential complementary 'projects' that make up a 'programme', and this needs managing.

This enterprise would not be possible without extensive and diverse contributions from many people and organisations, most of them on a voluntary, altruistic basis.

It is important that their contributions are recognised not just as a way of saying thank you but also to convey to the reader the project management community's ownership of the material and the status of the ongoing products that arise from their endeavours.

Firstly, we recognise all the authors of the reference materials and sources that have enriched the words and diagrams provided and that are integral layers within this *APM Body of Knowledge*.

Secondly, we would like to thank the many parties from a wide range of locations and industry sectors who responded to interviews and/or completed (extensive) questionnaires with thoroughness and patience.

Thirdly, we wish to acknowledge the many individuals who have contributed by writing or checking or commenting on draft sections. They have done this as individuals, on behalf of their organisations or in steering groups or working parties during 2004 and 2005.

Fourthly, we would also like to acknowledge the many organisations that have permitted or encouraged their staff to contribute as individuals and have provided collected corporate views and contributed funding to the process.

Fifthly, there are the editorial and production teams who have assembled and made available this edition and its supporting promotional and back-up material in attractive and accessible formats both in hard copy and electronic versions.

Finally, we thank Professor Peter Morris and his team for their continuing academically rigorous work from the fourth edition onwards through to this fifth edition. The APM sponsor for recent research efforts has been Miles Shepherd, currently vice president of APM and previous chairman.

Perhaps we should also acknowledge the diverse collection of end user people and organisations for the *APM Body of Knowledge*, who are addressed later in the Introduction and provide the essential demand to keep this material up to date and available.

Thank you to all participants and stakeholders in the *APM Body of Knowledge*.

Introduction

WELCOME

The *APM Body of Knowledge* is a well-established collection of project management knowledge, now in its fifth edition. Divided into sections and topics it provides introductions and common guides to those areas considered essential to the discipline of managing projects, and it is clearly structured with definitions, explanations and suggested further reading material. This information will direct and assist those interested in project management in their work, studies and learning for recognised qualifications.

In this fifth edition the authors and editors have retained many aspects familiar from previous editions but they have also made some changes. While the established primary structure remains the same, all topics have been reviewed and updated.

The *APM Body of Knowledge* identifies 52 areas of knowledge, each of which is covered in a topic. We have added 10 new topics and changed 16 topic titles in order to reflect current thinking. In this new edition we have made a change to the topic numbering system in order to improve clarity. Topics are thus numbered decimally by section (1.1, 1.2 and so on). Figures are numbered consecutively within each of the seven sections (6.1, 6.2, 6.3).

All the sections and topics have been reviewed to bring them up to date, to be consistent in the weighting and style of explanations, and to exist as stand-alone topics. Illustrations have been added as appropriate.

Multiple-author books and useful websites are listed in the first topic (1.1 – Project management) and have been suggested to provide an overview of the entirety of project management. The references for further reading within each topic have been updated, limiting the number for each topic and including only those that are readily available.

In presentation terms improvements have been made to ease access and navigation through the *APM Body of Knowledge* by the provision of a glossary, a list of acronyms and an index, as well as cross-referencing, section-coding and a word search facility (in the digital version).

The overall approach reflects the needs and understandings within the UK and for those interested in adopting a UK approach wherever they may live and work. However, we have tried to avoid creating undue difficulties for those living and working in other parts of the world or from other cultures.

The content retains the APM philosophy of a pan-sector approach for explanations and further reading. We fully recognise the interest in particular sectors and the growth of sector specific reference material and this is something we will continue to monitor and address for future knowledge provision.

The use of project management as a vehicle for change is becoming much more widespread and popular, in ever-widening applications. The historically established sectors of project management are also reassessing and developing their needs and contexts – in construction, information technology, engineering, energy, transport and defence. Many 'new' industries and sectors have been discovering and adapting project management more widely to suit their needs – banking, entertainment, human resources, leisure, event management, retail supply, disaster recovery, product launches, political conferences, legal processes and more.

APM has long recognised that project management is not simply a matter of applying some tools and techniques or a 'one-size-fits-all' formula.

It is within this broadening of project management applications, the deepening of project management related knowledge and increasing speed of access that a firm initial project management knowledge base is required. The *APM Body of Knowledge* aims to provide this initial base.

THE STRUCTURE OF THE *APM BODY OF KNOWLEDGE*

The primary structure of the text is well established in the following seven sections:

1. Project management in context
2. Planning the strategy
3. Executing the strategy
4. Techniques
5. Business and commercial
6. Organisation and governance
7. People and the profession

There is nothing absolutely fixed about this structure in its format or sequence; it does, however, have clarity and logic. Many of the topics addressed in each section are closely linked with others elsewhere, or are interdependent. However, they are treated separately due to their significance and to aid simplicity of presentation.

In reality many of the topics may fit into more than one section – as they may also be applicable to more than one phase of a project. For example, project risk management and project quality management are not to be treated as topics in isolation.

FROM GENERAL, TO DETAILED

The *APM Body of Knowledge* endeavours to convey the knowledge appropriate to the discipline of managing projects, rather than the processes and practices of project management.

Within the *APM Body of Knowledge* the topics are those that are 'generic' to project management; correspondingly the way they are presented here is also generic, and at a high level. Detailed descriptions and explanations of the topics can be found in the lists of suggested further reading, in teaching and research institutions and their outputs, in the libraries and collections of business and professional libraries – in the UK and around the world. The principal aim is to give an introduction and scoping guide to each of the topics that professionals in project management consider to be essential components of the discipline. The characteristics of project, programme and portfolio management are explored in Section 1; thereafter the topics pursue 'mainstream' project management scenarios. However, many aspects can be interpreted and applied to programme and portfolio management and specialisms by niche services or particular industry circumstances.

Despite established definitions for these three 'Ps', in, for example, the British Standard Project Management vocabulary, there is still a range of understandings on the similarities and differences between them:

- A *project* is a unique, transient endeavour undertaken to achieve a desired outcome.
- A *programme* is a group of related projects, which may include related business-as-usual activities, that together achieve a beneficial change of a strategic nature for an organisation.
- A *portfolio* is a grouping of projects, programmes and other activities carried out under the sponsorship of an organisation.

APM BODY OF KNOWLEDGE – NOT A SET OF RULES OR PRACTICES

This is a body of knowledge. It is not a fixed set of rules or practices, or a prescriptive method that will guide people, organisations and teams from A to Z, leading them to an inevitable achievement of their targets and success criteria, such as 'on time, within budget, to the agreed quality'. The range of applications of project management in the UK means that it is not credible to produce a universal guidebook that in a step-by-step, phase-by-phase mechanical manner will drive towards success in an assured fashion.

The *APM Body of Knowledge* adopts a consistent approach across all topics. The explanations for each topic are deliberately short, general and high level. This recognises that the context of the need for knowledge is variable, reflecting a wide spectrum of interests and needs by industry, sector, location, relationships, stages, complexity, value, criticality and so forth. The contents of the *APM Body of Knowledge* do not provide or seek to imply a mechanistic set of rules, processes or practices that must be followed or must be fully known about in order to deliver projects successfully (one can never be so assured) or to demonstrate unquestionable professional capability.

KNOWLEDGE, EXPERIENCE AND COMPETENCIES

Good effective project management requires appropriately balanced combinations of knowledge, experience and behaviour. Experience generates both explicit and tacit knowledge which is clearly reflected in this *APM Body of Knowledge* . Competencies can be assessed against the various sections and those in Section 7 in particular. Expertise can be readily assessed and measured against all the sections and their descriptions – areas of strength can be made stronger, less strong or weak areas can be identified and remedied, and efforts towards continuing professional development (CPD) can be prioritised.

USERS OF THE *APM BODY OF KNOWLEDGE*

The range of users of the *APM Body of Knowledge*   continues to grow. We recognise the following users:

- **Front line practitioners** and consultants/advisors undertaking project activities who wish to keep up to date with knowledge generally or to investigate particular elements to assist themselves or their teams.
- **Senior managers** of project-driven or project aware organisations who also want to keep abreast of current thinking and advise their teams and staff accordingly.
- The **Association for Project Management** itself uses the body of knowledge to maintain the currency of syllabuses for qualifications and to provide a structure for all project management knowledge collection and development.
- **APM-approved providers of development programmes (trainers)** will use the *APM Body of Knowledge*   as a guide to assess students and construct courses for APM (and other) examinations and qualifications. Similarly, project management tool developers may use the structure or aspects of the *APM Body of Knowledge*   for product development.
- **'Students'** of project management, including scholars and examination candidates of all ages, and the APM membership generally, at school, college, university or thereafter (not forgetting that seasoned practitioners are all always learning too) who will be assisted with their understanding of APM examinations and qualifications and provided with a reliable source of knowledge.
- **Researchers** at a higher level who are studying aspects of project management for academic or commercial purposes or by location, sector or subject and are searching for definitive reference materials will find them directly or indirectly via the *APM Body of Knowledge*   (and the ever-growing collection of articles in APM's collection of periodicals, publications and referenced websites).
- **Authors and publishers** of books and articles who wish to reference their material within a recognised source.

- **Fellow member bodies of the International Project Management Association (IPMA)** and their individual members, and other bodies with an interest in project management will find the *APM Body of Knowledge* valuable as an explanation of a UK approach.
- **Librarians, information and knowledge managers** will find the *APM Body of Knowledge* useful as a source of classification and definition and as a wider reference tool.
- **Potential project managers** and potential members of the APM will find the *APM Body of Knowledge* to be an accessible introduction and indispensable primer.

CONTRIBUTORS TO THE *APM BODY OF KNOWLEDGE*

One of the main attributes of the *APM Body of Knowledge* is that it has been written by the project management community for the project management community.

The contributors to this latest edition are as knowledgeable as ever and now represent even greater diversity and wider consultation.

Contributors include cross-sectional representatives of:

- experienced practitioners;
- academic scholars;
- current authors and researchers;
- front line training providers;
- established project management organisations.

Specifically there have been:

- extensive peer group reviews of individual sections and of the document overall, including over forty structured interviews and data-gathering meetings from a range of industry sectors;
- a web-enabled questionnaire, that received over 400 responses, and which has been considered and incorporated as appropriate;
- workshop reviews with senior executives.

All of these resources have been combined to produce a strong, well-established, up-to-date *APM Body of Knowledge*.

AND FINALLY

On the inside of the front cover of this book there is some guidance on how to use this *APM Body of Knowledge*.

On the reverse of the back flaps of this book there are itemised lists of topics which can be folded out to provide easy navigation in using the document.

Best wishes to all readers, users, interested parties and organisations.

Section 1

Project management in context

Project management fits within the general framework of business and management, and is used to bring about change. Project management is a management discipline that is differentiated from the management of an organisation's business-as-usual by the fact that a project has a clear objective and deliverables,[1] with a defined start and end, that must be completed on time, within budget (cost) and to the agreed quality[2] and, of course, it must deliver the agreed benefits.

In order to understand project management in context it is important to appreciate:

- the boundaries of project management and where it fits in the general framework of business and management (Topic 1.1 – Project management);
- how projects can be delivered within a programme (Topic 1.2 – Programme management);
- how organisations manage projects, programmes and related operational activities as a portfolio of investment opportunities (Topic 1.3 – Portfolio management);
- that projects are not undertaken in vacuums and there needs to be an awareness of the environment in which they are undertaken (Topic 1.4 – Project context);
- that projects need direction and support from within an organisation, which is provided by a sponsor (Topic 1.5 – Project sponsorship);
- that within organisations there can be centres of project management expertise that assist both the organisation and the project manager (Topic 1.6 – Project office).

---

[1] Deliverable is the term used to describe the outputs of the project both during the project and at the end. To many people, deliverables and products are synonyms. A deliverable may not be a physical outcome.

[2] Quality is the term used to describe the performance of the delivery and the deliverables (outputs) of the project. To many people, quality and performance are synonyms.

1

1.1

Project management

Project management is the process by which projects are defined, planned, monitored, controlled and delivered such that the agreed benefits are realised. Projects are unique, transient endeavours undertaken to achieve a desired outcome. Projects bring about change and project management is recognised as the most efficient way of managing such change.

Organisations[1] have structures in place for the ongoing and routine management of business-as-usual.[2] Project management works across these structures drawing on the expertise and knowledge of the organisation, as well as external third parties if appropriate, to deliver a project. Essentially, project management achieves this by:

- understanding the need, problem or opportunity that the project will address;
- determining the business case, success criteria and benefits of the proposed project;
- defining what has to be accomplished and delivered, typically stated in terms of scope, time, cost and quality;
- developing a plan[3] to achieve the deliverables and then implementing the plan, ensuring that progress is maintained in line with objectives;
- utilising resources[4] as and when required in a team environment, under the direction of a project manager who is accountable for the successful delivery of the project in terms of time, cost and quality;
- ensuring that the sponsor is accountable for achievement of the defined benefits;
- using appropriate mechanisms, tools and techniques.

Project management should be applied throughout the project life cycle[5] (Topic 6.1). There are generic project management processes that need to be applied to each phase of the project life cycle. These may be described as:

---

[1] Organisation is used to describe an entity that is undertaking the project or providing services to a project.

[2] Also referred to as day-to-day business or operations.

[3] In the *APM Body of Knowledge* a plan is the project management plan – see Topic 2.4. In some industries and business sectors a plan is another way of referring to the schedule, which is incorrect.

[4] Resources are all those items required to undertake a project and include people, finance and materials.

[5] A project life cycle is a series of phases that all projects pass through.

- a starting or initiating process;
- a defining and planning process;
- a monitoring and controlling process;
- a learning and closing process.

The project management process provides the single point of integrative responsibility. It achieves this by defining the required inputs and outputs while taking into account all relevant constraints and mechanisms, as illustrated in Figure 1.1.

Project management expertise is spread across the project team. Project management capability and maturity exist at an individual and an organisational level. At an organisational level various project management capability maturity models have been developed that allow organisations to continuously improve their project management processes and procedures. Such models typically define the lowest level as an organisation that uses project management in an *ad hoc* manner through to an organisation that continually improves its project management capability.

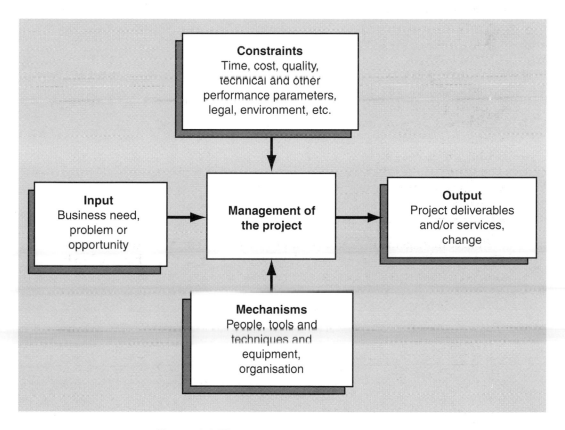

Figure 1.1 The project management process

A large project may be divided into subprojects each with their own unique deliverables that contribute to the overall project deliverable. It is possible for several projects to each produce their own unique deliverables, which then collectively contribute to a greater goal or benefit. Such projects are brought together under a programme and managed using programme management (Topic 1.2).

Further reading

British Standards Institution (2000–2002) BS 6079–1–3 Project Management. Guides, BSI, London

Buttrick, R. (2005) *The Project Workout*, 3rd edn, FT Prentice Hall, London, ISBN 0–273–68181–8

Hamilton, A. (2004) *Handbook of Project Management Procedures*, Thomas Telford, London, ISBN 0–72773258–7

Meredith, J. R. and Mantel, S. M. (2003) *Project Management: A Managerial Approach*, Wiley, Chichester, ISBN 0–471–07323–7

Office of Government Commerce (2005) *Managing Successful Projects with PRINCE2*, Stationery Office, London, ISBN 0–11–330946–5

Turner, J. R. (1998) *The Handbook of Project-Based Management*, 2nd edn, McGraw-Hill Education, New York, ISBN 0–07709161–2

The books and websites cited here are relevant to most, if not all, of the topics in the *APM Body of Knowledge*   and have been placed in the first topic simply for convenience.

Multiple-author books

Cleland, David I. and Ireland, Lewis R. (eds) (2002) *Project Management: Strategic Design and Implementation*, 4th edn, McGraw-Hill, New York, ISBN 0–07–139310–2
Morris, P. W. G. and Pinto, J. K. (eds) (2004) *The Wiley Guide to Managing Projects*, Wiley, Chichester, ISBN 0–471–23302–1
Stevens, M. (ed) (2002) *Project Management Pathways*, Association for Project Management, Princes Risborough, ISBN 1–903494–01–X
Turner, J. R. and Simister, S. J. (eds) (2000) *The Gower Handbook of Project Management*, 3rd edn, Gower, Aldershot, ISBN 0–566–08138–5

Useful websites

Association for Project Management – www.apm.org.uk
International Project Management Association – www.ipma.ch
Office of Government Commerce – Successful Delivery Toolkit – www.ogc.gov.uk/sdtoolkit
Project Management Institute – www.pmi.org
UK Ministry of Defence – Acquisition Management System – www.ams.mod.uk

1.2

Programme management

Programme management is the co-ordinated management of related projects, which may include related business-as-usual activities that together achieve a beneficial change of a strategic nature for an organisation. What constitutes a programme will vary across industries and business sectors but there are core programme management processes.

Senior management defines an overall strategy for the organisation. This will set a number of objectives and targets for the organisation. Members of the management team will identify how the objectives and targets will be achieved. This may lead to the initiation of projects and programmes.

Senior management will analyse, select and prioritise the programmes and projects through portfolio management[1] (Topic 1.3) to make an optimal contribution to the achievement of the organisation's strategic objectives.

Those programmes that are selected will be undertaken through the definition, delegation and delivery of related projects. The programme manager must monitor the projects in terms of time, cost, quality, risks and issues, and interdependencies with other related projects and business-as-usual activities, and delegate responsibility for the successful completion of individual projects to project managers.

Individual projects should have a benefits management function. A distinctive feature of programmes is that the related projects must be managed together if the desired strategic benefits are to be achieved. Therefore a principal responsibility of the programme manager is to maintain a focus on the delivery of agreed strategic benefits, as illustrated in Figure 1.2. Individual projects outside a programme may also contribute to a strategic benefit.

Typically, the desired benefits will be identified within a business case, which includes a specification of what the programme is expected to achieve. Programmes will evolve over time and therefore will have to be redefined to take account of the changing business environment.

There are differences of opinion as to what constitutes programme management. However, applicable to all programmes are:

- accelerating, decelerating, redefining, terminating and initiating projects within the programme;
- managing interdependencies between projects and between projects and business-as-usual activities;
- managing resources available to the programme and resource conflicts;

[1] Portfolio management is the selection and management of all projects' programmes and related business-as-usual activities within an organisation.

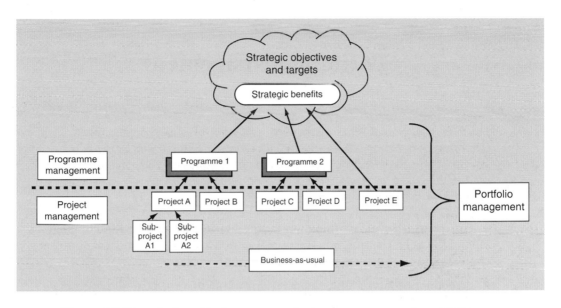

Figure 1.2 The relationship between project, programme and portfolio management

- managing risks, issues and changes at a programme level;
- defining and realising the strategic benefits.

Further reading

Bartlett, J. (2002) *Managing Programmes of Business Change*, Project Manager Today Publications, Bramshill, Hants, ISBN 1–900391–08–2

British Standards Institution (2004) BS EN 9200: 2004 Programme Management. Guidelines for project management specification, BSI, London

Office of Government Commerce (2002) *Managing Successful Programmes*, Stationery Office, London, ISBN 0–11–330016–6

Reiss, G. (1996) *Programme Management Demystified*, Spon, London, ISBN 0–419–21350–3

Springer, M. (2005) *A Concise Guide to Program Management: Fundamental Concepts and Issues*, Purdue University Press, ISBN 1–55753–376–8

Williams, D. and Parr, T. (2004) *Enterprise Programme Management: Delivering Value*, Palgrave Macmillan, Basingstoke ISBN 1–4039–1700–0

1.3

Portfolio management

Portfolio management is the selection and management of all of an organisation's projects, programmes and related business-as-usual activities taking into account resource constraints. A portfolio is a group of projects and programmes carried out under the sponsorship of an organisation. Portfolios can be managed at an organisational, programme or functional level.

There are differences of opinion as to what constitutes portfolio management. However, the common theme is that portfolio management within the context of project management involves:

- screening, analysis and financial appraisal of project and programme characteristics (resources, schedules, cash flows, risks, benefits and so on) in relation to the organisation's strategy;
- prioritisation and/or selection of projects or programmes within the organisation's portfolio, given the resources available, likely returns and risks;
- continued monitoring of the portfolio characteristics as projects and programmes develop;
- adjustment of the portfolio with regard to the constraints, risks and returns anticipated, and in the light of developing circumstances around the portfolio.

Portfolio management is particularly concerned with the interdependencies between projects and programmes in terms of:

- scarce or limited resources;
- balance within the portfolio between risks and return;
- timing;
- capacity bottlenecks.[1]

Organisations seek a mixture of projects and programmes that fulfil their strategic objectives. When a fixed resource pool has to be shared amongst a number of projects and programmes some form of prioritisation has to take place. This allows the more important projects and programmes to access the required resources and to move forward in accordance with their plans. Projects and programmes that are deemed low priority may have to revise their plans to take account of the reduced level of resources they potentially might receive, and those that no longer support the portfolio may need to be

---

[1] The term 'capacity bottleneck' is used to describe a situation where several projects all need access to a limited resource at the same time.

terminated. This aspect of portfolio management is often a subset of corporate governance (Topic 6.10) and thus is the responsibility of senior management. Senior management may be assisted in its deliberations by a project office (Topic 1.6) which collects and presents appropriate information on all projects and programmes to allow meaningful comparisons to be made.

Project and programme management have an important role to play in ensuring that portfolio management is provided with accurate up-to-date information, particularly on status. Project and programme managers may also have a significant role in influencing the portfolio prioritisation process, vying for the resources their projects or programmes may need at various stages of their life cycles.

Further reading

Benko, C. and McFarlane, W. (2003) *Connecting the Dots: Aligning Your Project Portfolio with Corporate Objectives*, Harvard Business School Press, Boston, MA, ISBN 1–57851–877–6

Dye, L. D. and Pennypacker, J. S. (eds) (1999) *Project Portfolio Management*, Center for Business Practices, Havertown, PA, ISBN 1–92957616–1

Kendall, G. I. and Rollins, S. C. (2003) *Advanced Project Portfolio Management and the PMO: Multiplying ROI at Warp Speed*, J. Ross Publishing, Fort Lauderdale, FL, ISBN 1–932159–02–9

Pennypacker, J. S. and Dye, L. D. (eds) (2002) *Managing Multiple Projects: Planning, Scheduling, and Allocating Resources for Competitive Advantage*, Marcel Dekker, New York, ISBN 0–8247–0680–3

1.4

Project context

Project context refers to the environment within which a project is undertaken. Projects do not exist in a vacuum and an appreciation of the context within which the project is being performed will assist those involved in project management to deliver a project.

A project will be managed differently according to a wide range of factors, including the industry or business sector in which it is based, geographical location, use of virtual teams, technical complexity or financial impact. The tools and techniques of project management should be applied in a manner that is appropriate to their context. Context covers both the external and internal environments and must consider the interests and influences of stakeholders (Topic 2.2). The major elements of the environment are often based on the acronym PESTLE (**P**olitical, **E**conomic, **S**ociological, **T**echnical, **L**egal and **E**nvironmental). Other factors to consider are organisational capability and maturity, structure and processes and individual resource capability and availability.

Industry and business sector practices provide some of the context within which project management is practised. The following are examples of context:

- Procurement practices, such as the various standard forms of construction contract or the application of partnering, can shape organisational structures and ways of working.
- Project management in drug development or the nuclear sector is strongly shaped by the regulatory requirements of licensing approval processes as well as by the scientific culture of the industry.
- Projects within the UK government sector have to follow particular practices such as OGC Gateway®[1] and take account of political influences.
- The use of publicly available methods such as PRINCE2 can have a huge effect on practice.

Variations in context make the application of appropriate project management practices challenging. Their appropriateness will vary according to the contextual variables described above.

All the above affect the context of the project and shape the environment that the sponsor, project manager and project team have to deal with, and may assist or restrict the attainment of the objectives, deliverables and

---

[1] The Office of Government Commerce examines a programme or project at critical points in its life cycle to provide assurance that it can progress successfully to the next phase.

benefits of the project. The successful accomplishment of a project generally requires a significant sensitivity to, and understanding of, the context in which it is based.

Further reading

Crawford, L., Hobbs, J. B. and Turner, J. R. (2005) Project Categorization Systems and their Use in Organisations: An Empirical Study, in *Innovations: Project Management Research 2004* (eds D. P. Slevin, D. I. Cleland and J. K. Pinto), Project Management Institute, Newton Square, PA, ISBN 1–930–69959–X

Davies, A. and Hobday, M. (2005) *The Business of Projects*, Cambridge University Press, Cambridge, ISBN 0–521–84328–6

Newton, R. (2005) *The Project Manager: Mastering the Art of Delivery*, FT Prentice Hall, London, ISBN 0–273–70173–8

1.5

Project sponsorship

Project sponsorship is an active senior management role, responsible for iden-
tifying the business need, problem or opportunity. The sponsor ensures the
project remains a viable proposition and that benefits are realised, resolving any
issues outside the control of the project manager.

Projects implement change and that allows organisations to fulfil their
business objectives. This emphasises benefits realisation, rather than delivery
of deliverables. Consequently, the role of the sponsor[1] is to direct a project
with benefits in mind, as opposed to the project manager, who manages the
project with delivery in mind with consideration of the benefits to be realised.
Project sponsorship is therefore more pertinent to project effectiveness while
project management is more concerned with project efficiency.

The sponsor is the primary risk taker and owner of the project's business
case. The sponsor is tasked with ensuring that the benefits of a project are
realised and therefore needs to ensure that any obstacles faced by a project
are dealt with.

There should be only one sponsor per project. The sponsor chairs the
steering group[2] (Topic 6.8) and is the person to whom the project manager is
accountable. The relationship between sponsor and project manager is
based on a continuous dialogue, with a common understanding of the
project context, the benefits sought and the costs and risks of achieving
those benefits.

The sponsor needs to be:

- a business leader and decision maker who is able to work across functional boundaries within an organisation;
- an advocate for the project and the change it brings about;
- prepared to commit sufficient time and support to undertake the role;
- sufficiently experienced in project management to be able to judge
  whether the project is being managed effectively.

Without clear goals, direction and business leadership provided by the
sponsor even the best project manager and project team can struggle to
succeed. Similarly, without clear, timely decisions and support a project will
falter.

---

[1] Also referred to as the project executive, senior responsible officer, project director, project
champion or project owner.
[2] The steering group oversees a project and provides strategic guidance. Alternatively called the
steering committee or project board.

The more a project changes the status quo, the more likely it is that organisation boundaries will be crossed and the greater the likelihood that organisational politics will become apparent (Topic 1.4). The sponsor has to understand what motivates the various stakeholders and be prepared, empowered and capable of addressing their interests. Interpersonal skills are paramount, especially those concerned with influencing people.

The effectiveness of a sponsor is related to the project management maturity of an organisation. The more mature an organisation, the more likely it is that the sponsorship role and hence benefits-driven projects will succeed.

Further reading

APM GoPM Specific Interest Group (2005) *Directing Change: A Guide to Governance of Project Management*, 2nd edn, Association for Project Management, Princes Risborough, ISBN 1–903494–15–X

Bennis, W. and Goldsmith, J. (2003) *Learning to Lead: A Workbook on becoming a Leader*, Basic Books, New York, ISBN 0–738–20905–8

Buttrick, R. (2003) *The Role of the Executive Project Sponsor*, Financial Times Executive Briefing, London, ISBN 0–273–65945–6

Buttrick, R. (2005) *The Project Workout*, 3rd edn, FT Prentice Hall, London, ISBN 0–273–68181–8

1.6

Project office

A project office serves the organisation's project management needs. A project office can range from simple support functions for the project manager to being responsible for linking corporate strategy to project execution.

A project office[1] provides supporting project management services. Not all organisations or projects will have a project office. Where a project office does not exist the services it provides must be undertaken by project managers.

As a minimum the project office should provide:

- administrative support and assistance to project managers;
- collection, analysis and reporting of project information;
- assurance of project management processes.

A project office can fulfil a number of additional roles:

- Where the project office is the functional home for project managers the project office allocates project management resources to projects and is responsible for the professional development of project management professionals.
- Where the project office contains project support experts it provides a service to projects by ensuring they have the tools, techniques and information they need. This can be in the form of either coaching and mentoring sponsors and project managers or doing the support work for them.
- Where the project office instigates improvements to the way the organisation runs projects it enables and drives lessons learned from projects to be implemented on future projects.
- Where the project office is responsible for excellence in project execution this frees the sponsor and the organisation's senior management to make business decisions and concentrate on exception management for the projects.
- Where the project office has a strategic role it is responsible for the execution of corporate strategy through projects and programmes. This project office acts as developer and repository of the standards, processes and methods that improve individual project performance. It also facilitates the organisation's ability to manage its entire collection of projects and programmes as one or more portfolios and serves as a single source of information on project activity and data across the enterprise. This type of

---

[1] Project office has been used as a generic term. Specific terms include project support office, project management office, project and programme support office, portfolio support office, enterprise programme management office.

project office can be referred to as the enterprise project management office (EPMO).

Additionally, a project office can provide the infrastructure to support communities of practice. These are informal networks of individuals within an organisation who have an interest in learning and best practice of a particular area of project management.

The main advantage in the drawing together of project management talent into any form of project office is the development of a centre of excellence allowing the organisation to learn, lead, grow and develop its project management potential.

Further reading

Bolles, D. (2002) *Building Project-Management Centers of Excellence*, American Management Association, New York, ISBN 0–8144–0717–X

Englund, R. L, Graham, R. J. and Dinsmore, P. C. (2003) *Creating the Project Office: A Manager's Guide to Leading Organizational Change*, Jossey-Bass, San Francisco, CA, ISBN 0–7879–6398–4

Hill, G. M. (2003) *The Complete Project Management Office Handbook*, Auerbach Publications, Boco Raton, FL ISBN 0–8493–2173–5

Kendall, G. I. and Rollins, S. C. (2003) *Advanced Project Portfolio Management and the PMO: Multiplying ROI at Warp Speed*, J. Ross Publishing, Fort Lauderdale, FL, CA, ISBN 1–932159–02–9

Marsh, D. (2000) *Project and Programme Support Office Handbook*, vols 1 and 2: *Foundation* and *Advanced*, Project Manager Today Publications, Branshill, Hants ISBN 1–900391–05–8 and ISBN 1–900391–06–6

Miranda, Eduardo (2003) *Running the Successful Hi-Tech Project Office*, Artech House, Norwood, MA, ISBN 1–58053–373–6

Section 2

Planning the strategy

The unique, transient nature of projects means that a strategy, and a plan for their execution, has to be developed. A project that is properly planned will have a far greater chance of success than a poorly planned project. A number of processes can be used to enable a project to be planned that will allow the sponsor to achieve the agreed benefits.

In order to plan the strategy, consideration should be given to:

- the need to understand how the success of the project will be measured from the project manager's, sponsor's and stakeholders' perspectives (Topic 2.1 – Project success and benefits management);
- the importance of managing all those with an interest in the project (Topic 2.2 – Stakeholder management);
- how the project will deliver value (Topic 2.3 – Value management);
- how the plans for implementing the project should be combined and then approved (Topic 2.4 – Project management plan);
- the importance of proactive risk management (Topic 2.5 – Project risk management);
- the need for a quality management process that is applied throughout the project (Topic 2.6 – Project quality management);
- the working environment and health and safety factors (Topic 2.7 – Health, safety and environmental management).

2.1

Project success and benefits management

Project success is the satisfaction of stakeholder needs and is measured by the success criteria as identified and agreed at the start of the project. Benefits management is the identification of the benefits at an organisational level and the monitoring and realisation of those benefits.

The sponsor may view success as the project having achieved stated benefits as defined in the business case. From the project manager's perspective success may mean meeting agreed scope, time, cost and quality objectives as defined in the project management plan (Topic 2.4). However, stakeholders will have differing views of the project's success which must be taken into account.

It is possible to have a successful project that fails to deliver expected benefits or a project that delivers significant benefits but is considered a failure. Therefore project success and benefits need to be considered together because it is the organisational impact of deliverables that produces benefits. Stakeholders must agree how success for the project is defined, and the benefits the organisation wants to achieve by investing in the project.

Benefits management involves identifying and agreeing the benefits and how they will be measured, monitored and managed throughout the project until they are realised. Benefits can be measured quantitatively, such as financially, by market share or by output capacity, and qualitatively, such as improving security, increasing staff satisfaction or achieving a higher brand position.

At handover and closeout, it will be known whether a project has achieved its success criteria,[1] whereas benefits may not be realised until after handover and closeout. Therefore ownership of benefits realisation rests with the sponsor rather than with the project manager.

For the project manager to understand what success is, success criteria must be agreed with stakeholders during the concept phase (Topic 6.2) but may be changed at any time in the project's life cycle via change control (Topic 3.5). Success criteria require quantitative measures against which to judge their success. Key performance indicators (KPIs) are measures of success criteria. Tracking KPIs ensures that the project is progressing towards achievement of success criteria, enabling corrective action to be taken. Examples of success criteria are the achievement of deliverables on time or

---

[1] Terminology in this area is fluid. Success criteria can be called many things in different environments including key result areas (KRAs) or critical success factors (CSFs).

the recruitment of skilled resources; associated KPIs might be performance against the schedule and rate of recruitment.

Success factors are elements of the project context or management process that should be controlled or influenced, and will increase the likelihood of a successful project. The presence of these factors does not guarantee project success, but their absence may contribute to failure. Examples of success factors include senior management support, clear goals and objectives or a motivated project team.

Further reading

Buttrick, R. (2005) *The Project Workout*, 3rd edn, FT Prentice Hall, London, ISBN 0–273–68181–8

Johnson, G., Scholes, K. and Whittington, R. (2004) *Exploring Corporate Strategy*, FT Prentice Hall, London, ISBN 0–273–68789–5

Morris, P. W. G. and Jamieson, H. A. (2004) *Translating Corporate Strategy into Project Strategy*, Project Management Institute, Newton Square, PA, ISBN 1–930–69937–9

Office of Government Commerce (2002) *Managing Successful Programmes*, Stationery Office, London, ISBN 0–11–330016–6

2.2

Stakeholder management

Stakeholder management is the systematic identification, analysis and planning of actions to communicate with, negotiate with and influence stakeholders. Stakeholders are all those who have an interest or role in the project or are impacted by the project.

Stakeholders have a key role in defining the success criteria used to judge the success of the project and their interest and power should not be overlooked. Stakeholders must be identified, their level of interest (positive or negative) and power to influence the success of the project analysed, and plans devised for their management. Stakeholder management is an iterative process which starts during project concept.

Stakeholder identification requires consideration of who is involved in, affected by or can affect the project. Brainstorming of potential stakeholders may identify:

- resources needed for the project;
- organisations or people who will be affected by the project;
- organisations or people on the sidelines of the project who will influence attitudes and behaviours;
- statutory and regulatory bodies.

Once stakeholders have been identified stakeholder analysis is used to establish their position in relation to the project. Questions to consider are as follows:

- Do they have an interest in the project succeeding?
- Will they be openly supportive of the project as it progresses?
- Is the stakeholder ambivalent about the project?
- Could the stakeholder have a negative view about what the project will deliver?
- What are their expectations and how can these be managed?

A tool to further understand a stakeholder's position in relationship to the project is a stakeholder grid (Figure 2.1). Considering a stakeholder's placement on this grid will help to determine stakeholder management actions.

The stakeholder analysis will need to be validated against the project context as it often provides a good pointer towards how organisations and people will relate to the project outcomes. Stakeholders must be managed to ensure that their positive interest in the project is utilised and maintained or that their negative interest is removed or minimised. Stakeholders who are

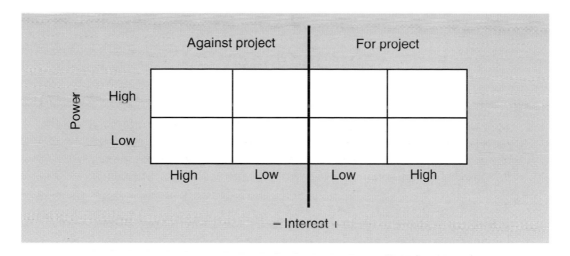

Figure 2.1 A stakeholder grid

'for' the project and in a position of high power can be used to influence stakeholders who are 'against' the project.

Stakeholder management becomes more complex when stakeholders' views are not consistent throughout the life cycle of the project as changes occur in their opinions, roles, views regarding the project and allegiances. The stakeholder analysis will need to be reviewed throughout the life cycle.

The project's communication plan should be employed as a tool for stakeholder management. It may include who the stakeholders are and their communication needs, and who is responsible for their management and planned responses.

Further reading

Johnson, G., Scholes, K. and Whittington, R. (2004) *Exploring Corporate Strategy*, FT Prentice Hall, London, ISBN 0–273–68789–5

Neely, A., Adams, C. and Kennerley, M. (2002) *Performance Prism: The Scorecard for Measuring and Managing Stakeholder Relationships*, FT Prentice Hall, London, ISBN 0 273 65334 2

Phillips, R. (2003) *Stakeholder Theory and Organizational Ethics*, McGraw-Hill Education, London, ISBN 1–57675268–2

Young, T. L. (2003) *The Handbook of Project Management. A Practical Guide to Effective Policies and Procedures*, Kogan Page, London, ISBN 0–7494–3965–3

2.3

Value management

Value management is a structured approach to defining what value means to the organisation and the project. It is a framework that allows needs, problems or opportunities to be defined and then enables review of whether the initial project objectives can be improved to determine the optimal approach and solution.

Value management uses proven methods that are systematically brought together to identify and deliver better value from projects. The key to the process is the involvement of stakeholders and their understanding of the function and value a project must deliver. Value management is concerned with motivating people, developing skills, advancing teams and promoting innovation, in order to optimise the overall performance of a project. For project managers, value management is concerned with improving the decision-making framework for the project within the project context.

Value is subjective and may be defined in a number of ways, such as worth, satisfaction of needs and benefits. In BS EN 12973:2000 value is defined as the ratio of 'satisfaction of needs' over 'use of resources', as shown in Figure 2.2: the fewer the resources used or the greater the function achieved, the greater

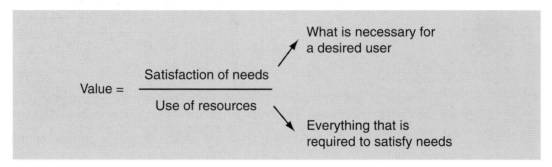

Figure 2.2 The definition of value as per BS EN 12973:2000

the value.

Value management has evolved out of a number of techniques, such as value analysis and functional analysis and system technique (FAST), that are based on the concept of value and functional approach. The value management approach[1] involves three root principles:

- A continuous awareness of value for the project, establishing measures or estimates of value, monitoring and controlling them.
- A focus on the objectives and targets before seeking solutions.
- A focus on function, providing the key to maximise innovative and practical outcomes.

The structured approach of value management is used to define what value means in the process of delivering the specified project deliverables. This is undertaken by gaining a consensus about the project deliverables and how these will be achieved by the project. The process is strategic and iterative and involves challenging the requirements and confirming the project's success criteria.

While value management is concerned with the optimisation of the strategy and business objectives, value engineering is concerned with optimising the conceptual, technical and operational aspects of a project's deliverables (Topic 4.5).

Further reading

British Standards Institution (2000) BS EN 12973:2000 Value Management, European Committee for Standardisation (CEN) Technical Committee CEN/TC 279, BSI, London

Dallas, M. F. (2005) *Value and Risk Management: A Guide to Best Practice*, Blackwell, Oxford, ISBN 1–405–12069–X

Kelly, J., Male, S. and Graham, D. (2004) *Value Management of Construction Projects*, Blackwell, Oxford, ISBN 0–632–05143–4

Society of American Value Engineers (SAVE) (1998) *Value Methodology Standard*, Northbrook, IL, SAVE International (available online from www.value-eng.org)

Thiry, Michel (1997) *Value Management Practice*, Project Management Institute, Newton Square, PA, ISBN 1–88010–14–1

Woodhead, R. M. and McCuish, J. D. (2002) *Achieving Results: How to Create Value*, Thomas Telford, London, ISBN 0–7277–3184–X

---

[1] BS EN 12973:2000 Value Management defines this approach.

2.4

Project management plan

The project management plan brings together all the plans for a project. The purpose of the project management plan (PMP) is to document the outcomes of the planning process and to provide the reference document for managing the project. The project management plan is owned by the project manager.

The project management plan[1] (PMP) confirms the agreements between the sponsor and other stakeholders and the project manager. It is approved by the sponsor, representing the organisation, and the project manager, representing the project team. Sharing the PMP with stakeholders is important in establishing common agreement of the contents, especially as the stakeholders' expectations of the project may have changed during the planning process. Although the project manager owns the PMP it should be developed with the project team; this removes ambiguity, develops commitment and assists in effective handover of the project.

The PMP documents how the project will be managed in terms of why, what, how (and how much), who, when and where:

- The 'why' is a statement of the change to be delivered by the project which includes a definition of the need, problem or opportunity being addressed. This is frequently developed in the business case.
- The 'what' describes the objectives, a description of the scope, the deliverables and their acceptance criteria. It also describes the success criteria for the project and the KPIs used to measure success. The 'what' needs to take into account the project's constraints, assumptions and dependencies.
- The 'how' defines the strategy for management, the handover of the project, the tools and techniques, monitoring and control, and reporting arrangements.
- 'How much' defines the project budget and the budgeting and cost management process.
- The 'who' includes a description of key project roles and responsibilities and the plan for all the resources that will be required.
- 'When' defines the timescales, including milestones and any arrangement for phasing, which must also then be reflected in the 'how much'.
- 'Where' defines the geographical location(s) where the work is performed, which impacts on costs and personnel factors.

---

[1] The project management (PMP) plan is sometimes referred to as a project execution plan, a project implementation plan, a project plan or simply a plan. In PRINCE2 the PMP is called the project initiation document (PID). It also brings together all the plans in one document allowing formal project authorisation.

The PMP also describes the policies and plans for managing changes, communication, configuration, governance, health, safety and environment issues, procurement, quality and risk.

The PMP is progressively developed during the planning process and is managed as a live, configuration-controlled document. In order to develop the PMP, scope management (Topic 3.1), scheduling (Topic 3.2), resource management (Topic 3.3) and budgeting and cost management (Topic 3.4) will be required. Once agreed, the PMP provides a baseline description of how the project will be managed, which is then periodically reviewed and updated through change control. The PMP will itself be the baseline document upon which changes are considered.

Further reading

British Standards Institution (2002) BS 6079–1:2002 Guide to Project Management, BSI, London

Kerzner, H. (2004) *Advanced Project Management: Best Practices on Implementation*, Wiley, Chichester, ISBN 0–471–47284–0

Lester, Albert (2004) *Project Planning and Control*, 4th edn, Butterworth Heinemann, Oxford, ISBN 0–750–65843–6

Neiman, Robert A. (2004) *Execution Plain and Simple: Twelve Steps to Achieving any Goal on Time and on Budget*, McGraw-Hill, New York, ISBN 0–07–143888–2

Office of Government Commerce (2005) *Managing Successful Projects with PRINCE2*, Stationery Office, London, ISBN 0–11–330946–5

2.5

Project risk management

Project risk management is a structured process that allows individual risk events and overall project risk to be understood and managed proactively, optimising project success by minimising threats and maximising opportunities.

All projects are inherently risky, because they are unique, constrained, complex, based on assumptions and performed by people. As a result, project risk management must be built into the management of projects, and should be used throughout the project life cycle.

Traditionally risk has been viewed as exclusively negative, but in project management it is defined as 'an uncertain event or set of circumstances that, should it occur, will have an effect on achievement of one or more project objectives', with the clear understanding that risks can affect achievement of project objectives either positively or negatively. The term 'risk event' is therefore used to cover both opportunities and threats, and both can be managed through a single risk management process.

It is also possible to define a higher level of 'project risk' which is 'exposure of stakeholders to the consequences of variation in outcome', arising from an accumulation of risk events together with other sources of uncertainty to the project as a whole.

The risk management process as illustrated in Figure 2.3 requires an initiation step to define scope and objectives, after which risks can be identified. The relative significance of identified risks is assessed using qualitative techniques to enable them to be prioritised for further attention. Quantitative risk analysis may also be used to determine the combined effect of risks on overall project outcome. A range of techniques are available, such as Monte Carlo simulation, decision trees and influence diagrams.

The process continues with risk response planning, aiming to avoid, reduce, transfer or accept threats as well as to exploit, enhance, share or accept opportunities, with contingency[1] for risks which cannot be handled proactively. The next step is implementation of agreed responses, followed by iterative identification, review and update throughout the project life cycle to maintain awareness of current risk exposure.

It is also important to identify and manage behavioural influences on the risk process, both individual and group, since these can have a significant impact on risk management effectiveness.

Risk management within a project must not be conducted in isolation, but must interface with the organisation. This includes escalation of risks to programme and portfolio levels, as well as contributing to business risk assessments and corporate governance requirements.

---

[1] Contingencies can include time, cost, resources and course of action.

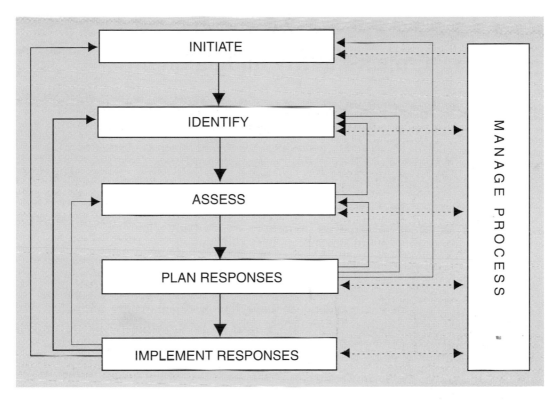

Figure 2.3 The risk management process (Source: APM (2004) *Project Risk Analysis and Management Guide*, 2nd edition)

Further reading

Association for Project Management (APM) (2004) *Project Risk Analysis & Management (PRAM) Guide*, 2nd edn, APM Publishing, Princes Risborough, ISBN 1–903494–12–5

Chapman, C. B. and Ward, S. C. (2003) *Project Risk Management: Processes, Techniques and Insights*, 2nd edn, Wiley, Chichester, ISBN 0–471–85355–7

Hillson, D. A. (2003) *Effective Opportunity Management for Projects: Exploiting Positive Risk*, Marcel Dekker, New York, ISBN 0–8247–4808–5

Hillson, D. A. and Murray-Webster, R. (2005) *Understanding and Managing Risk Attitude*, Gower, Aldershot, ISBN 0–566–08627–1

Institute of Risk Management (IRM), National Forum for Risk Management in the Public Sector (ALARM) and Association of Insurance and Risk Managers (AIRMIC) (2002) *A Risk Management Standard*, IRM/ALARM/AIRMIC, London, ISBN 0–11–330909–0

Office of Government Commerce (2002) *Management of Risk: Guidance for Practitioners*, Stationery Office, London, ISBN 0–11–330909–0

2.6

Project quality management

Project quality management is the discipline that is applied to ensure that both the outputs of the project and the processes by which the outputs are delivered meet the required needs of stakeholders. Quality is broadly defined as fitness for purpose or more narrowly as the degree of conformance of the outputs and process.

Quality management covers four processes: quality planning, quality assurance, quality control and continuous improvement.

The requirements for quality, expressed in measurable terms as acceptance criteria, form the foundation for quality management for the project. Quality planning prepares to achieve those requirements, enabling the project manager to manage the trade-off between scope, time, cost and quality. Outputs and processes can only be fit for purpose if the purpose is understood.

Quality assurance (QA) provides confidence to stakeholders that requirements for quality will be achieved. QA validates the consistent use of procedures and standards, supported by independent reviews and quality audits. QA will also be a source of lessons learned and ideas for improvement.

Quality control (QC), consisting of inspection, testing and quality measurement, verifies that the project deliverables conform to specification, are fit for purpose and meet stakeholder expectations.

The success of QA and QC can be enhanced by using a number of tools and techniques including project risk management (Topic 2.5), modelling and testing (Topic 4.6) and configuration management (Topic 4.7). Configuration management will support the effective control of documentation and physical items.

Concepts that further define quality are 'right first time' and 'zero defects', for re-work costs the project time and money and reduces stakeholder confidence. Accepting outputs to a reduced specification may allow the project to meet requirements for time and cost, but is poor project quality management. Delivering results to a higher specification, sometimes called 'gold-plating', is also poor quality.

Organisations that achieve project quality demonstrate a continual systematic approach to improvement, i.e. continuous improvement, that is focused on specifying requirements tightly and meeting them without wasting time or resources in the process. The practices encompassed in 'total quality management' (TQM), 'six sigma' and 'lean' are designed to achieve results as efficiently and effectively as possible.

The drive for 'total' quality has led to the development of maturity models designed to measure attainment and provide the motivation and a mechanism for objectively achieving improvement. Models such as the EFQM excellence model, the project excellence model, and a wide range of other capability maturity models also allow benchmarking between organisations and wider improvement across an organisation or sector.

Further reading

Bartlett, John (2005) Right First and Every Time: *Managing Quality in Projects and Programmes*, Project Manager Today Publications, Bramshill, Hants, ISBN 1–900391–13–9

British Standards Institution (2000) BS EN ISO 9000:2000 Quality Management Systems. Fundamentals and vocabulary, BSI, London

British Standards Institution (2000) BS EN ISO 9001:2000 Quality Management Systems. Requirements, BSI, London

British Standards Institution (2000) BS EN ISO 9004:2000 Quality Management Systems. Guidelines for performance improvements, BSI, London

British Standards Institution (2003) BS EN ISO 10006:2003 Quality Management Systems. Guidelines for quality management in projects, BSI, London

Rose, Kenneth (2005) *Project Quality Management*, J. Ross Publications, Fort Lauderdale, FL, ISBN 1–932159–48–7

2.7

Health, safety and environmental management

Health, safety and environmental management is the process of determining and applying appropriate standards and methods to minimise the likelihood of accidents, injuries or environmental impact both during the project and during the operation of its deliverables.

The management of health, safety and environmental factors is important in projects. It is a major component of construction, communications, energy, nuclear, food, pharmaceutical, transportation, waste and other sectors that operate under strict regulatory control. For example safety management impacts on the quality requirements of safety-critical software in many industries.

At a project level such management requires a working knowledge of the legal and organisational policies and procedures that apply to the project, including an understanding of the requisite health, safety and environmental regulations.

Legislation[1] influences the project manager's responsibility towards the people in the project team. For example the project manager may have to ensure that reasonable adjustment to physical premises has been made in order to avoid discrimination against an employee in their project team.

Organisations also have a legal duty to ensure employees are not made ill by their work. This includes taking steps to prevent physical and mental illness brought about by stress. The project manager must be aware of how the organisation's policy impacts on their project, for example by monitoring that excessive hours are not worked.

Environmental legislation is subject specific. Requirements for noise, dust, protection of flora and fauna, waste and sustainability, for example, must be proactively incorporated within project planning, including any disposal activities, to comply with these regulations.

UK and EU legislation demands that health and safety risk assessment and management is carried out for most commercial activities, including projects, in order to reduce health and safety risk to an acceptable level. There are a number of techniques and processes that cover these activities, including hazard and operability (HAZOP), hazardous condition (HAZCON), defect

---

[1] Examples of UK legislation and regulations include the Health and Safety at Work Act, the Management of Health and Safety at Work Regulations, Construction (Design and Management) Regulations, Display Screen Regulations and the Disability Discrimination Act.

reporting and corrective action (DRACAS) and as low as reasonably practicable (ALARP).

The project manager is expected to ensure that the project has a plan or plans including health, safety and environmental management, organisation, health and safety risk management, training, auditing and reporting.

The project manager owes a duty of care[1] to all those involved in the project. Likewise all those involved in the project have a duty of care to themselves and others to act responsibly and upon the project manager's instructions.

Further reading

British Standards Institution (2004) BS EN ISO 14001:2004 Environmental Management Systems. Requirements with guidance for use, BSI, London

Health and Safety Executive (2001) *Managing Health and Safety in Construction: Approved Code of Practice and Guidance for the Construction (Design and Management) Regulations*, HSE Books, London, ISBN 0-7176-21391

Stranks, J. (2001) *Health and Safety Law*, Prentice Hall, London, ISBN 0–273–65452–7

Stowe, J. (2002) *How to Develop an Effective Safety Policy*, Stationery Office, London, ISBN 0–1170–2824–X

---

[1] Duty of care in many instances is a legal responsibility.

Section 3

Executing the strategy

After the strategy and plan for the project have been agreed the strategy can be executed. Execution is far more than just implementing the project management plan (PMP). The context in which the project is executed has to be monitored and controlled. The constituent plans contained within the PMP have to be developed further and then used to monitor and control the project. Any changes to the plans whether internal or external to the project must be formally managed by change control.

The first four topics in this section are used in preparation of the PMP and have to be performed before it is baselined. After approval of the PMP these topics may be further performed to develop the plans to the level required to implement the project. These topics are performed in order that:

- the complete scope of the project is defined (Topic 3.1 – Scope management);
- the schedule within which the scope must be delivered is determined (Topic 3.2 – Scheduling);
- the resources required to deliver the scope are understood (Topic 3.3 – Resource management);
- the necessary budget to deliver the scope is agreed (Topic 3.4 – Budgeting and cost management).

The final four topics deal with change, monitoring and control:

- The need to allow for and formally manage change against an agreed baseline is fundamental to project success (Topic 3.5 – Change control).
- The ongoing measurement and management of the project's performance is essential (Topic 3.6 – Earned value management).
- Projects create large volumes of information which need to be managed. This management includes formal reporting (Topic 3.7 – Information management and reporting).
- Project managers need to ensure that issues are managed (Topic 3.8 – Issue management).

3.1

Scope management

Scope management is the process by which the deliverables and work to produce them are identified and defined. Identification and definition of the scope must describe what the project will include and what it will not include, i.e. what is in and out of scope.

The scope comprises the project deliverables and the work associated with producing those deliverables. It is important to also define what is outside of scope, i.e. the deliverables that the project will not provide. Scope management is continually applied throughout the project life cycle.

A high-level statement of scope is documented in the business case. This will describe the breadth of the scope. The depth of the scope is described at differing levels of detail as the project progresses. Scope is refined as part of requirements management (Topic 4.1) and also in the production of the project management plan (PMP) (Topic 2.4).

The scope in the PMP is refined using a product breakdown structure (PBS) and work breakdown structure (WBS):

- The PBS defines all the products (deliverables) that the project will produce. The lowest level of a PBS is a product (deliverable).
- The WBS defines the work required to produce the deliverables. The lowest level of detail normally shown in a WBS is a work package.[1] Acceptance criteria for each work package must be established as part of the ongoing project quality management process.

The organisational breakdown structure (OBS) is created to reflect the strategy for managing and handover of the project. The OBS shows the hierarchical management structure for the project, the communication routes and reporting links.

The WBS and OBS can be combined to create a responsibility assignment matrix (RAM), which correlates the work packages in the WBS to the people, organisations or third parties responsible for accomplishing the assigned work.

The cost breakdown structure (CBS) shows either the costs assigned to work packages using the WBS, or the costs assigned to functional areas and third parties using the OBS. The scope is used as input to the estimating and scheduling processes.

---

[1] In BS 6079 the lowest level of detail is an activity. Activities may not be shown on the WBS if this is considered to be too great a level of detail.

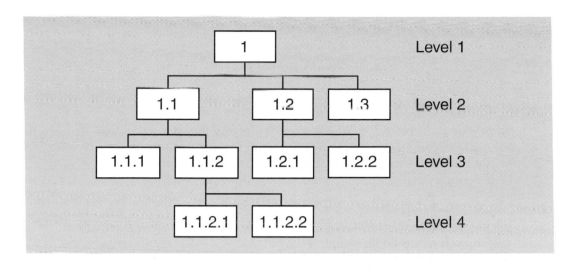

Figure 3.1 An example of a hierarchical structure

The PBS, WBS, OBS and CBS are hierarchical structures. An example is shown in Figure 3.1, where sequential numbering is used to differentiate the levels of detail.

When the final scope has been agreed with the sponsor it is baselined. This baseline is used to measure any changes and for the effective implementation of earned value management (Topic 3.6). The scope is monitored to ensure that scope creep does not occur. Change control (Topic 3.5) is used to manage any required changes in the scope.

Further reading

APM Earned Value SIG (2002) *Earned Value Management: APM Guidelines*, APM Publishing, Princes Risborough, ISBN 1–903494–26–5

Harrison, F. and Lock, D. (2004) *Advanced Project Management: A Structured Approach*, Gower, Aldershot, ISBN 0–566–07822–8

Haugan, Gregory T. (2001) *Effective Work Breakdown Structures*, Management Concepts, Vienna, VA, ISBN 1–56726–135–3

Kerzner, H. (2003) *Project Management: A Systems Approach to Planning, Scheduling and Controlling*, 8th edn, Wiley, Hoboken, NJ, ISBN 0–471–22577–0

Lewis, James P. (2005) *Project Planning, Scheduling and Control*, 4th edn, McGraw-Hill, New York, ISBN 0–07–146037/3

Project Management Institute (2001) *Project Management Institute Practice Standard for Work Breakdown Structures*, Project Management Institute, Newton Square, PA, ISBN 1–880410–81–8

3.2

Scheduling

Scheduling is the process used to determine the overall project duration and when activities and events are planned to happen. This includes identification of activities and their logical dependencies, and estimation of activity durations, taking into account requirements and availability of resources.

Scheduling[1] requires the identification of the activities in a project. These are all the activities necessary to complete the work packages as defined in the work breakdown structure (WBS) (Topic 3.1). The granularity of the schedule allows activities to be shown at differing levels of detail. A high-level schedule is often called a master schedule, which would highlight project milestones.

The logical dependencies between the activities must be defined. There are two principal methods of illustrating output: network diagrams and Gantt charts.[2] Activity-on-node[3] network diagrams show activities at the nodes and the links between the nodes represent the dependencies, also called logic.

Estimates of activity durations are produced taking account the resources required and their availability and productivity. Incorporation of activity durations into the network allows the overall project duration, critical path and float[4] to be determined. The critical path is the longest sequence of activities through a network from start to finish, the sum of whose durations determines the overall project duration. There may be more than one such path. Activities on the critical path must be completed on time or the project end date will be delayed. As part of an iterative process the overall project duration can be reduced using techniques such as fast-tracking and concurrent engineering.

A refinement of the network diagram is the program evaluation review technique (PERT) which uses a weighted three-point estimate of activity duration in place of a single-point estimate.

The network diagram can be displayed as a Gantt chart. A Gantt chart allows the activities to be represented against a calendar and the length of the

---

[1] The schedule is sometimes wrongly referred to as the plan (project plan).

[2] Gantt charts are sometimes referred to as bar charts.

[3] Also called precedence diagrams. An alternative notation used for a network diagram is activity-on-arrow.

[4] There are two main types of float: total float, i.e. the amount of time by which an activity can be delayed or extended without affecting the end date of the project, and free float, i.e. the amount of time by which an activity can be delayed or extended without affecting the start date of any subsequent activity. Float is also called slack.

bar represents the activity duration with logic links shown between the bars. Software tools have caused a rise in the use of the Gantt chart at the expense of the network diagram.

In addition to the detailed scheduling of activities, the project's overall time constraints have to be considered and the schedule revised until these can be met. This is an iterative process until the project manager and sponsor reach agreement when the schedule is then baselined. This baseline can be used to measure any changes and for the effective implementation of earned value management (Topic 3.6).

Scheduling continues throughout the project life cycle. Changes to the schedule that have an impact on milestones should only be undertaken as part of change control (Topic 3.5).

An innovation to the scheduling process is the critical chain approach, which combines:

- a more integrated approach to resourcing;
- centralised management of contingencies as a buffer;
- avoidance of multi-tasking.

Further reading

APM Earned Value SIG (2002) *Earned Value Management: APM Guidelines*, APM Publishing, Princes Risborough, ISBN 1–903494–26–5

Burke, R. (2003) *Project Management: Planning and Control Techniques*, 4th edn, Wiley, Hoboken, NJ, ISBN 0–470–85124–4

Gordon, J. and Lockyer, K. (2005) *Project Management and Project Planning*, FT Prentice Hall, London, ISBN 0–273–69378–6

Kerzner, H. (2003) *Project Management: A Systems Approach to Planning, Scheduling and Controlling*, 8th edn, Wiley, Hoboken, NJ, ISBN 0–471–22577–0

Lester, Albert (2004) *Project Planning and Control*, 4th edn, Butterworth-Heinemann, Oxford, ISBN 0–750–65843–6

Leach, L. P. (2005) *Critical Chain Project Management*, 2nd edn, Artech House, Norwood, MA, ISBN 1–58053–903–3

3.3

Resource management

Resource management identifies and assigns resources to activities so that the project is undertaken using appropriate levels of resources and within an acceptable duration. Resource allocation, smoothing, levelling and scheduling are techniques used to determine and manage appropriate levels of resources.

Resource management ensures that an appropriate level of resources is used on the project. Two types of resources are used on projects:

- Replenishable: when absent or used up, fresh supplies can be obtained. Raw materials and money are common examples.
- Re-usable: when no longer needed, these resources become available for other uses. Accommodation, machines, test equipment and people are re-usable.

Projects consume resources that have to be available at the right time, in the right quantities and of the right quality. The challenge for resource management is determining what is 'right'. It is often the case that projects do not own resources; they have to work with resource providers to obtain the resources needed by the project. Resource management includes resource allocation, resource smoothing, resource levelling and resource scheduling.

Resource allocation is the process by which resources are mapped against activities, often shown as aggregated resource histograms against a timescale.

Resource smoothing[1] can be applied to ensure that resources are used as efficiently as possible. This involves utilising float within the project or increasing or decreasing the resources required for specific activities, so that any peaks and troughs of resource usage are smoothed out. It does not affect the project duration.

Resource levelling[2] can be applied when there are resource constraints. Resource levelling forces the amount of work scheduled to not exceed the limits of resources available. This results in either activity durations being extended or entire activities being delayed to periods when resources are available. Resource levelling often results in a longer project duration.

Resource scheduling ensures that resources are available when needed and where possible are not underutilised.

Resource allocation and resource smoothing or levelling are iterated until a balance between resource availability and required project duration is achieved.

---

[1] Also called time-limited scheduling.
[2] Also called resource-limited scheduling.

Changes to the project will require the impact on resources to be considered as part of change control (Topic 3.5).

Effective resource management ensures:

- efficient utilisation of resources;
- confidence that the schedule is realistic in terms of the required and available resources;
- the early identification of resource capacity bottlenecks and conflicts.

Further reading

Bower, Joseph L. and Gilbert, Clark G. (2005) *From Resource Allocation to Strategy*, Oxford University Press, Oxford, ISBN 0–19–927744–3

Burke, R. (2003) *Project Management: Planning and Control Techniques*, 4th edn, Wiley, Hoboken, NJ, ISBN 0–470–85124–4

Devaux, S. A. (1999), *Total Project Control: A Manager's Guide to Integrated Project Planning, Measurement and Tracking*, Wiley, New York, ISBN 0–471–32859–6

Lock, D. (2003) *Project Management*, 8th edn, Gower, Aldershot, ISBN 0–566–08551–8

Pennypacker, J. S. and Dye, L. D. (2002) *Managing Multiple Projects: Planning, Scheduling and Allocating Resources for Competitive Advantage*, Marcel Dekker, New York, ISBN 0–8247–0680–3

Schwindt, Christoph (2005) *Resource Allocation in Project Management*, Springer, Berlin, ISBN 3–540–25410–2

3.4

Budgeting and cost management

Budgeting and cost management is the estimating of costs and the setting of an agreed budget, and the management of actual and forecast costs against that budget.

An initial cost estimate is included in the business case, and used as part of the investment appraisal of the project. This initial cost estimate is refined in line with scope, schedule and resources. The results of this refinement will produce an overall cost estimate that should include an allowance for risk and contingency. The cost estimate will need to be iteratively revised to suit the constraints of the business case. When the cost estimate has been agreed with the sponsor, this becomes the budget.

For effective cost management, costs incurred should be directly attributable to a budget item. This alignment between budget and cost is usually achieved through the use of a cost breakdown structure (CBS).

The budget is phased over time to give a profile of expenditure. This is an important part of the budgeting process as the profile of expenditure is used in project financing and funding. It will allow a cash flow forecast for the project to be developed, and a drawdown of funds to be agreed with the organisation.

Cost management is the monitoring and control of costs against the budget. Cost management will require the recording and monitoring of the following:

- Commitment: this reflects the placement of an order for work to be done, and is the amount of money removed from the budget represented by this order.
- Accrual: work done for which payment is due but has not been made.
- Actual expenditure: the money that has already been paid.
- Forecast out-turn cost: the total of actual expenditure, accruals, commitments and the estimate of the costs to complete the work to the end of the project.

As part of monitoring, the performance of a project is reviewed at regular intervals. Reviews should consider non-financial information such as scope and schedule, to assist with the assessment of cost performance. By comparing actual cost against total budget and the expenditure profile, trends may be identified that can be extended to determine the forecast out-turn cost. Identifying and taking corrective action to minimise adverse variances against budget is necessary for effective control. Such reviews form part of earned value management (Topic 3.6).

The budget should be reviewed at appropriate points, for example as part of periodic reporting and at gate reviews, and any change to the budget should only be undertaken as part of change control (Topic 3.5).

Further reading

APM Earned Value SIG (2002) *Earned Value Management: APM Guidelines*, APM Publishing, Princes Risborough, ISBN 1–903494–26–5

Cappels, Thomas (2003) *Financially Focused Project Management*, J. Ross Publishing, Fort Lauderdale, FL, ISBN 1–932159–09–6

Goldsmith, Larry (2005) *Project Management Accounting: Budgeting, Tracking, and Reporting Costs and Profitability*, Wiley, Chichester, ISBN 0–471–71184–5

Rad, P. F. (2001) *Project Estimating and Cost Management*, Management Concepts, Vienna, VA ISBN 1–56726–144–2

Stenzel, Catherine and Stenzel, Joe (2002) *Essentials of Cost Management*, Wiley, New York, ISBN 0–471–22734–X

Taylor, J. C. (2005) *Project Cost Estimating Tools, Techniques and Perspectives*, St Lucie Press, Boca Raton, FL, ISBN 1–57444–342–9

3.5

Change control

Change control is the process that ensures that all changes made to a project's baselined scope, time, cost and quality objectives or agreed benefits are identified, evaluated, approved, rejected or deferred.

Robust procedures are used to produce a baseline definition of project plans, which are encompassed in the project management plan (PMP). Any proposed changes to this baseline need to go through a similarly robust procedure to ensure that changes to the project are identified, evaluated, approved, rejected or deferred.

A change may be proposed by any project stakeholder. Change may be unavoidable or highly desirable; it may equally be unnecessary and not useful. Any proposed change to the project must be formally controlled. The project team, with the appropriate support of relevant stakeholders including the sponsor, should therefore review changes fully before their approval and actioning. The impact of changes on all aspects of the project should be carefully assessed as well as their impact on business-as-usual and other projects. All approved changes should be fully documented and efficiently communicated.

The project must have an effective change control process in operation and the project team should be familiar with its operation. It is the project manager's responsibility to ensure that a change control process is used in the project.

A change control process should include the following:

- Change request: a stakeholder who is requesting change provides relevant information on the nature of the change.[1] The change is entered into a change log, which is[2] a register of all changes that have been requested whatever their status, for example pending, approved, rejected or deferred.
- Initial evaluation: the change is reviewed to consider if it is worthwhile evaluating it in detail. The evaluation of change consumes resources, which in itself is a deviation from the project plan. The proposed change may be rejected without further evaluation.
- Detailed evaluation: the change is evaluated to consider the impact on the project's baselined scope, time, cost or quality objectives or agreed benefits.

[1] This may be described on a change request form.
[2] In PRINCE2 all potential changes are entered into an issue log not a change log.

- Recommendation: a recommendation is made as to whether the change should be approved, rejected or deferred. The sponsor has ultimate authority to act on the recommendation. The decision must be communicated.
- Update plans: if a change is approved, all plans are updated to reflect the change.
- Implement: the necessary actions to implement the change are undertaken.

If an unauthorised change is identified it should be retrospectively put through the change control process.

Change control is intrinsically linked to configuration management. Any changes will need to be fed back into the project's configuration (Topic 4.7).

In certain circumstances, it is appropriate to have a change freeze on a project where no further changes will be considered as to do so would jeopardise the achievement of the project objectives.

Further reading

APM Earned Value SIG (2002) *Earned Value Management: APM Guidelines*, APM Publishing, Princes Risborough, ISBN 1–903494–26–5

Field, M. and Keller, L. (1997) *Project Management*, Thomson Learning, London, ISBN 1–86152–274–6

Office of Government Commerce (2005) *Managing Successful Projects with PRINCE2*, Stationery Office, London, ISBN 0–11–330946–5

3.6

Earned value management

Earned value management (EVM) is a project control process based on a struc-tured approach to planning, cost collection and performance measurement. It facilitates the integration of project scope, time and cost objectives and the estab-lishment of a baseline plan for performance measurement.

EVM is used to inform management decisions on a project. It necessitates the integration of project scope, time and cost objectives and the establish-ment of baselined plans against which physical performance can be meas-ured during the execution of a project. Furthermore, it provides a sound basis for problem identification, corrective actions and replanning as required.

The fundamental elements of project management that need to be in place for EVM to be used are as follows:

- A work breakdown structure (WBS) to define the work.
- Organisational responsibility for work accomplishment defined in an organisational breakdown structure (OBS), drawing information from the WBS.
- The budget distributed in the WBS.
- All authorised work scheduled.
- A method of measuring achievement.
- The budget phased over time against the schedule to provide a profile of expenditure.
- Baselined plans: this may require an integrated baseline review (IBR) to be held following the establishment of the initial baseline.
- Costs identified as either direct or indirect costs, and all direct costs recorded.[1]
- Performance data collected and analysed on a periodic basis.
- Forecasts for the remaining work produced.
- Any changes to the baseline managed through a change control process.

Conventional scheduling and also budgeting and cost management will inform the project manager what budget has been spent and what activities have been completed or are in progress. However, this does not provide a per-formance measure. EVM provides this measure of performance and allows future performance to be predicted based on current variances and trends.

The purpose of measuring earned value is to provide information in order to determine:

---

[1] Earned value management is associated with physical work and therefore only direct costs are relevant.

- what has been achieved of the planned work;
- what it has cost to achieve the planned work;
- whether the work achieved is costing more or less than was planned;
- whether the project is ahead or behind the planned schedule.

Using this measure of earned value, EVM will provide:

- ongoing performance measurement;
- variance and trend analysis;
- measures of efficiency;
- prediction of outturn cost and final duration;
- information to assess whether corrective actions are required.

EVM will accurately show deviations from the baselined plans, but it may not be immediately evident that the plan is flawed. Accurate management information can only be extracted if accurate management information is in place from the start of the project.

Further reading

APM Earned Value SIG (2002) *Earned Value Management: APM Guidelines*, APM Publishing, Princes Risborough, ISBN 1–903494–26–5

British Standards Institution (2002) BS 6079–1: 2002 A Guide to Project Management, BSI, London

Fleming, Quentin W. and Koppelman, Joel M. (2000) *Earned Value Project Management*, 2nd edn, Project Management Institute, Newton Square, PA, ISBN 1–880410–27–3

Wake, S. (2004) *Earned Value Analysis in the UK*, 7th edn, (available from the author)

Webb, Alan (2003) *Using Earned Value: A Project Manager's Guide*, Gower, Aldershot, ISBN 0–566–08533–X

3.7

Information management and reporting

Information management is the collection, storage, dissemination, archiving and appropriate destruction of project information. Information reporting takes information and presents it in an appropriate format which includes the formal communication of project information to stakeholders.

Projects generate, utilise and absorb significant quantities of information. It is important that there is an appropriate process in place to manage the information. In managing information, consideration also needs to be given to communication (Topic 7.1) and formal reporting to stakeholders.

Without the availability of appropriate, timely and accurate information,[1] projects would necessarily be chaotic and any decisions taken would be merely arbitrary, even capricious.

Information is collected in order to provide a central repository for the project, and a means of controlling information flow. Information may need to be actively sought, rather than being automatically delivered into the project.

A decision is made as to what information it is appropriate to store, and how to store it so that it can be readily accessed and retrieved by relevant people or systems. Information that is collected but does not need to be stored is destroyed in accordance with an agreed procedure.[2]

Dissemination involves the distribution of existing information and the conversion of data to information for distribution. Data converted into information and disseminated in the form of reports is part of reporting. Reporting is the process by which stakeholders are kept informed about the project, as included in the communication plan (Topic 7.1). Reports will include reports of progress, quality, audit, project reviews, risk assessment and finances. To reduce the burden of reporting the use of exception reports should be considered.

Information is archived throughout the project life cycle. This allows for information to be removed from immediately accessible storage to an archive where it is no longer as readily accessible.

Information management changes during the project life cycle in terms of understanding what is needed, who to disseminate information to, when to

---

[1] A distinction can be made between document management, i.e. how information is created and shared, and records management, which is ensuring that the project observes necessary policy, legislative or regulatory requirements.
[2] Careful consideration should be given to the destruction of information; for example, can paper be recycled or must it be destroyed to protect confidentiality?

issue information and when to destroy it. However, pertinent information must adhere to the communication plan.

Further complexity arises when considering commercial confidentiality and statutory obligations such as information security and freedom of information. Information management in a project needs to integrate with the organisation's information management process.

A decision must be made as to the granularity of information that should be collected, stored and archived. Information that is no longer required can be destroyed in accordance with an agreed procedure.

The use to which information will be put post-project should be considered. It will be the case that some information generated during the project will be beneficial to the organisation in its following business-as-usual activities and when undertaking similar projects.

Further reading

Buttrick, R. (2005) *Project Workout: A Toolkit for Reaping the Rewards of All Your Business Projects*, 3rd edn, FT Prentice Hall, London, ISBN 0–273–68181–8

Gardiner, P. (2005) *Project Management: A Strategic Management Approach*, Palgrave Macmillan, Basingstoke, ISBN 0–333–98222–3

International Standards Organization (2002) ISO/IEC 15288-System Life Cycle Processes, BSI, London

Laudon, Kenneth C. and Laudon, Jane P. (2003) *Management Information Systems*, 8th edn, Prentice Hall, London, ISBN 0–131–01498–6

3.8

Issue management

Issue management is the process by which concerns that threaten the project objectives and cannot be resolved by the project manager are identified and addressed to remove the threats they pose.

An issue[1] is defined as a threat to the project objectives that cannot be resolved by the project manager. Issues should be differentiated from problems, which are concerns that the project manager has to deal with on a day-to-day basis. Risks should not be confused with issues. Risks are uncertain in that an event may not occur, whereas issues have already occurred and are therefore not uncertain (Topic 2.5).

The importance of issue management in projects is that issues are outside the direct control of the project manager. The project manager must ensure that issues are escalated to the sponsor who may in turn escalate them to the project steering group so that resolution can be reached. Issues that remain unaddressed or unresolved are the cause of many project failures. Consequently, the project manager must ensure that issues are identified, escalated appropriately and resolved. Stakeholder management (Topic 2.2) is used to formulate and present issues in ways that the owner (not necessarily the project manager) of the issue can recognise and thus assists them in issue resolution.

An issue log is used to track the progress of the issue from identification to resolution. For each issue, the issue log should describe the issue, who raised it, the date the issue was formally raised, possible consequences or impacts on the project, possible resolution and the resolution owner, the final outcome and date the issue is closed.

Issue resolution is one of the fundamental purposes of a project steering group (Topic 6.8). The appropriateness of the constituency of the project steering group can be judged by whether its members are capable of dealing with the issues as they arise. Monitoring and reporting to the project steering group the 'ageing' of issues is an activity performed by or for the project manager.

Common failures in the management of issues are:

- wrongly identifying as issues project problems that are the responsibility of the project manager. This diverts attention away from handling genuine issues;

---

[1] There are alternative definitions of an issue, for example 'any major problem that the project team has to deal with'. In PRINCE2 an issue is a term used to cover any concern, query, request for change, suggestion or off-specification raised during a project, and an issue can be about anything to do with the project.

■ failing to further escalate an issue when the owner of the issue resolution has not resolved it in a timely manner.

Further reading

Buttrick, R. (2005) *Project Workout: A Toolkit for Reaping the Rewards of All Your Business Projects*, 3rd edn, FT Prentice Hall, London, ISBN 0–273–68181–8

Maylor, H. (2005) *Project Management*, FT Prentice Hall, London, ISBN 0–273–70431–1

Office of Government Commerce (2005) *Managing Successful Projects with PRINCE2*, Stationery Office, London, ISBN 0–11–330946–5

Section 4

Techniques

In project management a number of techniques are used to assist in the successful delivery of project objectives. Some of these techniques are equally applicable to all projects while others are more suited to specific types of projects.

The techniques that are described here enable the project manager to:

- fully define users' requirements (Topic 4.1 – Requirements management);
- take an initial, preferred solution and refine it into an optimal solution (Topic 4.2 – Development);
- estimate the project's cost and time objectives (Topic 4.3 – Estimating);
- use technology appropriately throughout the project life cycle (Topic 4.4 – Technology management);
- ensure the continued application of best value (Topic 4.5 – Value engineering);
- model and test deliverables prior to handover and closeout of the project (Topic 4.6 – Modelling and testing);
- ensure that a project's deliverables are developed in such a way that their configuration is clearly controlled (Topic 4.7 – Configuration management).

4.1

Requirements management

Requirements management is the process of capturing, analysing and testing the documented statement of stakeholder and user wants and needs. Requirements are a statement of the need that a project has to satisfy, and should be comprehensive, clear, well structured, traceable and testable.

In a project, the stakeholders' and, in particular, users' wants and needs are documented as requirements. A clear and agreed expression of requirements and their acceptance criteria is essential for success as this manages stakeholder expectations and provides a measure against which project success can be judged.

Requirements should have an emphasis on 'what' is required, rather than 'how' it will be achieved. High-level requirements are documented during the concept phase of the project life cycle; they are further developed and agreed during the definition phase. The preferred solution that meets the need, problem or opportunity is tested against the requirements' acceptance criteria for fitness for purpose or conformance.

Requirements management includes the following:

- Capture: eliciting, structuring and documenting the requirements and related acceptance criteria.
- Analysis: agreeing the priority of requirements, taking into consideration benefits, business priorities, availability of resources and budget. The prioritised requirements should be evaluated to ensure that they meet the project objectives and will deliver the benefits that justify proceeding with the project.
- Testing: the structure and content of the documented requirements need to appeal to different people, with an expectation that testing of the requirements through reviews will be undertaken.

The primary factors used to structure the content of the requirements are as follows:

- Value – the size of the benefit associated with each requirement.
- Priority – stakeholders agree the priority ordering of requirements.
- Time – business time imperatives drive the ordering of the requirements.
- Process – the way the solution is to be built, particularly important where subcontractors will be used to build some components.

The agreed requirements are used as a baseline for change control, and as the basis for implementing the solution. Proposed changes should be reviewed and documented, where accepted as a change. Configuration management needs to take into account changes in requirements.

A common understanding of the requirements by the project manager and project team is fundamental to ensuring that the wants and needs are captured and clearly articulated, and that solutions are developed to meet those needs.

Further reading

Alexander, I. and Stevens, R. (2002) *Writing Better Requirements*, Addison-Wesley, Boston, MA, ISBN 0–321–13163–0

Blyth, A. and Worthington, J. (2001) *Managing the Brief for Better Design*, Spon, London, ISBN 0–419–25130–8

Forsberg, K., Mooz, H. and Cotterman, H. (2000) *Visualizing Project Management: A Model for Business and Technical Success* 2nd edn, Wiley, New York, ISBN 0–471–35760–X

Office of Government Commerce (2005) *Managing Successful Projects with PRINCE2*, Stationery Office, London, ISBN 0–11–330946–5

Robertson, S. and Robertson, J. (2004) *Requirements-led Project Management: Discovering David's Slingshot*, Addison-Wesley, Boston, MA, ISBN 0–321–18062–3

Robertson, S. and Robertson, J. (1999) *Mastering the Requirements Process*, Addison-Wesley, Boston, MA ISBN 0–201–36046–2

4.2

Development

Development is the progressive working up of a preferred solution to an opti-mised solution during the definition and implementation phases. The opti-mised solution is refined with the stakeholders against the requirements.

Alternative designs to meet the preferred solution will be developed using an iterative approach. The project team should work to shape the proposed solution in ways that optimise satisfaction of the requirements and their acceptance criteria, and help to achieve project success. The project manager should ensure that the correct processes and practices are being followed and that the impact on scope, time, cost and quality is being managed.

Engagement with stakeholders and users throughout the development process is essential to maintain commitment and manage expectations as the solution develops.

Uncertainties and technical innovations in the solution need to be consid-ered. These can increase risk and may result in delays, increased cost or unworkable solutions. Strategies to support innovation include: pilots or prototyping, where the innovation is explored without impacting the opera-tional environment and to minimise risk to the project; the use of modelling and simulations; and phased implementations of new technology.

As the project proceeds from definition to implementation, application of a phased development approach should be used with design documentation reviews, quality reviews, lessons learned reviews and validations against the requirements.

There are a number of structured methodologies to assist in the develop-ment of an optimised solution. For example development of information systems offers a variety of development methodologies:

- The structured systems analysis and design methodology (SSADM) uses modelling techniques to identify, model and document the solution in a waterfall model.
- The dynamic systems development method (DSDM) advocates an itera-tive approach. An iteration involves timeboxing, prototyping, workshops and testing.
- Agile development methodologies are a family of methodologies where the development emphasises real time communication and software.

In the construction industry[1] the development approach is iterative. A client brief containing requirements and high-level solutions is prepared and

---

[1] The Office of Government Commerce has produced a series of guides called Achieving Excellence in Construction which aims at improving government performance.

agreed. The project team uses techniques such as value management and value engineering to optimise the solutions into detailed design drawings and specifications. Optimisation will be undertaken on an iterative basis, with solutions being refined with the stakeholders.

For all projects, progressive testing of the emerging solution against the requirements ensures continual management of the solution development. Validation against overall requirements and verification against specifications and designs are both important. Verification ensures the deliverable is being built right; validation ensures that the right deliverable is being built.

Further reading

Augustine, S. (2005) *Managing Agile Projects*, Prentice Hall PTR, London, ISBN 0–131–24071–4

Mooz, H., Horsberg, K. and Cotterman, H. (2003) *Communicating Project Management: The Integrated Vocabulary of Project Management and Systems Engineering*, Wiley, Hoboken, NJ, ISBN 0–471–26924–7

Stapleton, J. (2002) *DSDM: A Framework for Business Centred Development*, Addison Wesley, Boston, MA, ISBN 0–321–11224–5

Weaver, P., Lambrou, N. and Walkley, M. (2002) *Practical Business Systems Development using SSADM: A Complete Tutorial Guide*, FT Prentice Hall, London, ISBN 0–273–65575–2

Wells, T. (2002) *Dynamic Software Development: Managing Projects in Flux*, CRC Press, Boca Raton, FL, ISBN 0–8493–1292 2

4.3

Estimating

Estimating uses a range of tools and techniques to produce estimates. An estimate is an approximation of project time and cost targets that is refined throughout the project life cycle.

At the concept phase of a project establishing cost and time targets is difficult due to lack of detailed information. It is important that targets are based on a rationale that is informed by a structured reasoning process or methodology.

There are three primary methods of estimating:

- bottom-up;
- comparative;
- parametric.

The bottom-up (analytical) method uses the project work breakdown structure (WBS) derived to a level of detail that allows estimates of cost and time for the project activities to be provided. Once estimates for each activity have been agreed and contingencies applied the overall project targets can be established.

Comparative or analogous estimating uses historic data from similar projects to determine the most appropriate cost and time. The data are compared by scaling of size, complexity and type of technology employed to determine a more informed estimate of the project's budget and schedule parameters.

Parametric estimating uses defined parameters by which a project can be measured, for example the cost or time to build a single deliverable, with this figure then being multiplied depending on the number of such parameters required. This method of estimating is typically used in statistical modelling.

Estimating can be presented in different ways. Single or deterministic estimates do not account for estimating error, human influence or data inconsistencies. A three-point estimate accepts variation in project values starting with the most likely mid-range value, setting an aggressive optimistic target as the minimum end of range value and a pessimistic view as the maximum end of the range.

An estimate is about a future event and therefore involves uncertainty. Some estimates have a contingency associated with them to cover risks and uncertainties. As the project develops and additional information about the requirements and circumstances become available, uncertainty will decrease, the estimate can be refined[1] and contingencies may be released.

---

[1] This progressive reduction in uncertainty may be described using the concept of the estimating funnel.

Estimating is not an activity restricted to the early phases of a project life cycle. Estimates of the impact of change requests, the cost and time to complete the project and risk responses will be required later in the project life cycle.

Further reading

Lewis, J. P. (2005) *Project Planning, Scheduling and Control*, 4th edn, McGraw Hill, New York, ISBN 0–07–146037–3

Rad, P. F. (2001) *Project Estimating and Cost Management*, Management Concepts, Vienna, VA, ISBN 1–56726–144–2

Stutzke, R. (2005) *Software Project Estimation: Projects, Products, and Processes*, Addison Wesley, Boston, MA, ISBN 0–201–70312–2

Taylor, J. C. (2005) *Project Cost Estimating Tools, Techniques and Perspectives*, St Lucie Press, Boco Raton, FL, ISBN 1–57444–342–9

4.4

Technology management

Technology management is the management of the relationship between available and emerging technologies, the organisation and the project. It also includes management of the enabling technologies used to deliver the project, technologies used to manage the project and the technology of the project deliverables.

Technology and its uses evolve at a rapid pace and there are multiple types of technologies, for example computer operating systems, mobile telephones, and Web enabled business processes. Different technology can create opportunities for new approaches and products but can also introduce threats, both of which must be managed.

The organisation's strategic objectives take account of available and emerging technologies both inside and outside the organisation. Organisational strategy will determine how best to align with these technologies.

Technology management for projects can occur at different levels, for example:

- as part of the organisation's strategic objectives, and the translation of these into the project's objectives;
- to deliver the project, for example enabling technology such as software and equipment used by the project;
- to manage the project, for example tools for reporting, scheduling and risk management;
- as the technological deliverables resulting from the project and written into its requirements.

Failure in technology management at any of these levels may have an impact on the project and organisation.

If the project has not been aligned to the organisation's strategic objectives for technology management, the project may achieve its acceptance criteria, but will not realise long-term benefits for the organisation.

An initial assessment will be made as to the most suitable enabling technologies to use on a project. This selection will take into account factors such as cost, time and availability of skills to use the technology. Any failure in the enabling technology may result in the project not meeting its objectives. For example scarcity of skills may result in the technology being unusable or used incorrectly.

Technologies used to manage the project can be important in monitoring and controlling progress, information management and reporting. Failure in these managerial technologies can also result in the project being poorly managed and the organisation not recognising the project's true status.

All projects plan for success. However, when using innovative technologies there is uncertainty as to whether success can be achieved. At handover the deliverables may not be able to enter the operational phase due to a failure of technology. When a new technology product is the deliverable of the project, a failure of the technology generally results in a failure overall.

Further reading

Flyvbjerg, B., Bruzelius, N. and Rothengatter, W. (2003) *Megaprojects and Risk: An Anatomy of Ambition*, Cambridge University Press, Cambridge, ISBN 0–521–80420–5

Liefer, R. *et al.* (2001) *Radical Innovation: How Mature Companies can Outsmart Upstarts*, Harvard Business Press, Boston, MA, ISBN 0–87584–903–2

Webb, A. (2000) *Project Management for Successful Product Innovation*, Gower, Aldershot, ISBN 0–566–08262–4

4.5

Value engineering

Value engineering is concerned with optimising the conceptual, technical and operational aspects of a project's deliverables. Value engineering utilises a series of proven techniques during the implementation phase of a project.

Value engineering is a subset of value management (Topic 2.3) and deals with the generation or revision of technical solutions, i.e. the 'how' as in how to achieve the desired functionality at an appropriate cost. Value management is concerned with the optimisation of strategic requirements issues and the 'what', i.e. what needs to be improved, what change is required.

The value engineering process, as illustrated in Figure 4.1, incorporates the following activities:

- Functional analysis: to identify and select the functional attributes of different solutions.
- Detailed design: to evolve a small number of alternative solutions for delivering the functional attributes.

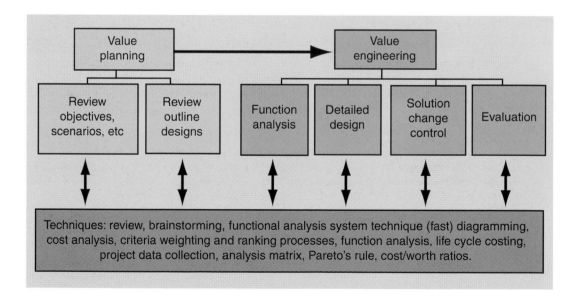

Figure 4.1 The value management process BS EN 12973:2000 (*reproduced with the permission of the BSI*)

- Solution change control: analysis and evaluation of alternative solutions that arise during the implementation stage as new information becomes available, and the control of any solution changes.
- Evaluation: of the outcome and the contribution of the value management process, including whether the objectives defined were achieved, where the most improvements were made in functionality and identification of any lessons for the future.

The process may be applied as a series of workshops or studies at key points in the project. Considered, rightly, as an attitude of mind, formal value engineering involves a formal approach to the improvement of solutions (see requirements management (Topic 4.1) and development (Topic 4.2)). It is achieved through teamwork in a workshop environment, using a plan of work based on problem-solving and creative thinking. The format of each of these workshops can be subdivided into the following distinct value engineering phases:

- Information – confirm the project time, cost and quality objectives.
- Function analysis – agree the project function and available resources.
- Speculation – idea generation to identify value opportunities.
- Idea evaluation – rank the identified opportunities according to their appropriateness.
- Idea development – develop the evaluated opportunities to understand their benefits and costs.
- Implementation – decision building and action-planning to establish the way forward.

Further reading

British Standards Institution (1997) BS EN 1325–1:1997 Value Management. Value analysis, functional analysis vocabulary, BSI, London

British Standards Institution (2000) BS EN 12973:2000 Value Management, European Committee for Standardisation (CEN) Technical Committee CEN/TC 279, BSI, London

Office of Government Commerce (2002) *Value for Money Evaluation in Complex Procurements*, OGC, Norwich (available free – OGC publication code: CPO033)

Office of Government Commerce (2003) Achieving Excellence in Construction, No 6 Risk and Value Management, Stationery Office, London

Woodhead, R. M. and McCuish, J. D. (2002) *Achieving Results. How to Create Value*, Thomas Telford, London, ISBN 0–7277–3184–X

4.6

Modelling and testing

Modelling and testing are used to provide a representation and assurance of whether the project objectives can be achieved. Modelling is the process of creating and using a device that duplicates the physical or operational aspects of a deliverable. Testing is the process of determining how aspects of a deliverable perform when subjected to specified conditions.

Modelling may be either physical or virtual. Physical models represent the three-dimensional, solid aspects of a deliverable and can be used to display its features or potentially test aspects of it. Virtual models provide a visual representation of a deliverable and can also be used to test its operational performance. Virtual models can be essential to the development of dynamic systems particularly if continuous human interaction with a computerised system is required, for example a flight simulator. Models can also be useful when communicating the appearance or functioning of a deliverable to a wide audience whose support or contribution may be necessary for the project to succeed.

Testing is the activity performed to ensure that the deliverables will meet their acceptance criteria. Testing may be performed on the actual deliverable, on a test deliverable or on a model. Testing can be used to verify whether deliverables meet requirements and to validate that the final deliverable is fit for purpose.

Testing will not provide a complete answer to uncertainty. Test plans are normally designed around the extremes of certain aspects and conditions that a deliverable might have to perform and be subjected to, and other aspects based on a reasoned assessment of what might occur. Failures in operation can still happen if conditions arise that are outside of those considered reasonable or were not recognised as significant at the time tests were conducted.

All project plans must include the need for testing in terms of criteria, responsibilities, budgets and time provisions where areas of uncertainty exist. A project plan must ensure that knowledge is gained through testing in a logical manner and that design decisions taken at one stage are based on information discovered in earlier stages. A robust and logical approach can be generated to manage technical, cost and schedule risks.

Modelling and testing may not be a matter over which the project manager has discretion; for many projects, certain testing is mandatory or regulatory.

Modelling and testing are fundamental aspects of quality management. They form an integral part of quality control and quality assurance (Topic 2.6).

Further reading

Black, R. (2002) *Managing the Testing Process: Practical Tools and Techniques for Managing Hardware and Software Testing*, 2nd edn, Wiley, New York, ISBN 0–471–22398–0

Pidd, M. (2004) *Systems Modelling: Theory and Practice*, Wiley, Chichester, ISBN 0–470–86731–0

Williams, T. (2002) *Modelling Complex Projects*, Wiley, New York, ISBN 0–471–89945–3

4.7

Configuration management

Configuration management comprises the technical and administrative activities concerned with the creation, maintenance and controlled change of the configuration throughout the project life cycle.

A configuration is the functional and physical characteristics of the final deliverable as defined in technical documents and achieved in the execution of project plans. These plans should contain all items that can be identified as being relevant to the project and that should only be modified after relevant authorisation.

Configuration management can therefore be regarded as asset control and is essential whether one or more versions of a deliverable will be created. At its simplest, configuration management must involve version control.

Five activities are performed within a configuration management process:

- Configuration management planning: a configuration management plan should describe any project-specific procedures and the extent of their application during the life cycle of the project. The plan should also identify roles and responsibilities for carrying out configuration management.
- Configuration identification: involves breaking down the project into component parts or configuration items and creating a unique numbering or referencing system for each item, and establishing configuration baselines.
- Configuration control: ensures that all changes to configuration items are controlled. An important aspect is being able to identify the interrelationships between configuration items.
- Configuration status accounting: provides records and reports that relate to a deliverable and its configuration information during the life cycle of the project. It also enables traceability of configuration items throughout their development.
- Configuration audit: is used to determine whether a deliverable conforms to its requirements and configuration information. Typically an audit is a review undertaken at the end of a phase or stage and at the end of the handover and closeout phase of the project.

The configuration management process must be closely aligned to the change control process (Topic 3.5) as a key aspect is the ability to identify, track and protect different versions of a deliverable. Together, these aspects will have a significant impact on the quality of a project's deliverables (Topic 2.6).

Configuration management is an invaluable tool to the project manager to provide control of the project deliverables and to avoid mistakes and misunderstandings. It is an integral part of a project's quality plan.

Further reading

British Standards Institution (2003) BS ISO 10007:2003 Quality management systems. Guidelines for configuration management, BSI, London

Field, M. and Keller, L. (1997) *Project Management*, Thomson Learning, London, ISBN 1–86152–274–6

Office of Government Commerce (2005) *Managing Successful Projects with PRINCE2*, Stationery Office, London, ISBN 0–11–330946–5

Section 5

Business and commercial

It is important to take account of the business and commercial environment within which a project operates. This environment can be set by the project or imposed on it by the organisation's standard practices.

The business and commercial environment is established by considering and understanding a number of aspects:

- How an organisation ensures that the benefits generated by a project will be commensurate with their investment (Topic 5.1 – Business case).
- How project management professionals can market and sell their project to decision makers to secure a competitive advantage (Topic 5.2 – Marketing and sales).
- How a project can acquire the necessary financing and funding (Topic 5.3 – Project financing and funding).
- How to develop and implement a strategy to procure resources for the project (Topic 5.4 – Procurement).
- An awareness of a range of legal issues (Topic 5.5 – Legal awareness).

5.1

Business case

The business case provides justification for undertaking a project, in terms of evaluating the benefit, cost and risk of alternative options and rationale for the preferred solution. Its purpose is to obtain management commitment and approval for investment in the project. The business case is owned by the sponsor.

The business case sets out the justification and the strategic rationale for the project, and provides a framework for informed decision-making in planning and managing the project and its subsequent benefits realisation. Its basis is an evidence-based evaluation of the benefit, costs and risk of a solution to a need, problem or opportunity identified by the sponsor and approved by the funding organisation.

The business case must clearly articulate the balance between the benefits sought and the costs and risks of achieving those benefits. The benefits should relate to the level of risk and the cost of the project that the organisation is willing to accept. A high-risk project is only worth doing if the benefits are proportionally high: for a given level of benefits there is a limit on the level of risk that could be sustained and the cost of the project should be proportional to the expected benefits.

The business case is owned by the sponsor and is created during the concept phase of the project life cycle. It should be kept up to date and used as the basis for decisions as to whether to continue with the project at gates and project reviews.

The contents of the business case will include:

- reason for the project;
- high level description of the project scope;
- evaluation of options, including the 'do nothing' option;
- benefits;
- risks;
- estimated costs;
- target schedule;
- investment appraisal;
- assumptions;
- constraints;
- dependencies;
- project success criteria;
- impact on business-as-usual.

In practice it is good to evaluate more than one viable alternative solution and compare the benefits capable of being delivered by each solution. The evaluation process may include the use of investment appraisal techniques such as payback, internal rate of return (IRR), discounted cash flow (DCF) and net present value (NPV) to provide a like-for-like comparison of options.

The project manager may not be involved in the preparation of the business case but should have an understanding of it and be able to convey this understanding to the project team.

Further reading

Buttrick, R. (2005) *Project Workout: A Toolkit for Reaping the Rewards of All Your Business Projects*, 3rd edn, FT Prentice Hall, London, ISBN 0-273-68181-8

Graves, Samuel B. and Ringuest, Jeffrey L. (2002) *Models & Methods for Project Selection: Concepts from Management Science, Finance and Information Technology*, Springer, Berlin ISBN: 1-4020-7280-5

H. M. Treasury (2003) *The Green Book: Appraisal and Evaluation in Central Government*, Stationery Office, London, ISBN 0-11-560107-4

Manganelli, R. and Hagen, B. (2003) *Solving the Corporate Value Enigma: A System to Unlock Shareholder Value*, AMACOM, New York, ISBN 0-8144-0692-0

Rogers, M. (2001) *Engineering Projects Appraisal*, Blackwell Science, Oxford, ISBN 0-632-05606-1

Scholes, K., Johnson, G. and Whittington, R. (2004) *Exploring Corporate Strategy: Text and Cases*, FT Prentice-Hall, London, ISBN 0-273-68789-5

5.2

Marketing and sales

Marketing involves anticipating the demands of users and identifying and satisfying their needs by providing the right project at the right time, cost and quality. Sales is a marketing technique used to promote a project. Marketing and sales needs to be undertaken internally and possibly externally to an organisation.

The project team will be involved in both marketing and selling the project to the organisation. If there is a need to market and sell the project outside the organisation, team members may again be involved.

As the advocate for the project the sponsor must market and promote the project to the organisation. This could require influencing a project's position in the organisation (Topic 1.3) or assisting in securing appropriate resources (Topic 3.3).

The project manager needs to use selling techniques to achieve buy-in from stakeholders, the project team and users for the project's approach and decisions made. In selling the project strategy to the organisation the project manager will use negotiation and influencing skills. Effective communication is fundamental, and consideration must be given to the audience, objectives, timing and method of communication, which will be described in the communication plan.

The project may need to be marketed outside the organisation to sell the deliverables to the external market. The project manager may need to draw on marketing expertise available within the organisation or externally to do this work. One of the deliverables of the project may then be a marketing strategy.

The marketing strategy may be based on market research, and empirical knowledge of the environment. The external and internal environment is understood in terms of project context (Topic 1.4). The marketing strategy defines the emphasis and allocation of resources to best meet the objectives of the organisation within project constraints, for example time, cost, quality and resources.

Marketing and sales activities are helpful in understanding the organisation and its relationship to the project. These activities can assist in satisfying the needs of internal and external stakeholders. The success of many of the deliverables of a project relies on their performance within a competitive environment. Understanding how marketing can be applied facilitates the promotion of these deliverables throughout the project's life cycle.

Further reading

Cova, B., Ghauri, P. and Salle, R. (2002) *Project Marketing: Beyond Competitive Bidding*, Wiley, Chichester, ISBN 0-471-48664-6

Emerick, Donald and Round, Kimberlee (2000) *Exploring Web Marketing and Project Management*, Prentice Hall PTR, Upper Saddle River, NJ, ISBN 0-13-016396-1

Kotler, P. (2001) *Kotler on Marketing*, Free Press, New York, ISBN 0-684-86047-3

Kotler, Philip, Bloom, Paul and Hayes, Thomas (2002) *Marketing Professional Services*, Prentice Hall, Upper Saddle River, NJ, ISBN, 0-7352-0179-X

Lancaster, Geoff and Jobber, David (2000) *Selling and Sales Management*, 5th edn, FT Prentice Hall, London, ISBN 0-273-642103

Young, Laurie (2005) *Marketing the Professional Services Firm: Applying the Principles and Science of Marketing to Professional Services*, Wiley, Chichester, ISBN 0-470-01173-4

5.3

Project financing and funding

*Project financing and funding is the means by which the capital to undertake
a project is initially secured and then made available at the appropriate time.
Projects may be financed externally, funded internally or a combination of
both.*

Securing the finance or funds for a project is usually the sponsor's responsibility. The project manager and project team should know, and be sensitive
to, how the project is financed and the particular requirements imposed on
the project by its financing.

The organisation will have to balance cash flow across its portfolio of
projects and programmes in order to meet the commitments it has made to
provide funding. Individual projects within the portfolio need to plan how
they drawdown monies against the agreed funding. Deviations from the
plan need to be reported to the organisation so that cash flow at portfolio
level can be adjusted. An understanding of the relationship between
management accounting and project budgeting and cost management is
necessary.

Potential currency fluctuations may affect the cash flow and drawdown
where some or all of the financing is in a foreign currency. For example the
project may receive funding in one currency and make payments to suppliers
in another currency.

During the concept phase the development of a business case will consume
resources that must be secured and financed. The ability of projects to acquire
initial or 'seed corn' financing during this phase is important.

Projects can be financed from many sources. They can be internally funded
or financed by external capital or a combination of both, which may be in the
form of loans or investment in the project's outcome. In the UK public sector
there are a number of financial arrangements that have been put in place by
government. These include the *private finance initiative* (PFI), *public private
partnership* (PPP) and *build, own, operate, transfer* (BOOT).

In circumstances where an organisation obtains a loan to undertake a
project, a bond may be required to secure the loan. The requirements of the
bond may be defined in terms of financial and performance measures. Guarantees can be provided so that if certain events occur, compensation becomes
due from those providing the bond.

Further reading

Euromoney Institutional Investor (2003) *Project Finance: The Guide to Value and Risk Management in PPP Projects*, Euromoney Institutional Investor, London, ISBN 1-85564-981-0

Grimsey, Darrin and Lewis, Mervyn K. (2004) *Public Private Partnerships: The Worldwide Revolution in Infrastructure Provision and Project Finance*, Edward Elgar, Cheltenham, ISBN 1-84064-711-6

Khan, Fouzul and Parra, Robert (2003) *Financing Large Projects: Using Project Finance Techniques and Practices*, Pearson Education Asia, Hong Kong, ISBN 0-13-101634-2

Yescombe, Edward (2002) *Principles of Project Finance*, Academic Press, London, ISBN 0-12-770851-0

5.4

Procurement

Procurement is the process by which the resources (goods and services) required by a project are acquired. It includes development of the procurement strategy, preparation of contracts, selection and acquisition of suppliers, and management of the contracts.

A procurement strategy should be prepared as part of the project management plan (PMP). The procurement strategy will set out how to acquire and manage the internal or external resources (goods and services) needed for the project.

The procurement strategy includes consideration of factors such as:

- the make-or-buy decision;
- use of a single integrated supplier or multiple discrete suppliers;
- required supplier relationships;
- supplier selection and sources;
- conditions and form of contract;
- types of pricing or methods of reimbursement.

In order to execute the procurement strategy various types of contractual arrangements can be used, for example:

- one comprehensive contract;
- a sequence of contracts;
- parallel contracts;
- sub-contracts.

When formulating the procurement strategy, consideration must be given as to what terms, including payment, are likely to motivate suppliers to achieve the objectives of the project. When preparing the contracts, terms and conditions must be agreed, including dispute resolution, termination, confidentiality, intellectual property rights (IPR) and contract payment methods such as fixed price, unit rate-based and cost-reimbursement.

Selection and acquisition of suppliers involves tendering and bidding. Suppliers should be chosen on a combination of capability, quality and price. Tendering is the preparation of tender documents, the solicitation of bids, the evaluation of bids and the award of contracts. Bidding is the submission of a bid by a potential supplier in response to a request for proposal (RFP).[1] Procured resources can represent the highest proportion of the project cost. Negotiation and subsequent acceptance of the tender or the bid locks these costs into the project as commitments.

---

[1] Also called invitation to tender (ITT) or invitation for bidding (IFB).

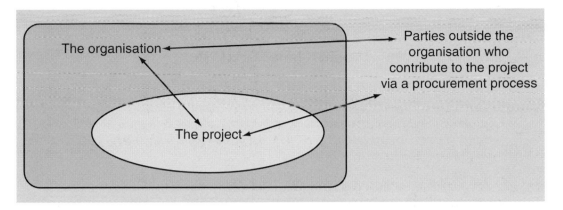

Figure 5.1 The interaction between the organisation and the project
procurement process

The organisation's procurement process includes consideration of partnering and alliances, and e-commerce. Partnering and alliancing are ways of creating long-term relationships for the mutual benefit of all parties involved in the arrangement. E-commerce is the use of internet-led IT to facilitate the buying and selling of goods and services, on either a business-to-business (B2B) basis or a business-to-consumer (B2C) basis.

A project needs to take into account the organisation's overall procurement policies and processes when developing its own project-specific procurement strategy (Figure 5.1). For example the project may only be able to use a supplier from the organisation's preferred list.

Ethical procurement is important. A project needs to be able to demonstrate that its procurement practices are ethical and transparent and that good governance, corporate accountability and probity are being observed, for example sustainability and employment practice.

Further reading

APM Publishing (1998) *Contract Strategy for Successful Project Management*, APM Publishing, Princes Risborough, ISBN 0-953159-01-9

APM Publishing and McKenna, Cameron (1998) *Standard Terms for the Appointment of a Project Manager*, APM Publishing, Princes Risborough, ISBN 0-953159-02-7

Davies, A. and Hobday, M. (2005) *The Business of Projects*, Cambridge University Press, Cambridge, ISBN 0-521-84328-6

Marsh, P. (2004) *Contract Negotiation Handbook*, 3rd edn, Gower, Aldershot, ISBN 0-566-08021-4

Ministry of Defence (MOD) (2005) *The Acquisition Handbook: A Guide to Achieving Defence Capability, 'Faster, Cheaper, Better and More Effectively Integrated'*, 6th edn, Ministry of Defence, London (available online from www.ams.mod.uk)

Scott, B. (2001) *Partnering in Europe*, Thomas Telford, London, ISBN 0-7277-2965-9

5.5

Legal awareness

Legal awareness provides project management professionals with an under-standing of the relevant legal duties, rights and processes that should be applied to projects.

Legal awareness includes an appreciation of the potential causes of claims, disputes (and the means of resolving them), liabilities, breaches of contract and the legal basis of industrial relations. This awareness entails knowing when to seek appropriate legal advice.

Essentially, there are two types of law – statute and common law.[1] Statute law is the written 'law of the land' consisting of Acts of Parliament (including those enacted under European legislation). Common law is based on precedent and provides a means of compensation for the failure of another party to comply with the requirements of statute law and for the failure to observe any duties that have been established by common practice. In both types, cases are judged by the facts and the law is determined by the interpretation of the courts and announced by way of a judgement.

A contract is an agreement between two parties under which one party promises to do something for the other in return for a consideration, usually a payment. A valid legal contract requires agreement (offer and unqualified acceptance), an intention to be legally bound, a consideration, competent parties, legality of purpose and certainty of terms. Commercial contracts will include:

- the contract agreement;
- a general specification and scope of work;
- general and special conditions of contract;
- administrative and coordination procedures.

Key provisions under the contract that a project manager may need to manage include:

- time – commencement, schedule, suspension and completion;
- payment provisions;
- incorporating change;
- performance indicators;

[1] Within the UK there are two distinct bodies of law: English and Scottish. There are fundamental differences as to how these bodies of law operate and for the purposes of brevity only English law will be considered here. Similarities with Scottish law do exist but alternative material should be consulted with regard to the specifics of the law in Scotland and indeed in other legal systems outside the UK.

- liquidated damages;
- termination;
- bonds, guarantees and insurances;
- giving valid instructions and decisions;
- remedies for breach of contract including claims and disputes.

A claim is an assertion under the contract of a right or entitlement that may lead to a demand or request, usually for extra payment and/or time. There should be clear processes described in the contract for the management of claims.

Disputes arise when the parties to a contract have a disagreement concerning a particular event. The contract should contain provisions for settling such disputes. There are a number of ways of settling disputes:

- Litigation: the dispute is heard in a court of law.
- Alternative dispute resolution (ADR) is the collective term for settling disputes with the help of an independent third party without a court hearing, for example arbitration, adjudication and mediation.
- Negotiation between the parties.

Further reading

APM Publishing (1998) *Contract Strategy for Successful Project Management*, APM Publishing, Princes Risborough, ISBN 0-953159-01-9

APM Publishing and McKenna, Cameron (1998) *Standard Terms for the Appointment of a Project Manager*, APM Publishing, Princes Risborough, ISBN 0-953159-02-7

Duxbury, R. (ed.) (2003) *Contract Law* (Nutshell series), 6th edn, Sweet & Maxwell, London, ISBN 0-421-78360-5

Elliott, C. and Quinn, F. (2005) *Contract Law*, 5th edn, Longman, Harlow, ISBN 1-405-80710-5

Mackie, Karl *et al.* (2000) *The ADR Practice Guide: Commercial Dispute Resolution*, 2nd edn, Butterworths, London, ISBN 0-406-91057-X

Tweeddale, A. and Tweeddale, K. (2005) *Arbitration of Commercial Disputes: International and English Law and Practice*, Oxford University Press, Oxford, ISBN 0-19-926540-2

Section 6

Organisation and governance

A project and its roles and responsibilities must be set out in a structured manner. This structure covers both the project life cycle and the organisational hierarchy and includes the procedures that must be followed.

The first five topics deal with the life cycle of a project from an initial idea through to the operational use of the deliverables it produces:

- The importance of the project life cycle and the description of a generic life cycle: concept, definition, implementation, handover and closeout (Topic 6.1 – Project life cycles).
- The identification of the need, problem or opportunity and the business case (Topic 6.2 – Concept).
- Planning the project and creating the project management plan (Topic 6.3 – Definition).
- Realising and delivering the plan (Topic 6.4 – Implementation).
- Putting the deliverables into operational use (Topic 6.5 – Handover and closeout).

It is important to review a project throughout its life cycle and at its completion (Topic 6.6 – Project reviews).

Project management needs to take into account the structure of the organisation carrying out the project (Topic 6.7 – Organisation structure) and how the project will work within that structure (Topic 6.8 – Organisational roles).

Successful project management is underpinned by structured and repeatable methods and procedures (Topic 6.9 – Methods and procedures). A further important aspect concerns the governance of project management (Topic 6.10 – Governance of project management).

6.1

Project life cycles

Project life cycles consist of a number of distinct phases. All projects follow a life cycle and life cycles will differ across industries and business sectors. A life cycle allows the project to be considered as a sequence of phases which provides the structure and approach for progressively delivering the required outputs.

Projects will always have a beginning and an end, as do phases, and how these points are defined will vary.[1] The project life cycle phases[2] will follow a similar high-level generic sequence: concept, definition, implementation and handover and closeout. In specific circumstances the project life cycle is replaced by an extended form. This extended life cycle[3] includes two further phases: operations and termination (Figure 6.1).

The concept phase (Topic 6.2) establishes the need, problem or opportunity for the project. The project's feasibility is investigated and a preferred

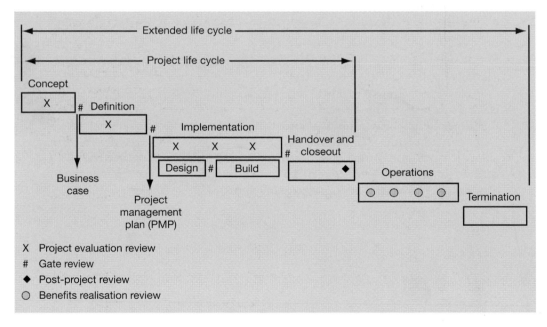

Figure 6.1 The project and extended life cycles

[1] There are also other life cycles such as those used in PFI and PPP arrangements.
[2] Each project life cycle phase needs to go through its own project management phases, such as starting or initiating, defining and planning, monitoring and controlling, learning and closing.
[3] The extended life cycle is also called a product life cycle or acquisition life cycle and is often the basis for through life-costing.

solution identified; if supported, the project continues to the definition phase.

The definition phase further evaluates the preferred solution and options to meet that solution, and prepares the plans necessary for implementation of the project (Topic 6.3).

The implementation phase implements the project strategy and plan (Topic 6.4). This phase can be divided into two or more stages.

The handover and closeout phase delivers the project to the sponsor and the organisation. The project is now complete in terms of delivery of a capability that will allow benefits to be achieved (Topic 6.5).

In the extended life cycle the operations phase will include the ongoing support and maintenance of the project's deliverables. The termination phase concludes the operational life of the deliverables and completes their disposal in an effective manner.

When considering the project life cycle the following must be taken into account:

- The potential to add value to the project reduces as the project progresses, and the cost of making changes or correcting errors increases.
- During the implementation phase, the consumption of resources will accumulate at their greatest rate.
- Planning and estimating should be carried out at an appropriate level to suit the phase.
- Resources should be identified early and therefore effectively utilised.
- Risks should be identified and responses targeted at distinct phases.
- Gates[1] should be established to allow effective end of phase reviews and to confirm that sufficient planning and preparation are in place to commence the next phase (Topic 6.6).
- Early phase successes should be used to reinforce stakeholder commitment.
- Lessons can be learned from earlier phases and applied to improve future performance and future projects.

All phases of the life cycle are important. No phase should be omitted but they may overlap.

Further reading

British Standards Institution (2000–2002) BS 6079-1–3 Project Management: Guides, BSI, London

Gordon, J. (2005) *Project Management and Project Planning*, FT Prentice Hall, London, ISBN 0-273-69378-6

Newton, R. (2005) *The Project Manager: Mastering the Art of Delivery*, FT Prentice Hall, London, ISBN 0-273-70173-8

[1] Also called stage gates and control gates. In UK Central Government there is a broader process known as OGC Gateway®.

6.2

Concept

Concept is the first phase in the project life cycle. During this phase the need, opportunity or problem is confirmed, the overall feasibility of the project is considered and a preferred solution identified. The business case for the project will be produced in this phase.

Organisational strategy and planning trigger and capture new needs, problems or opportunities. This pre-project activity is performed within organisational functions or departments as appropriate. The resources required to undertake the definition phase will be identified. Senior management will make a decision (possibly at a formal gate) to move the need, problem or opportunity into a project life cycle and authorise the resources required.

Concept is the first phase of the project life cycle. The need, problem or opportunity is confirmed and investigated. The project's feasibility is assessed and, if supported, the project continues to the definition phase.

As part of feasibility the project's fit with the organisation's strategic objectives is considered. The project's alignment with the organisation's portfolio or a programme will be reviewed if relevant. High-level risks will be identified and assessed to understand the impact on the organisation and the project.

A number of options are identified and evaluated at a high level to propose a preferred solution. Stakeholders will be identified and analysed. They will contribute to the high-level requirements that will be used in the consideration of options and the proposal of the preferred solution. The 'do nothing' option must always be considered. In proposing a preferred solution a financial appraisal may be undertaken to include payback and the discounted cash flow (DCF) method: net present value (NPV) and internal rate of return (IRR).

The rationale for the project is made in the business case (Topic 5.1) which is produced during this phase either by the sponsor or on behalf of the sponsor. The sponsor owns the business case. The level of detail in the business case needs to be sufficient for the organisation to formally sanction the project. If the business case is approved by the organisation the project will move into the definition phase. This decision is often taken at a formal gate through which the project must pass.

Further reading

British Standards Institution (2000–2002) BS 6079-1–3 Project Management. Guides, BSI, London

Buttrick, R. (2005) *The Project Workout*, 3rd edn, FT Prentice Hall, London, ISBN 0-273-68181-8

Office of Government Commerce (2005) *Managing Successful Projects with PRINCE2*, Stationery Office, London ISBN 0-11-330946-5

6.3

Definition

Definition is the second phase of the project life cycle. During this phase the pre-ferred solution is further evaluated and optimised. Often an iterative process, definition can affect requirements and the project's scope, time, cost and quality objectives. As part of this phase the project management plan (PMP) is pro-duced and the resources required during the implementation phase will be identified.

Information created during the concept phase is used as input to the defi-nition phase. In the definition phase the preferred solution that meets the need, problem or opportunity is tested against the high-level requirements for fitness for purpose or conformance. Alternative designs to meet the preferred solution can be developed using an iterative approach. These alter-natives can be modelled and tested and what-if assessments carried out as appropriate. The preferred solution will be agreed with the sponsor and stakeholders.

Plans are prepared, for example a risk management plan, a quality plan, a communication plan, a health and safety plan, based on the preferred solu-tion. The level of detail in the plans and the tolerance level of the estimates need to be sufficient for the organisation to formally sanction the project. The plans are drawn together and form the project management plan (PMP) (Topic 2.4). At this point the business case may require updating based on the plans produced. The updated business case may be incorporated in the PMP. The project manager owns the PMP.

If the PMP is agreed by the sponsor and other stakeholders and approved by the organisation then the project will move into the implemen-tation phase. This decision is often taken at a formal gate through which the project must pass. Once approved the PMP becomes the baseline for the project.

A process will be put in place to allow for the resources required during implementation to be secured. If external suppliers are used the process can be used to provide confirmation of estimates.

At the end of the definition phase there is a gate at which the organisation approves the project to move into the next phase, implementation. From this point the cumulative expenditure on the project increases at its greatest rate. This gate is the last point in the life cycle where the project can be terminated or modified without incurring further and more significant costs.

Further reading

Archibald, R. D. (2003) *Managing High-technology Programs and Projects*, 3rd edn, Wiley, Hoboken, NJ, ISBN 0-471-26557-8

Blyth, A. and Worthington, J. (2001) *Managing the Brief for Better Design*, Spon, London, ISBN 0-419-25130-8

Parnaby, J., Wearne, S. and Kochhar, A. (2003) *Support Tools and Techniques, Section 2: Design for Implementation, Managing by Projects for Business Success*, Professional Engineering Publishing, London, ISBN 1-86058-341-5

Webb, A. (2000) *Success By Design: Project Management for Successful Product Innovation*, Gower, Aldershot, ISBN 0-566-08262-4

6.4

Implementation

Implementation is the third phase of the project life cycle, during which the project management plan (PMP) is executed, monitored and controlled. In this phase the design is finalised and used to build the deliverables.

A start-up meeting at the beginning of this phase ensures a shared understanding of the project objectives, plans and how the project team will work together.[1]

There are two stages in this phase: design and build. In the design stage, the design is optimised and completed. The output of the design stage is the appropriate documentation, for example drawings, specifications, contracts, at the level of detail that is required to move into the build stage.

Once the design is substantially complete the sponsor will have the design approved at a gate and the project will move into the build stage and relevant activities undertaken.

The project manager monitors all implementation activities to ensure that the project remains on plan and will achieve its agreed scope, time, cost and quality objectives. Control actions are implemented by the project manager to correct deviations from the plan. Regular reports are produced by the project manager and communicated to the project team and stakeholders. A tool that can be used to monitor performance is earned value management (Topic 3.6).

The volume of activities and number of people involved are greatest during the implementation phase, which typically accounts for a high proportion of the total project budget and activity.

Risks identified in earlier phases that may occur during implementation need to be monitored. Issues that cannot be managed by the project team are more likely to arise and the project manager needs to escalate these to the sponsor for resolution. Configuration management is used to ensure that the integrity of the project's deliverables is maintained. Change control is the process used to manage the acceptance, rejection, or deferral of change to the project.

Ongoing procurement of external resources may be required throughout implementation. Procurement may also be required as a control action where a planned internal resource becomes unavailable.

The sponsor reviews the business case against the organisation and external environment on an ongoing basis. This will ensure that the benefits are still valid and the project should continue.

---

[1] The way that the project team will work together can be formally documented in a project charter.

The component deliverables are tested against agreed acceptance criteria as described in the quality plan. In this phase the component deliverables are not tested as an entity. Testing of the completed set of deliverables takes place during handover and closeout. The decision to enter the next phase of handover and closeout and enter an operational environment is taken at a gate.

Further reading

Archibald, R. D. (2003) *Managing High–Technology Programs and Projects*, 3rd edn, Wiley, Hoboken, NJ, ISBN 0-471-26557-8

Davies, A. and Hobday, M. (2005) *The Business of Projects*, Cambridge University Press, Cambridge, ISBN 0-521-84328-6

Gardiner, P. D. (2005) *Project Management: A Strategic Planning Approach*, Palgrave Macmillan, Basingstoke, ISBN 0-333-98222-3

Hamilton, A. (2004) *Handbook of Project Management Procedures*, Thomas Telford, London, ISBN 0-7277-3258-7

6.5

Handover and closeout

Handover and closeout is the fourth and final phase in the project life cycle. During this phase final project deliverables are handed over to the sponsor and users. Closeout is the process of finalising all project matters, carrying out final project reviews, archiving project information and redeploying the project team.

The most important aspect of this phase is allowing the project to enter into an operational environment. This decision will be based on the successful testing of the project to ensure deliverables meet the agreed acceptance criteria.

As part of the handover process the deliverables of the project are prepared for passing over to the sponsor and the user. Testing of component deliverables will have taken place as part of implementation in a safe, non-operational mode. Testing of the complete set of deliverables is carried out in an operational mode, usually with the people involved in business-as-usual activities. The purpose of this process is to set the deliverables to work safely in their final operational mode. If the deliverables meet the acceptance criteria, the project is ready to be formally accepted.

The sponsor and users accept responsibility for the project deliverables. This may be an instantaneous, gradual or phased process, depending on the nature of the deliverables. The purpose is to demonstrate that the deliverables meet performance requirements and are acceptable. Plans for acceptance and handover should be prepared and agreed in the project management plan.

The handover process may also include:

- acceptance of all pertinent documentation (containing all prescribed information relative to the deliverables, including guarantees and warranties);
- acceptance certificate(s) signed by the sponsor or users to confirm acceptance;
- transfer of responsibility for the deliverables from the project team to the sponsor or users;
- formal transfer of ownership.

The remaining project personnel must be redeployed in a controlled manner. Once the project deliverables have been handed over, the project manager needs to ensure that:

- any surplus project materials and facilities are disposed of;
- all contracts and purchase orders are finalised;
- all project accounts are finalised;

- all project documentation and records are completed and archived;
- a post-project review is undertaken in order that lessons are learned (Topic 6.6);
- performance appraisals of the project team are undertaken, which should include recognition of individual and team performances.

The capability is now in place for the benefits to be realised. The realisation of the benefits is the responsibility of the sponsor (Topics 1.5 and 2.1).

Further reading

Gardiner, P. D. (2005) *Project Management: A Strategic Planning Approach*, Palgrave Macmillan, Basingstoke, ISBN 0-333-98222-3

Kerzner, H. (2003) *Project Management: A Systems Approach to Planning, Scheduling and Controlling*, 8th edn, Wiley, Hoboken, NJ, ISBN 0-471-22577-0

Lock, D. (2003) *Project Management*, 8th edn, Gower, Aldershot, ISBN 0-566-08551-8

6.6

Project reviews

Project reviews take place throughout the project life cycle to check the likely or actual achievement of the objectives specified in the project management plan (PMP) and the benefits detailed in the business case. Additional reviews will take place following handover and closeout to ensure that the benefits are being realised by the organisation.

Reviews should be planned throughout the project life cycle. They allow the project manager and project team to reflect on the project and objectively review their work.

Project evaluation reviews are planned in the project life cycle by the project manager and are in addition to the ongoing monitoring and control process. The prime document to review against is the project management plan, although any impacts on the business case must be considered.

The aims of a project evaluation review are to:

- evaluate the project management processes used;
- establish lessons learned and actions arising from them;
- raise any concerns and agree corrective actions;
- review the likely technical success of the project;
- validate overall progress against the plan: schedule, budget, resources, quality;
- consider stakeholder relationships and perceptions.

A gate review will be undertaken at the end of a phase or stage of the life cycle to determine whether the project should move into the next phase or stage. This is a decision point for senior management to authorise continued investment in the project. The decision will be informed by outputs from the most recent project evaluation review, the completed deliverables of the current phase or stage, robust plans to perform the subsequent phase or stage, and any external changes of circumstance.

Audits are undertaken by a group outside the project team. This can be the project office, internal audit or a third-party organisation. The purpose of an audit is to provide an objective evaluation of the project.

The post-project review is undertaken after the project deliverables have been handed over but before final closeout. The purpose of this review is to learn lessons that will enable continuous improvement. All project documentation can be used as part of the review. The aims of the review are to:

- evaluate the project against its success criteria;

- determine what went right and what went wrong, distinguishing between causes and effects;
- recognise individual and team performance;
- evaluate the project management processes and any tools or techniques used.

A benefits realisation review is undertaken after a period of business-as-usual. The purpose of the review is to establish that the project benefits have or are being realised. The review is the responsibility of the sponsor. There may be a need for further benefits realisation reviews.

Further reading

Buttrick, R. (2005) *The Project Workout*, 3rd edn, Prentice Hall, London, ISBN 0-273-68181-8

Kerth, Norm (2001) *Project Retrospectives: A Handbook for Team Reviews*, Dorset House, New York, ISBN 0-932633-44-7

Love, Peter, Fong, Patrick and Irani, Zahir (2005) *Management of Knowledge in Project Environments*, Butterworth-Heinemann, Oxford, ISBN 0-750-66251-4

6.7

Organisation structure

The organisation structure is the organisational environment within which the project takes place. The organisation structure defines the reporting and decision-making hierarchy of an organisation and how project management operates within it.

Organisations have a number of functional departments within them such as finance, IT and human resources. These functions provide the structure within which resources and processes are brought together to perform work. Project management cuts across functional boundaries and the ease or difficulty with which this occurs is influenced by the way the organisation is structured.

Organisational structures lie on a continuum with functional at one extreme and project at the other (Figure 6.2). The relative level of authority between a functional manager and a project manager determines where the organisation lies on the continuum. In practice, organisations rarely adopt the extreme structures.

A functional organisation structure is used by organisations involved in routine operations and provides a stable structure for managing routine work.

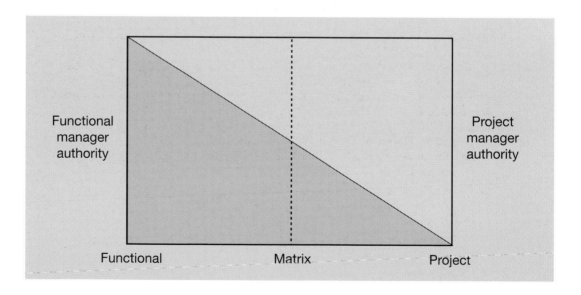

Figure 6.2 The organisational continuum

It supports the development of individuals and the growth of functional capabilities. However, this hinders integration in cross-functional projects.

In matrix organisation structures individuals stay within their functional departments while performing work on one or more projects. This provides a means of balancing project and functional objectives. However, people report to both functional heads and project managers, which can lead to conflict. This can be overcome by clear definition and understanding of roles, responsibilities and authority within the matrix. The project office can play a vital role in aiding communication, prioritisation and integration across projects.

The project organisation structure will afford the maximum authority to the project manager. This provides integration of functional capabilities within projects. However, this leads to duplication of facilities, and less efficient use of resources.

The organisation structure does not define who does the work in the project. This is the purpose of the project's organisational breakdown structure (OBS). The OBS is created to reflect the strategy for managing and handover of the project. It shows the hierarchical management structure for the project, the communication routes and reporting links. The project's work breakdown structure (WBS) and OBS can be combined to create a responsibility assignment matrix (RAM), which correlates the work packages in the WBS to the people, organisations or third parties responsible for accomplishing the assigned work (Topic 3.1).

The organisation structure for a project may change as the project progresses through its life cycle.

Further reading

Archibald, R. D. (2003) *Managing High-Technology Programs and Projects*, 3rd edn, Wiley, Hoboken, NJ, ISBN 0-471-26557-8

Capon, Claire (2003) *Understanding Organisational Context: Inside & Outside Organisations*, 2nd edn, Financial Times Management, London, ISBN 0-273-67660-1

Gardiner, P. D. (2005) *Project Management: A Strategic Planning Approach*, Palgrave Macmillan, Basingstoke, ISBN 0-333-98222-3.

Moore, David R. (2002) *Project Management: Designing Effective Organizational Structures in Construction*, Blackwell, Oxford, ISBN 0-632-06393-9

Thompson, Paul B. and McHugh, David (2003) *Work Organisations: Critical Introduction*, 3rd edn, Palgrave Macmillan, Basingstoke, ISBN 0-333-94991-9

6.8

Organisational roles

Organisational roles are the roles performed by individuals or groups in a project. Both roles and responsibilities within projects must be defined to address the transient and unique nature of projects and to ensure that clear accountabilities can be assigned.

Roles have to be defined for the unique circumstances of a project. These roles may differ from those that the individuals hold within the organisation. For example, a project manager's boss in the functional organisation may be a member of the project team and report to the project manager on all matters relating to the project.

There are a number of principal roles that may need to be defined on a project.

A steering group[1] provides overall strategic direction for the project. The steering group is chaired by the sponsor and consists of representatives from users and suppliers. Where a steering group is not required, the sponsor provides overall direction and management of the project.

The sponsor's role is to own the business case and be ultimately accountable for the project and for delivering the benefits.

The project manager manages the project on a day-to-day basis and is responsible for delivering the capability that allows the benefits to be realised.

Users represent the group of people who will benefit from the project. Users may also be subject matter experts who contribute to defining requirements and acceptance criteria.

Suppliers represent the people or organisations that will provide resources to the project. Suppliers can be internal or external to the organisation. They are responsible for producing the project's deliverables.

The project office provides support to the project manager and sponsor. The degree of this support may vary considerably (Topic 1.6).

Stakeholders are those with an interest in the project. A stakeholder may be an individual or group, either internal or external to the organisation. Stakeholders contribute to defining fitness for purpose for the project.

Project team members are accountable to the project manager. Team members ensure that the work assigned to them by the project manager is performed either by themselves or by others within a working group. In a working group work is delegated to individuals and the interrelationship between activities is managed through a single person, perhaps a member of the project team.

---

[1] The steering group may also be called the steering committee or project board.

Project assurance is the independent monitoring and reporting of the project's quality and deliverables. This role may report directly to the sponsor or steering group.

Further managerial roles that may be required are configuration manager, cost manager, project accountant, project planner, procurement manager, quality manager and resource manager.

It is the sponsor's and the project manager's responsibility to design an appropriate organisational structure for the project and keep it up to date.

Further reading

Boddy, D. (2002) *Managing Projects: Building and Leading the Team*, Prentice Hall, London, ISBN 0-273-65128-5

Brooks, Ian (2002) *Organisational Behaviour: Individuals, Groups and Organisation*, FT Prentice Hall, London, ISBN 0-273-65798-4

Buttrick, R. (2005) *Project Workout: A Toolkit for Reaping the Rewards of All Your Business Projects*, 3rd edn, FT Prentice Hall, London, ISBN 0-273-68181-8

Longman, A. and Mullins, Jim (2005) *The Rational Project Manager: A Thinking Team's Guide to Getting Work Done*, Wiley, Hoboker, NJ, ISBN 0-471-72146-8

Pande, Peter S., Neuman, Robert P. and Cavanagh, Roland (2002) *The Six Sigma Way Team Fieldbook: An Implementation Guide for Project Improvement Teams*, McGraw-Hill, New York, ISBN 0-07-137314-4

Redding, John C. (2000) *The Radical Team Handbook: Harnessing the Power of Team Learning for Breakthrough Results*, Jossey-Bass Wiley, San Francisco, CA, ISBN 0-7879-5161-7

6.9

Methods and procedures

Methods and procedures detail the standard practices to be used for managing projects throughout a life cycle. Methods provide a consistent framework within which project management is performed. Procedures cover individual aspects of project management practice and form an integral part of a method.

The use of a standard method or procedures has a variety of benefits, including:

- providing a consistent approach to all projects within the organisation, leading to better development of projects and governance of project management (Topic 6.10);
- an environment for developing continuous improvement in project management processes (Topic 2.6);
- common understanding of roles within the project team and stakeholders (Topic 6.8).

Without methods or procedures, project management is practised in an unpredictable manner and project managers will develop and use their own ways of working, leading to inefficiencies at an organisational level.

A method embodies best practice and provides consistent guidelines for people involved in the project. An example of an open method is PRINCE2, developed and maintained by the UK Government, which is used extensively in public and private sector projects. Many large organisations develop and utilise bespoke methods.

A method may be based around a project life cycle and includes:

- process descriptions for each phase of a project life cycle;
- inputs and outputs for each process;
- documentation guidelines and templates;
- guidelines for organisational design, accountability, responsibility and communication (Topics 6.7 and 6.8);
- role definitions for all those involved in the project, including the project team (Topic 6.8);
- procedures to be used throughout the life cycle, for example value management (Topic 2.3), project risk management (Topic 2.5) and project quality management (Topic 2.6), issue management (Topic 3.8), change control (Topic 3.5) and configuration management (Topic 4.7).

A procedure sets out the steps to follow in order to perform project management processes. Organisations that are new to project management may choose to develop a small number of procedures and add to these as their expertise grows.

The development and maintenance of methods and procedures may fall under the remit of the project office (Topic 1.6).

Further reading

Charvat, Jason (2003) *Project Management Methodologies: Selecting, Implementing, and Supporting Methodologies and Processes for Projects*, Wiley, Chichester ISBN 0-471-22178-3

Hamilton, A. (2004) *Handbook of Project Management Procedures*, Thomas Telford, London, ISBN 0-7277-3258-7

Office of Government Commerce (2005) *Managing Successful Projects with PRINCE2*, Stationery Office, London, ISBN 0-11-330946-5

Peters, Lawrence J. (2004) *Software Project Management: Methods and Techniques*, Software Consultants International, New York, ISBN 0-97448861-5

6.10

Governance of project management

Governance of project management (GoPM) concerns those areas of corporate governance that are specifically related to project activities. Effective governance of project management ensures that an organisation's project portfolio is aligned to the organisation's objectives, is delivered efficiently and is sustainable.

Effective governance of project management (GoPM) will align the interests of board directors, project teams and wider stakeholders, help improve corporate performance and reduce surprises at both boardroom level and for stakeholders.

Figure 6.3 illustrates that the governance of project management is a subset of the activities involved within corporate governance. It also shows that most of the activities involved with the management of projects lie outside

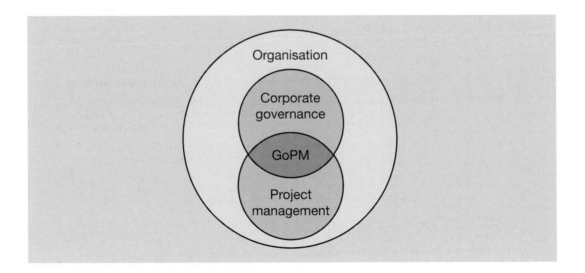

Figure 6.3 Governance of project management

the direct concern of corporate governance.

The best results from the governance of project management will come from the intelligent application of the principles set out below, combined with proportionate delegation of responsibility and the monitoring of internal control systems.

- The board[1] has overall responsibility for governance of project management.
- The roles, responsibilities and performance criteria for the governance of project management are clearly defined.
- Disciplined governance arrangements, supported by appropriate methods and controls, are applied throughout the project life cycle.
- A coherent and supportive relationship is demonstrated between the overall business strategy and the project portfolio.
- All projects have an approved plan containing authorisation points at which the business case is reviewed and approved. Decisions made at authorisation points are recorded and communicated.
- Members of delegated authorisation bodies have sufficient representation, competence, authority and resources to enable them to make appropriate decisions.
- The business case is supported by relevant and realistic information that provides a reliable basis for making authorisation decisions.
- The board or its delegated agents decide when independent scrutiny of projects and project management systems is required, and implement such scrutiny accordingly.
- There are clearly defined criteria for reporting project status and for the escalation of risks and issues to the levels required by the organisation.
- The organisation fosters a culture of improvement and of frank disclosure of project information.
- Project stakeholders are engaged at a level that is commensurate with their importance to the organisation and in a manner that fosters trust.

One method of examining the extent of application of these principles through an organisation is to ask a comprehensive set of questions in four component areas: portfolio direction, project sponsorship, project management, and disclosure and reporting. Positive answers to these key questions would indicate that current practice broadly fulfils the principles and meets appropriate governance requirements applied to the discipline of project management.

Further reading

APM GoPM Specific Interest Group (2005) *Directing Change: A Guide to Governance of Project Management*, 2nd edn, Association for Project Management, Princes Risborough, ISBN 1-903494-15-X

Comptroller and Auditor General (2004) *Improving IT Procurement*, Report HC877, National Audit Office, London ISBN 0102929165

Organization for Economic Cooperation and Development (2004) *Principles of Corporate Governance*, OECD Publications, Paris ISBN 9-264015-97-3

Turnbull, N. *et al.* (1999) *Internal Control: Guidance for Directors on the Combined Code*, Institute of Chartered Accountants, London, ISBN 1-84152-010-0

UK Financial Reporting Council (2003) *The Combined Code on Corporate Governance*, London ISBN 1-84140-406-3

[1] Board here refers to board of directors, rather than project board.

Section 7

People and the profession

People are the integral part of projects and project management. They both manage the project and perform the work and therefore projects succeed or fail through their involvement.

Important factors relating to people in project management are:

- the need for effective communication (Topic 7.1 – Communication);
- the contribution of teamwork (Topic 7.2 – Teamwork);
- the role of leaders (Topic 7.3 – Leadership);
- resolving conflict and how it can be managed to the benefit of the project (Topic 7.4 – Conflict management);
- negotiation between those involved in the project (Topic 7.5 – Negotiation);
- the understanding of human resource management practices (Topic 7.6 – Human resource management);
- the behavioural characteristics that a project management professional should ideally demonstrate (Topic 7.7 – Behavioural characteristics);
- the need for people and the organisation to learn and develop (Topic 7.8 – Learning and development);
- the professionalism of project management professionals and the ethics they should exhibit (Topic 7.9 – Professionalism and ethics).

7.1

Communication

Communication is the giving, receiving, processing and interpretation of information. Information can be conveyed verbally, non-verbally, actively, passively, formally, informally, consciously or unconsciously.

Effective communication is fundamental to project management. The primary objective of communication in project management is to gain a common understanding. Communication related to the project will be with different audiences, for example the project team, the sponsor, stakeholders, senior management and the organisation. The project manager should recognise that these different audiences have different communication needs in terms of volume, content, style, tone and medium, and tailor their communication to meet these needs.

Communication can affect understanding and feelings. The recipient's viewpoint, interests and cultural background[1] will affect how they interpret the communication. A communication may be open to different interpretation. Careful thought must be given to the choice of medium and its likely impact.

Active listening is a way of seeking feedback on the understanding of the transmitted communication. Confirming understanding assures that clarity is achieved.

Anticipating the impact of a communication is key. Communication is constant, and people continually interpret what they observe and experience.

Paying close attention to language, tone and body language can provide feedback regarding the impact of a communication on knowledge, understanding and feelings. Effective management of body language and verbal expression can enhance empathy and rapport where candour and a trusted and open exchange of views is encouraged.

Information that may be critical to the well-being of the project is often informally available before it is available through formal channels. The project manager must be sensitive to this and identify opportunities to exploit informal communication.

The project manager should be conscious of the project's context and communicate within the boundaries of what is sensitive or confidential to the organisation, and understand the effect of timing in the organisation.

Effective communication management throughout the life cycle is fundamental to the project. The project manager can choose to share, mask or

---

[1] Culture embraces social, organisational and ethnic considerations.

promote certain information. However, inappropriate style, tone, message and timing can have a negative impact on the project.

Formal and informal project communications should be captured in a communication plan which identifies what is to be communicated, why, the desired impact, when, how, where, through what channel and to whom (see stakeholder management (Topic 2.2)).

Further reading

Borg, James (2004) *Persuasion: The Art of Influencing People*, Prentice Hall, London, ISBN 0–273–68838–3

Brinkman, Rick and Kirschner, Rick (2002) *Dealing with People You Can't Stand: How to Bring Out the Best in People at their Worst*, McGraw-Hill Education, New York, ISBN 0–07–137944–4

Institute of Leadership & Management (ed.) (2003) *Project and Report Writing*, Pergamon, Oxford, ISBN 0–7506–5876–2

Maggio, Rosalie (2005) *The Art of Talking to Anyone: Essential People Skills for Success in Any Situation*, McGraw-Hill Education, New York ISBN 0–07–145229–X

Patterson, Kerry, Grenny, Joseph, McMillan, Ron and Switzler, A, (2002) *Crucial Conversations: Tools for Talking When Stakes are High*, McGraw-Hill Education, New York, ISBN 0–07–140194–6

7.2

Teamwork

Teamwork is when people work collaboratively towards a common goal as distinct from other ways that individuals can work within a group.

A project team consists of a number of people committed to a common goal that none can achieve alone, and where interrelationships between tasks are managed by collaboration. The project team can be supported by a working group. Within a working group, work is delegated to individuals and the interrelationship between activities is managed through a single person. It must be determined whether work is allocated to a team or to individuals within a working group; a distinction needs to be made as to whether at any one time people work as a member of a team or in a working group.

Regardless of whether they have input into team selection, the project manager should invest in building the team, ensuring appropriate communication to keep team members informed and motivated, and demonstrating leadership that the team can follow.

A group of people pass through a number of stages[1] of development before they can function as an effective team. The team may not evolve naturally or quickly so it is necessary to determine when action needs to be taken to promote transition through the stages. As the team develops it gathers a shared experience, language and culture, creating a high-performing, supportive and collaborative team environment.

The team may be cross-functional,[2] with varied experience and specialist skills. The project team will change throughout the project life cycle, with specialist skills required at certain phases and people continually joining or leaving the team. The team will be transient, being formed to create the project deliverables that will deliver the benefits to the organisation and disbanded when the project has completed its handover and closeout phase.

The project manager may facilitate the development of a charter that describes how the team will work together and their behaviours. The project manager must consider geographical, cultural and knowledge barriers that can disrupt team harmony, and use team discussions, communication, events, physical or virtual meetings to overcome these. The structure of the project team may be predefined by the organisation structure.

---

[1] There are a number of models of team development, such as Tuckman (forming, storming, norming, performing), Katzenbach and Smith (working group/high-performing team).
[2] The team may be drawn from different functions or departments of an organisation.

Individuals will perform better in a team context if they are performing in a role that plays to their strengths. Recognising and filling a variety of roles will strengthen the team.

The project manager needs to build and maintain a positive and effective team that encourages involvement, flexibility, efficiency, innovation and productivity to contribute to project success.

Further reading

Boddy, D. (2002) *Managing Projects: Building and Leading the team*, Prentice Hall, London, ISBN 0–273–65128–5

Jones, Robert, Oyung, Robert and Pace, Lise (2005) *Working Virtually: Challenges of Virtual Teams*, CyberTech, Hershey, PA, ISBN 1–59140–551–3

Katzenbach, J. R. and Smith, D. K. (2003) *The Wisdom of Teams*, HarperBusiness, New York, ISBN 0–06–052200–3

Lencioni, Patrick (2002) *The Five Dysfunctions of a Team: A Leadership Fable*, Jossey Bass Wiley, San Francisco, CA, ISBN 0–7879–6075–6

Nicholson, Nigel and West, Michael (eds) (2005) *Teamwork: How to use Teams to Enhance the Business*, Format, Norwich ISBN 1–90309134–9

7.3

Leadership

Leadership is the ability to establish vision and direction, to influence and align others towards a common purpose, and to empower and inspire people to achieve project success. It enables the project to proceed in an environment of change and uncertainty.

The role of leadership in a project is to maintain and promote the project vision, reinforce positive relationships, build an environment that supports effective teamwork, raise morale and empower and inspire the individual. Leaders require followers; leaders must also themselves be able to follow.

A leader ensures that exceptional events during the project life cycle are properly addressed and resolved. Projects do not always go well, and a leader who can see an opportunity rather than a threat will help to motivate the team through a challenging period.

Leadership should be exercised at all levels within the project. Team members will lead their colleagues to a successful result, which adds to the success of the project and has a positive impact on the functional area of the organisation that is providing resources. Within the context of a project team, responsibility for leadership can be exercised by all or some of the team all or some of the time. This presents those with nominated leadership roles the challenge of supporting and nurturing this attribute within the team.

A leader provides constructive and immediate feedback on the performance of individuals in the project, and encourages feedback on their own performance. To enable continual improvement, lessons learned will be shared, and success celebrated. Leaders can act as a coach and mentor to people working on the project in order to promote personal growth.

The leader represents and provides service to those they lead. Sensing what people need in order for them to perform most effectively is key to selecting which leadership style and activity is most appropriate. Projects have to respond to critical scrutiny. The leader protects the interests of the project and its people.

The project manager as leader has an impact on the organisation, in that they inspire trust, confidence and commitment when escalating or communicating upwards.

The project manager should focus on different aspects of leadership throughout the project life cycle and set the pace accordingly. Early phases of the project require expertise in influencing stakeholders and creating vision. As the project progresses, the leadership focus shifts to maintaining momentum, responding to ambiguity and change.

Further reading

Adair, J. (2005) *How to Grow Leaders: The Seven Key Principles of Effective Leadership Development*, Kogan Page, London, ISBN 0–7494–4363–4

Kleim, Ralph L. (2004) *Leading High Performance Projects*, J. Ross Publishing, Fort Lauderdale, FL, ISBN 1–932159–10–X

Kotter, J. (1999) John P. Kotter on What Leaders Really Do, Harvard Business School Press, Boston, MA, ISBN 0875848974

Lewis, James P. (2002) *Project Leadership*, McGraw-Hill, New York, ISBN 0–07–138867–2

Mann, Leon (2005) *Leadership, Management and Innovation in R&D Project Teams*, Greenwood, Westport, CN, ISBN 1–56720–398–1

Schein, H. (2004) *Organizational Culture and Leadership*, Jossey-Bass, San Francisco, CA, ISBN 0 7879-7597–4

7.4

Conflict management

Conflict management is the process of identifying and addressing differences that if unmanaged would affect project objectives. Effective conflict management prevents differences becoming destructive elements in a project.

There are differences of opinion and interpretation in projects, which are often resolved with discussion. New ideas and practices result from such debate. When agreement is not possible, differences must be resolved through conflict management. The project manager needs to recognise when a conflict may have a critical impact on the project and therefore requires a conflict management approach.

Conflict can arise among individuals, teams, stakeholders or at an organisational level, internally to the project or externally affecting the project. It may relate to interpersonal issues, interests, values, organisational cultures, technical opinion, politics and finance. The project manager needs to recognise the material and behavioural components of conflict.

A trend towards conflict is often identifiable. Indications may be obvious, such as open hostility or challenge, or more subtly expressed through changes in style or volume of communication, opting out, passive resistance, rumour-mongering or asides. An effective approach to conflict management can be to resolve differences before they give rise to conflict. The project manager's role is to anticipate and prepare, avoiding conflict escalation through skilful negotiation or appropriate use of authority.

Conflict management methods include:

- collaborating (confronting);
- compromising;
- accommodating (smoothing);
- competing (forcing);
- avoidance (withdrawal).

Conflict in a project can be constructive. Managed conflict brings concerns into the open, raises otherwise suppressed viewpoints and can clear up misunderstandings and uncertainty. This can enable positive working relationships to evolve.

Unresolved conflict can become expensive, increasing uncertainty and damaging morale. The project manager needs to identify the appropriate moment to intervene.

Distinguishing between the person and the position being taken can defuse tension and make the discussion more objective. While facts are easy to identify and address objectively, feelings are not. Conflict arising from people's feelings needs handling with sensitivity and empathy. The use of non-confrontational language and understanding the perspectives of adversaries are key. The project manager may have to adopt a position as advocate of one of the parties involved, or be perceived to be neutral.

Where conflict cannot be resolved, escalation to a higher authority may be required or specialists may be engaged to broker a resolution. If the effort required to resolve the conflict is disproportionate to the impact on the project, it may be necessary to reach a pragmatic resolution which may include agreeing to disagree.

Regardless of the approach used to manage and resolve conflict, the project manager should ensure that the outcome is communicated to all relevant stakeholders.

Further reading

Gardiner, P. D. (2005) *Project Management: A Strategic Planning Approach*, Palgrave Macmillan, Basingstoke, ISBN 0–333–98222–3

Masters, Marick F. and Albright, R. (2002) *The Complete Guide to Conflict Resolution in the Workplace*, Amacom, New York, ISBN 0–8144–0629–7

Mayer, Bernard S. (2000) *The Dynamics of Conflict Resolution: A Practitioner's Guide*, Jossey-Bass Wiley, San Francisco, CA, ISBN 0–7879–5019–X

Roberto, Michael A. (2005) *Why Great Leaders Don't Take Yes for an Answer: Managing for Conflict and Consensus*, Prentice Hall, London, ISBN 0–13–145439–0

Young, T. L. (2003) *Handbook of Project Management*, Kogan Page, London, ISBN 0–7494–3965–5

7.5

Negotiation

Negotiation is a search for agreement, seeking acceptance, consensus and alignment of views. Negotiation in a project can take place on an informal basis throughout the project life cycle, or on a formal basis such as during procurement, and between signatories to a contract.

A project has constraints such as time, cost and quality, and areas such as scope, requirements and technical discussions where people may have different agendas and interests and need to negotiate to reach agreement.

The project manager should be certain of their role in any negotiation, i.e. whether they are:

- the negotiator trying to reach agreement between two parties;
- a participant negotiating for their own desired situation; or
- an observer of the negotiation within the project.

To conclude a successful negotiation that maintains or enhances the relationship between the people involved, the project manager should aim to understand and address the underlying motivation, wants and needs of all parties, and separate the different views from the people involved. The people involved may be part of the project team or stakeholders whose ongoing support is essential.

The project manager prepares for a negotiation by understanding the different views involved, their authority, the relative power and influence of the parties involved, and the rationale for the tolerance or limit that is acceptable within the context of the project.

Resolution within tolerance may be deemed acceptable, whereas agreement outside this tolerance may require additional support (financial, time) from the sponsor or steering group. The project manager needs to select from a range of negotiating stances from adversarial through alliances to partnering.

The consequences of a failure to negotiate an agreement must be understood, such as the impact on time, cost and quality. The project manager must clarify the escalation route to use in the event of being unable to resolve the negotiation.

The negotiation itself can proceed through planning, discussing, proposing, trade-offs, bargaining and agreeing; this may be an iterative process. The project manager should consider fairness and ethics in the negotiation, as this helps to preserve the relationship between the people involved. The influence of culture on the people involved in the negotiation should also be considered. A specialist negotiator may be required where agreement is critical but difficult to achieve.

On resolution the outcome must be reviewed with the participants to achieve clarity and agreement, to clearly record the outcome to all parties and to incorporate the consequences into the project management plan.

Further reading

Borg, James (2004) *Persuasion: The Art of Influencing People*, Prentice Hall, London, ISBN 0–273–68838–3

Fisher, Roger and Shapiro, Daniel (2005) *Beyond Reason: Using Emotions as You Negotiate*, Viking Books, New York, ISBN 0–670–03450–9

Fisher, Roger, Ury, William and Patton, Bruce (2003) *Getting to Yes: The Secret to Successful Negotiation*, Random House, London, ISBN 1–8441–3146–7

HBS (2000) *Harvard Business Review on Negotiation and Conflict Resolution*, Harvard Business School Press, Boston, MA, ISBN 1–57851–236–0

Huczynski, Andrzej (2004) *Influencing Within Organizations*, rev. 2nd edn, Routledge, London, ISBN 0–415–31163–2

7.6

Human resource management

Human resource management (HRM) is the understanding and application of the policy and procedures that directly affect the people working within the project team and working group. These policies include recruitment, retention, reward, personal development, training and career development.

The project manager should understand the scope of their responsibility and authority to implement and conform with the human resource management (HRM) policies of the organisation, and any legal obligations. These include recruitment, redeployment and reduction of both permanent and contracted personnel, rewards and incentives, disputes, discipline, personal development, training, health and safety, and other conditions of work.

Many of these policies will be defined, owned by and supported elsewhere in the organisation. The project manager should identify the relevant functions and work effectively with them. Active pursuit of information relating to HRM is a primary duty of the project manager throughout the project life cycle. Effective collaboration between the project and HRM both leads to project success and enhances the human resources available to the organisation in the longer term.

HRM has a wider impact on the project than ensuring compliance with policies. Misuse or avoidance of policies can unsettle the people involved and result in disruption in the project team, with subsequent impact on time and performance, and a lack of confidence in the project from the stakeholders.

An induction process prepares people joining the project so that they will understand their roles and responsibilities, the goals and ethos of the project, and its working arrangements.

The transient nature of a project brings particular challenges for HRM. Among these are the need to manage information effectively, provide input to performance management processes and engage in long-term development of people and the organisation.

HRM specialists in the organisation may be available to the project. Their knowledge of employee relations, resourcing, organisation and legal factors can contribute to project success.

The development of human resources from the learning and experience gained by involvement in projects is also a source of competitive advantage. In this way the project manager contributes to HRM policies in their responsibility for talent management and social capital.

Further reading

Bratton, John and Gold, Jeffrey (2003) *Human Resource Management: Theory and Practice*, 3rd edn, Macmillan, Basingstoke, ISBN 0–333–99326–8

Buckingham, M. and Coffman, C. (1999) *First, Break All the Rules: What the World's Greatest Managers Do Differently*, Simon & Schuster, New York, ISBN 0–684–85286–1

Johnson, Mike (2004) *New Rules of Engagement: Life–Work Balance and Employee Commitment*, CIPD, London, ISBN 1–84398–072-X

Leary-Joyce, Judith (2004) *Becoming an Employer of Choice: Make Your Organisation a Place Where People Want to Do Great Work*, CIPD, London, ISBN 1–84398–057–6

Ulrich, Dave (1997) *Human Resource Champions*, Harvard Business Review Press, Boston, MA, ISBN 0–87584–719–6

7.7

Behavioural characteristics

Behavioural characteristics are the elements that separate and describe a person's preferred way of acting, interacting and reacting in a variety of situations. Behaviours complement knowledge and experience and are a function of values, beliefs and identity. They can be used in assessment, engagement and career advice.

Successful project management requires a combination of knowledge, experience and behaviour. Behaviours are closely associated with personality, but are not the same. It is far more difficult to understand or change personality than behaviour, which can be openly recognised and learned. Behaviour relates to use of language, perceptions from senses and movement (body language).

There are eight readily identified behavioural characteristics important for project management:

- *Attitude*: an open, positive 'can-do' attitude builds confidence and credibility both within the team and with other stakeholders, and sets the environment where collaboration can take place.
- *Common sense* : the ability to spot and adopt sensible, effective, straightforward solutions, i.e. 90 per cent right on time may be better than 100 per cent far too late! Common sense seeks to simplify rather than overcomplicate or over-engineer.
- *Open mindedness* : openness to new ideas, practices and methods, and in particular giving consideration to the plurality of views involved on the project.
- *Adaptability* : this is pragmatism, a propensity to be flexible where necessary and avoid rigid patterns of thinking or behaviour, to adapt to the requirements of the project, the needs of its sponsor, its environment and the people working on it – to ensure a successful outcome.
- *Inventiveness* : an ability to articulate innovative strategies and solutions either solo or with other members of the project, and to identify ways of working with disparate resources and interests to achieve project objectives.
- *Prudent risk taker* : a willingness and ability to identify and understand threats and opportunities.
- *Fairness* : a fair and open attitude, which respects all human values and reflects contract particulars, appointment conditions, legal agreements and legislation.

- *Commitment* : a focus on the project's objectives, user satisfaction and team-working. A strong orientation towards achievement of goals, targets and benefits, including scope, time, cost, and quality criteria.

Further reading

Archibald, R. D. (2003) *Managing High-technology Programs and Projects*, 3rd edn, Wiley, Hoboken, NJ, ISBN 0–471–26557–8

Arnold, John, Cooper, Cary L. and Robertson, Ivan T. (2004) *Work Psychology: Understanding Human Behaviour in the Workplace*, FT Prentice Hall, London, ISBN 0–273–65544–2

Barak, Michael Mor (2005) *Managing Diversity: Toward a Globally Inclusive Workplace*, Sage, London, ISBN 0–7619–2773–5

Skiffington, Suzanne and Zeus, Perry (2003) *Behavioral Coaching: Building Sustainable Personal and Organizational Strengths*, McGraw-Hill Education, New York ISBN 0–07–471328–0

7.8

Learning and development

Learning and development involves the continual improvement of competencies in the organisation. The identification and application of learning within projects develops the organisation's capability to undertake current and future projects.

The project manager should provide an environment that supports learning and development opportunities that meet the needs of the project, people and the organisation. People are responsible for their own learning and development and should ensure that the project manager is aware of their needs. In addition the project manager should also identify gaps in people's competencies and how best to address them.

The project manager needs to be aware of and comply with the organisation's policy on learning and development, collaborate with specialists that are responsible for learning and development, or share responsibility for the learning and development of people in the project.

Learning and development needs are determined through a process of performance management that relates people's ability to the organisation's expectation of performance. Performance management considers the immediate needs for capability to support projects and the longer term career development of people. Feedback on performance and behaviour contributes to the learning and development of people involved in the project. Feedback for the organisation, project manager and project team is frequently obtained and shared as lessons learned at a project evaluation review. Prompt and direct feedback has an immediate impact on the learning and development of the project team.

Coaching is a process for addressing a person's development needs and enhancing performance while fulfilling the work needed to complete the project. Coaches are sensitive to preferred learning styles. Mentoring is support, guidance and advice provided by one person that is not specific to particular work, but instead is related to a person's development in terms of significant transitions in knowledge, work or thinking.

Everyone in the project will encounter and should work towards creating opportunities for knowledge creation. In a project, knowledge is created by means of individual and organisational learning, achieved through socialisation, articulating what we and others know, embodying that through individual skills and work, and combining this into the technologies and other explicit expressions of knowledge that are common during projects.

Formal and informal networks offer the opportunity for sharing experience, tacit knowledge and lessons learned with peers. Project managers are part of a community of practice, which develops, promotes and advances best practice and standards. A community may be sector-specific, reflecting the fact that many project managers have or need specialist knowledge.

Learning is a lifelong activity. The project manager must be aware of the need to undertake continuing professional development (CPD) and keep pace with changing standards, techniques and methods.

Consideration of time and resources required to support learning and development must be taken into account in the project plans.

Further reading

Clutterbuck, D. and Maggerson, D. (2004) *Techniques for Coaching and Mentoring*, Butterworth Heinemann, Oxford, ISBN 0–750–65287-X

Krogh, G. Von, Ichijo, K., Nonaka, I. (2001) *Enabling Knowledge Creation: How to Unlock the Mystery of Tacit Knowledge and Release the Power of Innovation*, Oxford University Press, Oxford ISBN 0-195126165.

Parsloe, E. (1999) *The Manager as Coach and Mentor*, 2nd edn, CIPD, London, ISBN 0–85292–803–3

Wenger, E. (2002) *Cultivating Communities of Practice: A Guide to Managing Knowledge*, Harvard Business School Press, Boston, MA, ISBN 1–57851–330–8

7.9

Professionalism and ethics

Professionalism and ethics both relate to proper conduct. Professionalism is demonstrable awareness and application of qualities and competencies covering knowledge, appropriate skills and behaviours. Ethics covers the conduct and moral principles recognised as appropriate within the project management profession.

The features of a profession and professionalism may be summarised as follows:

- A profession creates and owns a distinctive, relevant body of knowledge.
- Members of the profession need to continue to practise and apply themselves to ongoing learning in order to maintain appropriate skills.
- Individual members should follow standards of professional ethics and behave in a manner appropriate to the profession.
- A profession should award certificates-to-practise based on examination of individuals' competence.

Project management has many of these features. A project manager who behaves in accordance with the features of a profession will provide a consistent, predictable standard and quality of work, have a responsibility to colleagues in project management to maintain these standards and will act as advocate for the profession.

The position of the project manager may be influenced by contractual requirements, but professionalism indicates that there remains a fiduciary relationship with the client which covers acting in equity, good faith and good conscience with due regard to the interests of the organisation or client.

The trust and respect of those they work for and with are key to the success of a project manager who wants to be regarded as a professional. This trust is gained by displaying a morally, legally and socially appropriate manner of behaving and working.

Ethical requirements are an integral part of the project manager's professional behaviour and require a fundamental understanding of the norms of the organisation's expectations, moral values and legal boundaries, which in turn vary by location, culture and sector. The ethics of the process by which the project deliverables are produced and the use to which the deliverables could be put should be considered. If a project manager believes that they have conflicts of interest or difficulties with professionalism or ethics in their activities then this should be escalated to a relevant authority, typically the sponsor or professional association for advice and direction.

The trend in recent decades has been for project management knowledge to become more comprehensive, formalised and recognised as a discipline. Organisations who have acknowledged this have expectations that project managers will behave professionally and ethically, to a consistent level of performance, creating a relationship that nurtures trust between the organisation and project manager in ways that transcend commercial agreements.

Further reading

Freidson, Eliot (2001) *Professionalism, the Third Logic: On the Practice of Knowledge*, University of Chicago Press, Chicago, IL, ISBN 0–226–26202–2

Harrison, M. (2005) *An Introduction to Business and Management Ethics*, Palgrave Macmillan, Basingstoke, ISBN 1–4039–0016–7

Malin, N. (ed.) (1999) *Professionalism, Boundaries and the Workplace*, Routledge, London, ISBN 0–415–19263–3

Trevino, L. and Nelson, K. (2005) *Managing Business Ethics*, 3rd edn, Wiley, Hoboken, NJ, ISBN 0–471–23054–5

Appendices

Comparison with the fourth edition of the *APM Body of Knowledge*

Fourth Edition 2000	Fifth Edition 2006	Comments
1 General	*1 Project management in context*	All topics renumbered. Section name changed
10 Project management	1.1 Project management	
11 Programme management	1.2 Programme management	
12 Project context	1.3 Portfolio management	New topic – Portfolio management split out of Programme management
	1.4 Project context	New topic
	1.5 Project sponsorship	New topic
	1.6 Project office	
2 Strategic	*2 Planning the strategy*	Section name changed
20 Project success criteria	2.1 Project success and benefits management	Topic name changed – benefits management added
21 Strategy/project management plan	2.2 Stakeholder management	New topic – previously covered within other topics
22 Value management	2.3 Value management	
23 Risk management	2.4 Project management plan	Topic name changed
24 Quality management	2.5 Project risk management	Topic name changed
25 Health, safety and environment	2.6 Project quality management	Topic name changed
	2.7 Health, safety and environmental management	Topic name changed
3 Control	*3 Executing the strategy*	Section name changed
30 Work content and scope management	3.1 Scope management	Topic name changed
31 Time scheduling/phasing	3.2 Scheduling	Topic name changed
32 Resource management	3.3 Resource management	
33 Budgeting and cost management	3.4 Budgeting and cost management	
34 Change control	3.5 Change control	
35 Earned value management	3.6 Earned value management	
36 Information management	3.7 Information management and reporting	Topic name changed – Reporting added
	3.8 Issue management	New topic

Fourth edition	New edition	Comment
4 Technical	*4 Techniques*	Section name changed
40 Design, implementation and handover management	4.1 Requirements management	Topic name changed; emphasis of topic changed also
41 Requirements management	4.2 Development	New topic added. Emphasis of topic changed
42 Estimating	4.3 Estimating	Emphasis of topic changed
43 Technology management	4.4 Technology management	
44 Value engineering	4.5 Value engineering	
45 Modelling and testing	4.6 Modelling and testing	
46 Configuration management	4.7 Configuration management	
5 Commercial	*5 Business and Commercial*	Section name changed
50 Business case	5.1 Business case	
51 Marketing and sales	5.2 Marketing and sales	
52 Financial management	5.3 Project financing and funding	Topic name changed
53 Procurement	5.4 Procurement	
54 Legal awareness	5.5 Legal awareness	
6 Organisational	*6 Organisation and Governance*	Section name changed
60 Life cycle design & management	6.1 Project life cycles	Topic name changed
61 Opportunity	6.2 Concept	Topic name changed
62 Design and development	6.3 Definition	Topic name changed
63 Implementation	6.4 Implementation	
64 Hand-over	6.5 Handover and closeout	Topic name changed
65 (Post) project evaluation review [O&M/ILS]	6.6 Project reviews	Topic name changed
66 Organisation structure	6.7 Organisation structure	
67 Organisational roles	6.8 Organisational roles	
	6.9 Methods and procedures	New topic
	6.10 Governance of project management	New topic
7 People	*7 People and the Profession*	Section name changed
70 Communication	7.1 Communication	
71 Teamwork	7.2 Teamwork	
72 Leadership	7.3 Leadership	
73 Conflict management	7.4 Conflict management	
74 Negotiation	7.5 Negotiation	
75 Personnel management	7.6 Human resource management	Topic name changed
	7.7 Behavioural characteristics	Transferred from 4th edition preface
	7.8 Learning and development	New topic
	7.9 Professionalism and ethics	New topic

Glossary of project management terms

This glossary is made up of terms used in the fifth edition of the *APM Body of Knowledge* plus many other terms used in the wider application of project management. Terms in bold within the definition are also listed.

Accept A response to a risk (**threat** or **opportunity**) where no course of action is taken.

Acceptance The formal process of accepting delivery of a **deliverable** or a product.

Acceptance criteria The requirements and essential conditions that have to be achieved before project **deliverables** are accepted.

Acceptance test* A formal, predefined test conducted to determine the compliance of the **deliverable**(s) with the **acceptance criteria**.

Accrual Work done for which payment is due but has not been made.

Accrued costs* Costs that are earmarked for the project and for which payment is due, but has not been made.

Acquisition strategy The establishment of the most appropriate means of procuring the component parts or services of a project.

Activity* A task, job, operation or process consuming time and possibly other resources. (The smallest self contained unit of work used to define the logic of a project).

Activity duration The length of time that it takes to complete an activity.

Activity ID A unique code identifying each activity in a project.

Activity network *See* **network diagram.**

Activity-on-arrow network* Arrow diagram – a **network diagram** in which the arrows symbolise the activities.

Activity-on-node network* Precedence diagram – a **network diagram** in which the nodes symbolise the activities.

Activity status The state of completion of an activity.

Actual cost* The incurred costs that are charged to the project budget and for which payment has been made, or accrued.

Actual cost of work performed (ACWP)* A term used in **earned value management**. Cumulative cost of work accrued on the project in a specific period or up to a specific stage. Note: for some purposes cost may be measured in labour hours rather than money. *See* **actual cost.**

Actual dates The dates on which activities started and finished as opposed to planned or forecast dates.

*Asterisks indicate definitions that are also published in BS6079–2: 2000. Permission to reproduce extracts of BS 6079–2: 2000 is granted by BSI. British Standards can be obtained from BSI customer services, 389 Chiswick High Road, London, W4 4AL, tel.: +44(0)20 89969001. Email: cservices@bsi-global.com

Actual expenditure   The money that has already been paid.

Actual finish   The date on which an activity was completed.

Actual start   The date on which an activity was started.

Actual time expended The elapsed time from the beginning of an activity to date.

Adjudication   The legal process by which an arbiter or other independent third party reviews evidence and argumentation, including legal reasoning, set forth by opposing parties to come to a decision or judgement which determines rights and obligations between the parties involved.

Agile development   A family of methodologies where the development emphasises real time communication and software.

Alliancing   An arrangement whereby two or more organisations agree to manage a contract or range of contracts between them jointly. *See* **partnering**.

Alternative dispute resolution (ADR) The collective term for settling **disputes** with the help of an independent third party without a court hearing. For example **arbitration**, **adjudication** and **mediation**.

Arbitration   The process of using a third party appointed to settle a **dispute**.

Arrow*   A direct connecting line between two nodes in a network.

Arrow diagram*   *See* **activity-on-arrow network**.

Arrow diagram method (ADM)   One of two conventions used to represent an activity in a **network diagram**. Also known as activity-on-arrow method.

As late as possible (ALAP)   An activity for which the early start date is set as late as possible without delaying the early dates of any successor.

Associated revenue*   That part of a project cost that is of a revenue nature and therefore charged as incurred to the profit and loss account.

As soon as possible (ASAP)   An activity for which the early start date is set to be as soon as possible. This is the default activity type in most project scheduling systems.

Assumptions   Statements that will be taken for granted as fact and upon which the project business case will be justified.

Assurance   The process of examining with the intent to verify. *See* **quality assurance**.

Audit*   The systematic retrospective examination of the whole, or part, of a project or function to measure conformance with predetermined standards.

Authorisation points   The points at which the business case is reviewed and approved.

Avoid   A response to a **threat** that eliminates its probability or impact on the project.

Backward pass*   A procedure whereby the latest event times or the latest finish and start times for the activities of a network are calculated.

Balanced matrix An organisational matrix where **functions** and projects have the same priority.

Bar chart*   A chart on which activities and their durations are represented by lines drawn to a common timescale. *See* **Gantt chart**.

Base date   A reference date used as a basis for the start of a project **calendar**.

Baseline* The reference levels against which the project is monitored and controlled.

Baseline cost(s) The amount of money a project or activity was intended to cost when the project plan was baselined.

Baseline date(s) The original planned start and finish dates for a project or an activity when the schedule was baselined.

Baseline plan The fixed **project plan**. It is the standard by which performance against the project plan is measured.

Baseline schedule The fixed **project schedule**. It is the standard by which project schedule performance is measured.

Behavioural characteristics The elements that separate and describe a person's preferred way of acting, interacting and reacting in a variety of situations.

Benchmarking A review of what other organisations are doing in the same area. For those organisations who appear to be particularly successful in what they do and how they do it and are taken to be examples to be emulated, i.e. used as benchmarks.

Benefit The quantifiable and measurable improvement resulting from completion of project **deliverables** that is perceived as positive by a **stakeholder**. It will normally have a tangible value, expressed in monetary terms, that will justify the investment.

Benefits framework An outline of the expected benefits of the project (or **programme**), the business operations affected and current and target performance measures. The totality of plans and arrangements to enable the organisation to realise the defined benefits

from a project or programme of projects.

Benefits management The identification of the benefits (of a **project** or **programme**) at an organisational level and the tracking and realisation of those benefits.

Benefits management plan A plan that specifies who is responsible for achieving the benefits set out in the **benefits profiles** and how achievement of the benefits is to be measured, managed and monitored.

Benefits profile A representation of when the benefits are planned to be realised.

Benefits realisation The practice of ensuring that the outcome of a project produces the projected benefits.

Benefits realisation review A review undertaken after a period of operations of the project **deliverables**. It is intended to establish that project benefits have or are being realised.

Bid A tender, quotation or any offer to enter into a contract.

Bid analysis An analysis of bids or tenders.

Bidding The process of preparing and submitting a bid or tender.

Bid list A list of contractors or suppliers invited to submit bids for goods or services.

Blueprint A document defining and describing what a **programme** is designed to achieve in terms of the business vision and the operational vision.

Body of Knowledge An inclusive term that describes the sum of knowledge within the profession of **project management**. As with other professions, such as law and medicine, the body of knowledge rests with the practitioners and academics that apply and advance it.

Bond Security against a loan or investment.

Bottleneck A process constraint that determines the capacity or capability of a system and restricts the rate, volume or flow of a process.

Bottom-up estimating An estimating technique based on making estimates for every work package (or activity) in the **work breakdown structure** and summarising them to provide a total estimate of cost or **effort** required.

Brainstorming The unstructured generation of ideas by a group of people in a short space of time.

Branching logic* Conditional logic. Alternative paths in a **probabilistic network**.

Breaches of contract A legal concept in which a binding agreement (contract) is not honoured by one of the parties to the contract, by non-performance or interference with the other party's performance.

Breakdown structure A hierarchical structure by which project elements are broken down, or decomposed. *See* **cost breakdown structure** (CBS), **organisational breakdown structure** (OBS), **product breakdown structure** (PBS), **risk breakdown structure** (RBS) **and work breakdown structure** (WBS).

Brief A high–level outline (strategic specification) of **stakeholders**' (customers/clients) needs and requirements for a project.

Budget* The agreed cost of the project or a quantification of resources needed to achieve an activity by a set time, within which the activity owners are required to work.

Budget at completion (BAC) The sum total of the time-phased budgets.

Budget cost The cost anticipated at the start of a project.

Budgeted cost of work performed (BCWP) A term used in **earned value management**. The planned cost of work completed to date. BCWP is also the 'earned value' of work completed to date. *See* **earned value**.

Budgeted cost of work scheduled (BCWS) A term used in **earned value management**. The planned cost of work that should have been achieved according to the project **baseline** dates. *See* **planned cost**.

Budget element Budget elements are the same as resources, the people, materials or other entities needed to do the work. They are typically assigned to a **work package**, but can also be defined at the **cost account** level.

Budget estimate An approximate estimate prepared in the early stages of a project to establish financial viability or to secure resources.

Budgeting Time-phased financial requirements.

Budgeting and cost management The estimating of costs and the setting of an agreed budget and the management of actual and forecast costs against that budget.

Buffer A term used in **critical chain** for the centralised management of **contingencies**.

Build, own, operate, transfer (BOOT) A situation whereby a private operator builds, owns, operates and then transfers a facility to another party after a specific period.

Build (stage) A stage within the **implementation** phase where the project **deliverables** are built or constructed.

Business-as-usual An organisation's normal day-to-day operations.

Business case The business case provides justification for undertaking a project, in terms of evaluating the benefit, cost and risk of alternative options and the rationale for the preferred solution. Its purpose is to obtain management commitment and approval for investment in the project. The business case is owned by the **sponsor**.

Business change manager(s) The role responsible for **benefits management** from identification through to realisation and ensuring the implementation and embedding of the new capabilities delivered by projects. May be more than one individual.

Business objectives The overall objectives of the business as opposed to the project.

Business risk assessment The assessment of risk to business objectives rather than risk to achieving project objectives.

Business to business (B2B) The exchange of services, information and products from a business to another business – generally undertaken electronically using the World Wide Web.

Business to consumer (B2C) The exchange of services, information and products from a business to a consumer – generally undertaken electronically using the World Wide Web.

Calendars A project calendar lists time intervals in which activities or resources can or cannot be scheduled. A project usually has one default calendar for the normal workweek (Monday through Friday, for example), but may

have other calendars as well. Each calendar can be customised with its own holidays and extra work days. Resources and activities can be attached to any of the calendars that are defined.

Capability A project capability (or outcome) that enables a benefit to be achieved. Alternatively having the necessary attributes to perform or accomplish.

Capability maturity models An organisational model that describes a number of evolutionary levels in which an organisation manages its processes, from *ad hoc* use of processes to continual improvement of its processes.

Capital Monetary investment in the project. Alternatively wealth used or available for use in the production of more wealth.

Capital cost* The carrying cost in a balance sheet of acquiring an asset and bringing it to the point where it is capable of performing its intended function over a future series of periods. *See* **revenue cost**.

Capital employed* The amount of investment in an organisation or project, normally the sum of fixed and current assets, less current liabilities at a particular date.

Capital expenditure (CapEX) The long-term expenditure for property, plant and equipment.

Cash flow* Cash receipts and payments in a specified period.

Cash flow forecast A prediction of the difference between cash received and payments to be made during a specific period or for the duration of the project.

Central repository A central location where data and information is stored. This can be a physical location, such as a filing cabinet, or a virtual location, such as a dedicated drive on a computer system.

Champion An end user representative often seconded into a **project team**. Someone who acts as an advocate for a proposal or project. Someone who spearheads an idea or action and 'sells it' throughout the organisation. A person within the parent organisation who promotes and defends a project.

Change A change to a project's baseline **scope**, cost, time or quality objectives.

Change authority An organisation or individual with power to authorise changes on a project.

Change control A process that ensures that all changes made to a project's baseline **scope**, cost, time or quality objectives are identified, evaluated, approved, rejected or deferred.

Change control board A formally constituted group of **stakeholders** responsible for approving or rejecting changes to the project **baselines**.

Change freeze A point on a project after which no further changes will be considered.

Change log A record of all project changes, proposed, authorised, rejected or deferred.

Change management The formal process through which changes to the project plan are approved and introduced. Also the process by which organisational change is introduced.

Change register *See* **change log**.

Change request A request to obtain formal approval for changes to the **scope**, design, methods, costs or planned aspects of a project.

Charter A document that sets out the working relationships and agreed behaviours within a **project team**.

Claim A written demand or assertion by a contracting party seeking as a matter of right financial adjustment or interpretation of an existing contract subject to the terms of the contract's dispute clause.

Client The party to a contract who commissions work and pays for it on completion.

Client brief *See* **brief**.

Closeout The process of finalising all project matters, carrying out final project reviews, archiving project information and redeploying the remaining project team. *See* **handover** and **closeout**.

Closure The formal end point of a project, either because it has been completed or because it has been terminated early.

Code of accounts Any numbering system, usually based on corporate code of accounts of the primary performing organisation, used to monitor project costs by category.

Commissioning* The advancement of an installation from the stage of static completion to full working order and achievement of the specified operational requirements. *See* **mechanical completion** and **pre-commissioning**.

Commitment A binding financial obligation, typically in the form of a purchase order or contract. The amount of money removed from the budget by this obligation.

Committed costs* Costs that are legally committed even if delivery has not taken place with invoices neither raised nor paid.

Common law Common law is the tradition, custom and especially precedent of previous judgements.

Communication The giving, receiving, processing and interpretation of information. Information can be conveyed verbally, non-verbally, actively, passively, formally, informally, consciously or unconsciously.

Communication plan A document that identifies what information is to be communicated to whom, why, when, where, how, through which medium and the desired impact.

Communication planning The establishment of project **stakeholders'** communication and information needs.

Comparative estimating An estimating technique based on the comparison with, and factoring from, the cost of a previous similar project or operation.

Competitive tendering A formal **procurement** process whereby vendors or contractors are given an equal chance to tender for the supply of goods or services against a fixed set of rules.

Completion When it is agreed that a project or part of a project has been completed in accordance with all requirements.

Completion date The calculated date by which the project could finish, following careful estimating and scheduling.

Community of practice A special type of informal network that emerges from a desire to work more effectively or to understand work more deeply among members of a particular speciality or work group.

Concept (phase) Concept is the first phase in the **project life cycle**. During this phase the need, opportunity or problem is confirmed, the overall feasibility of the project is considered and a preferred solution identified.

Concession The acceptance of something that is not within specified requirements.

Concurrent engineering The systematic approach to the simultaneous, integrated design of products and their related processes, such as manufacturing, testing and supporting.

Configuration* Functional and physical characteristics of a **deliverable** (product) as defined in technical documents and achieved in the product.

Configuration audit A check to ensure that all **deliverables** (products) in a project conform with one another and to the current specification. It ensures that relevant **quality assurance** procedures have been implemented and that there is consistency throughout project documentation.

Configuration control A system to ensure that all changes to **configuration** items are controlled. An important aspect is being able to identify the interrelationships between configuration items.

Configuration identification The unique identification of all items within the **configuration**. It involves breaking down the project into component parts or configuration items and creating a unique numbering or referencing system for each item and establishing configuration **baselines**.

Configuration item A part of a **configuration** that has a set function and is designated for **configuration management**. It identifies uniquely all items within the configuration.

Configuration management* Technical and administrative activities concerned with the creation, maintenance and controlled change of **configuration** throughout the project or product **life cycle**. See BS EN ISO 10007 for guidance on configuration management, including specialist terminology.

Configuration status accounting A record and report of the current status and history of all changes to the **configuration**. It provides a complete record of what has happened to the configuration to date.

Conflict management The process of identifying and addressing differences that if unmanaged would affect **project objectives**. Effective conflict management prevents differences becoming destructive elements in a project.

Conformance audit An audit of the operation of the **programme** or project management or other process to identify whether the defined processes are being adhered to.

Consideration In contract law – something of value. It may be money, an act or a promise. It is one of the key elements required to have a binding contract.

Constraints Things that should be considered as fixed or must happen. Restrictions that will affect the project.

Consumable resource A type of resource that only remains available until consumed (for example a material). *See* **replenishable resource**.

Context *See* **project context**.

Contingency The planned allotment of time and cost or other resources for unforeseeable risks within a project. Something held in reserve for the unknown.

Contingency budget The amount of money required to implement a **contingency plan**.

Contingency plan* Alternative course(s) of action to cope with project risks or if expected results fail to materialise.

Continuing professional development (CPD) A personal commitment made by an individual to keep their professional knowledge up to date and improve their capability, with a focus on what the person learns and how they develop throughout their career.

Continuous improvement Continuous improvement is a business philosophy popularised in Japan where it is known as Kaizen. Continuous improvement creates steady growth and improvement by keeping a business focused on its goals and priorities. It is a planned systematic approach to improvement on a continual basis.

Contract A mutually binding agreement in which the contractor is obligated to provide services or products and the buyer is obligated to provide payment for them.

Contractor A person, company or firm who holds a contract for carrying out the works and/or the supply of goods or services in connection with the project.

Contract price The price payable by the customer under the contract for the proper delivery of supplies and services specified in the **scope of work** of the contract.

Contract target cost The negotiated costs for the original defined contract and all contractual changes that have been agreed and approved, but excluding the estimated cost of any authorised, unpriced changes.

Contract target price The negotiated estimated costs plus profit or fee.

Control charts Control charts display the results, over time, of a process. They are used in quality management to determine if the process is in need of adjustment.

Coordination Coordination is the act of ensuring that work carried out by different organisations and in different places fits together effectively.

Corrective action Changes made to bring future project performance back into line with the plan.

Cost account A cost account defines what work is to be performed, who will perform it and who is to pay for it. Another term for cost account is control account.

Cost account manager (CAM) A member of a functional organisation responsible for cost account performance, and for the management of resources to accomplish such activities.

Cost–benefit analysis* An analysis of the relationship between the costs of undertaking an activity or project, initial and recurrent, and the benefits likely to arise from the changed situation, initially and recurrently.

Cost breakdown structure* (CBS) The hierarchical breakdown of a project into cost elements.

Cost budgeting The allocation of cost estimates to individual project activities or **deliverables**.

Cost centre* A location, person, activity or project in respect of which costs may be ascertained and related to cost units.

Cost code* A unique identity for a specified element of work. A code assigned to activities that allows costs to be consolidated according to the elements of a code structure.

Cost control system Any system of keeping costs within the bounds of bud-

gets or standards based upon work actually performed.

Cost curve A graph plotted against a horizontal timescale and cumulative cost vertical scale.

Cost estimating The process of predicting the costs of a project.

Cost incurred A cost identified through the use of the accrued method of accounting or a cost actually paid. Costs include direct labour, direct materials and all allowable indirect costs.

Cost management *See* **budgeting and cost management**.

Cost performance index (CPI)* A term used in **earned value management**. A measure, expressed as a percentage or other ratio of actual cost to budget plan. The ratio of work accomplished versus work cost incurred for a specified time period. The CPI is an efficiency rating for work accomplished for resources expended.

Cost performance report A regular cost report to reflect cost and schedule status information for management.

Cost plan A budget that shows the amounts and expected dates of incurring costs on the project or on a contract.

Cost plus fixed fee contract A type of contract where the buyer reimburses the seller for the seller's allowable costs plus a fixed fee.

Cost plus incentive fee contract A type of contract where the buyer reimburses the seller for the seller's allowable costs and the seller earns a profit if defined criteria are met.

Cost-reimbursement type contracts A category of contracts based on payments to a contractor for allowable estimated costs, usually requiring only a 'best efforts' performance standard from the contractor.

Cost/schedule planning and control specification (C/SPCS) The United States Air Force initiative in the mid-1960s which later resulted in their cost/schedule control systems criteria, C/SCSC.

Cost–time resource sheet (CTR) A document that describes each major element in the **work breakdown structure** (WBS), including a **statement of work** (SOW) describing the work content, resources required, the time frame of the work element and a cost estimate.

Cost variance* A term used in **earned value management**. The difference (positive or negative) between the actual expenditure and the planned/budgeted expenditure.

Critical activity An activity is termed critical when it has zero or negative **float**. Alternatively an activity that has the lowest float on the project.

Critical chain A networking technique based on Goldratt's **theory of constraints** that identifies paths through a project based on resource dependencies as well as technological precedence requirements.

Criticality index Used in **risk analysis**, the criticality index represents the percentage of **simulation** trials that resulted in the activity being placed on the critical path.

Critical path* A sequence of activities through a **project network** from start to finish, the sum of whose durations determines the overall project duration. There may be more than one such path. The path through a series of activities, taking into account interdependencies, in which the late completion of activities will have an impact on the project end date or delay a **key milestone**.

Critical path analysis* (CPA) The procedure for calculating the **critical path** and **floats** in a network.

Critical path method (CPM) A technique used to predict project duration by analysing which sequence of activities has the least amount of scheduling flexibility.

Critical success factor *See* **success factors**.

Culture The attitudes and values that inform those involved in a project.

Current dates The planned start and finish dates for an activity according to the current schedule.

Cut-off date The end date of a reporting period.

Dangle An activity in a **network diagram** that has either no predecessors or no successors. If neither, it is referred to as an isolated activity.

Decision tree A pictorial (tree-like) representation of the alternatives and outcomes in a decision situation.

Definition (phase) Definition is the second phase of the **project life cycle**. During this phase the preferred solution is further evaluated and optimised. Often an iterative process, definition can affect requirements and the project's **scope**, time, cost and quality objectives.

Delegation The practice of getting others to perform work effectively that one chooses not to do oneself. The process by which authority and responsibility is distributed from **project manager** to subordinates.

Deliverables* The end products of a project or the measurable results of intermediate activities within the project organisation. *See* **product**.

Delphi technique A process where a consensus view is reached by consultation with experts. Often used as an estimating technique.

Demobilisation The controlled dispersal of personnel when they are no longer needed on a project.

Dependencies* Something on which successful delivery of the project critically depends, which may often be outside the sphere of influence of the **project manager**, for example another project. Alternatively, dependency, a precedence relationship: a restriction that means that one activity has to precede, either in part or in total, another activity.

Dependency arrow* A link arrow used in an **activity-on-node network** to represent the interrelationships of activities in a project.

Design authority The person or organisation with overall design responsibility for the products of the project.

Design (stage) A stage within the **implementation** phase where the design of project **deliverables** is finalised.

Detailed design The in-depth design of the chosen solution, ready for full implementation.

Deterministic Something that is predetermined, with no possibility of an alternative outcome.

Deterministic estimate A predetermined estimate with no possibility of an alternative outcome.

Development The working up of a preferred solution to an optimised

solution during the **definition** and **implementation** phases of a project.

Deviations Departure from the established plan or requirements.

Direct costs* Costs that are specifically attributable to an activity or group of activities without apportionment. The cost of resources expended in the achievement of work that are directly charged to a project, without the inclusion of **indirect costs**.

Direct labour Labour that is specifically identified with a particular activity. It is incurred for the exclusive benefit of the project.

Discipline An area of expertise. *See* **function**.

Discounted cash flow (DCF)* The concept of relating future cash inflows and outflows over the life of a project or operation to a common base value thereby allowing more validity to comparison of projects with different durations and rates of cash flow.

Dispute A dispute is where parties disagree concerning a particular event.

Dispute resolution The process of resolving disputes between parties.

'Do nothing' option The result or consequence of taking no action, i.e., doing nothing to correct a problem, satisfy a need or seize an opportunity.

Drawdown The removal of funds from an agreed source resulting in a reduction of available funds.

Dummy activity (in activity-on-arrow network) A logical link that may require time but no other resource. An activity representing no actual work to be done but required for reasons of logic or nomenclature.

135

Duration The length of time needed to complete the project or an activity.

Duration compression Often resulting in an increase in cost, duration compression is the shortening of a project schedule without reducing the project **scope**.

Duty of care A duty of care is owed to persons who are so closely and directly affected by an individual's acts that they ought reasonably to have had them in contemplation as being affected when directing their mind to the acts or omissions that are called into question.

Dynamic systems development method (DSDM) A non-proprietary, **agile development** method for developing business solutions within tight time frames commonly used in IT projects.

Earliest finish date The earliest possible date by which an activity can finish within the logical and imposed constraints of the network.

Earliest start date The earliest possible date when an activity can start within the logical and imposed constraints of the network.

Earned hours The time in standard hours credited as a result of the completion of a given activity or a group of activities.

Earned value* The value of the useful work done at any given point in a project. The value of completed work expressed in terms of the budget assigned to that work. A measure of project progress. Note: the budget may be expressed in cost or labour hours.

Earned value analysis An analysis of project progress where the actual money, hours (or other measure) budgeted and spent is compared to the value of the work achieved.

Earned value management A project control process based on a structured approach to planning, cost collection and performance measurement. It facilitates the integration of project **scope**, time and cost objectives and the establishment of a **baseline plan** for performance measurement.

E-commerce Business that is conducted over the Internet using any of the applications that rely on the Web, such as e-mail, instant messaging, shopping carts and Web services.

Effectiveness A measure of how well an action meets its intended requirements.

Effort The number of labour units necessary to complete the work. Effort is usually expressed in labour hours, labour days or labour weeks and should not be confused with **duration**.

Effort-driven activity An activity whose duration is governed by resource usage and availability.

Effort remaining The estimate of **effort** remaining to complete an activity.

EFQM Excellence Model A model for diagnosing organisational excellence.

Elapsed time The total number of calendar days (excluding non-work days such as weekends or holidays) that is needed to complete an activity.

End activity An activity with no logical successors.

End user The person or organisation that will use the facility produced by the project or the products produced by such a facility.

Enhance A response to an **opportunity** that increases its probability, impact or both on the project.

Environment The project environment is the context within which the project is formulated, assessed and realised. This includes all external factors that have an impact on the project.

Escalate *See* **escalation**

Escalation The process by which aspects of the project such as issues are drawn to the attention of those senior to the project manager, such as the sponsor, steering group or project board.

Estimate An approximation of project time and cost targets, refined throughout the **project life cycle**.

Estimate at completion (EAC) A value expressed in money and/or hours to represent the projected final costs of work when completed. (Also referred to as projected **outturn cost**.)

Estimated cost to complete (ECC) The value expressed in either money or hours developed to represent the cost of the work required to complete an activity.

Estimating The use of a range of tools and techniques to produce estimates.

Ethical procurement Procurement that is in accordance with established ethics or moral values.

Event* State in the progress of a project after the completion of all preceding activities, but before the start of any succeeding activity. (A defined point that is the beginning or end of an activity).

Exception management An approach to management that focuses on drawing attention to instances where planned and actual results are expected to be, or are already, significantly different. Exceptions can be better than planned or worse than planned.

Exception report* A focused report drawing attention to instances where planned and actual results are expected to be, or are already, significantly different.

Exceptions Occurrences that cause deviation from a plan, such as **issues**, **change requests** and **risks**. Exceptions can also refer to items where the **cost variance** and **schedule variance** exceed predefined thresholds.

Expected monetary value The product of an event's probability of occurrence and the (financial) gain or loss that will result. Hence if there is a 50 per cent probability of rain and the rain will result in a £1000 increase in cost, the EMV will be $0.5 \times £1000$, i.e. £500.

Expediting The facilitation and acceleration of progress by the removal of obstacles (particularly used in **procurement** management).

Expended hours The hours spent to achieve an activity or group of activities.

Expenditure A charge against available funds, evidenced by a voucher, claim or other document. Expenditures represent the actual payment of funds.

Exploit A response to an **opportunity** that maximises both its probability and impact on the project.

Extended life cycle A **life cycle** model that includes the operational life and termination, including disposal of the project **deliverables**.

External constraint A **constraint** from outside the project.

External environment The environment in which the project must be undertaken that is external to the organisation carrying out the project.

External suppliers Suppliers external to the organisation carrying out the project.

Facility The final result, outcome or **deliverable** of the project.

Factors Situations that affect or influence **outcomes**.

Fast-tracking* The process of reducing the duration of a project usually by overlapping phases or activities that were originally planned to be done sequentially. The process of reducing the number of sequential relationships and replacing them typically with parallel relationships, usually to achieve shorter overall durations but often with increased risk.

Feasibility study* An analysis to determine if a course of action is possible within the terms of reference of the project. Work carried out on a proposed project or alternatives to provide a basis for deciding whether or not to proceed.

Final account The account that finally closes a purchase order or contract.

Financial appraisal An assessment of the financial aspects of a project or programme.

Financing and funding *See* **project financing and funding**.

Finish-to-finish lag The finish-to-finish lag is the minimum amount of time that must pass between the finish of one activity and the finish of its successor(s).

Finish-to-start lag The finish-to-start lag is the minimum amount of time that must pass between the finish of one activity and the start of its successor(s).

Firm fixed price contract A contract where the buyer pays a set amount to the seller regardless of that seller's cost to complete the contract.

Fitness for purpose The degree to which the project management process and project deliverables satisfy stakeholder needs. *See* **quality.**

Fixed date A calendar date (associated with a schedule) that cannot be moved or changed during the project.

Fixed price contracts A generic category of contracts based on the establishment of firm legal commitments to complete the required work. A performing contractor is legally obligated to finish the job, no matter how much it costs to complete.

Float *See* **free float** and **total float**.

Flow diagram A graphic representation of workflow and the logical sequence of the work elements without regard to a timescale. It is used to show the logic associated with a process rather than duration for completion of work.

Force-field analysis A technique used to identify the various pressures promoting or resisting change.

Forecast Estimates or prediction of future conditions and events based on information and knowledge available when the estimate was prepared.

Forecast costs A projection of future costs that the project will incur.

Forecast final cost *See* **estimate at completion**.

Forecast out-turn cost The cost of actual expenditure, accruals and the estimate of the costs to complete the work to the end of the project.

Form of contract The type of contract to be used. This could be a standard form of contract relevant to the business or industry sector.

Forward pass* A procedure whereby the earliest event times or the earliest start and finish times for the activities of a network are calculated.

Free float* Time by which an activity may be delayed or extended without affecting the start of any succeeding activity.

Function A specialist department that provides dedicated services, for example accounts department, production department, marketing department or IT.

Functional analysis The identification and analysis of the functional attributes of different solutions.

Functional analysis and system technique (FAST) An evolution of the value analysis process. FAST permits people with different technical backgrounds to effectively communicate and resolve issues that require multi-disciplined considerations. FAST builds on value analysis by linking the simply expressed, verb-noun functions to describe complex systems.

Functional departments *See* **function.**

Functional manager The person responsible for the business and technical management of a functional group.

Functional organisation (structure) A functional management structure where specific functions of a business are grouped into specialist departments that provide a dedicated service to the whole of the organisation, for example accounts department, production department, marketing department or IT.

Functional specification A document specifying in some detail the functions that are required of a system and the constraints that will apply.

Funding The actual money available for expenditure on the project.

Funding profile An estimate of funding requirements over time.

Gantt chart* A particular type of **bar chart** used in project management showing planned activity against time. A Gantt chart is a time-phased graphic display of activity durations. Activities are listed with other tabular information on the left side with time intervals over the bars. Activity durations are shown in the form of horizontal bars.

Gate review A formal point in a project where its expected worth, progress, cost and execution plan are reviewed and a decision is made whether to continue with the next phase or stage of the project.

Goal A one-sentence definition of specifically what will be accomplished, incorporating an event signifying completion.

Gold plating Completing deliverables to a higher specification than required to achieve acceptance criteria. Exceeding specification or grade and therefore adding cost that does not contribute to value.

Governance of project management (GoPM) GoPM concerns those areas of corporate governance that are specifically related to project activities. Effective governance of project management ensures that an organisation's project **portfolio** is aligned to the organisation's objectives, is delivered efficiently and is sustainable.

Guarantees Legally enforceable assurance of performance of a contract by a supplier or contractor.

Hammock* An activity joining two specified points that span two or more activities. Its duration is initially unspecified and is only determined by the durations of the specified activities. A group of activities, **milestones** or other hammocks aggregated together for analysis or reporting purposes. This term is sometimes used to describe an activity such as management support that has no duration of its own but derives one from the time difference between the two points to which it is connected.

139

Handover The point in the **life cycle** where **deliverables** are handed over to the **sponsor** and users. *See* **handover and closeout**.

Handover and closeout (phase) Handover and closeout is the fourth and final phase in the **project life cycle**. During this phase final project **deliverables** are handed over to the **sponsor** and users. Closeout is the process of finalising all project matters, carrying out final project reviews, archiving project information and redeploying the **project team**.

Hazards Potential sources of harm.

Health and safety plan The plan that identifies the health and safety strategies and procedures to be used on the project.

Health and safety risk assessment A legislative requirement placed on all employers and the self-employed.

Health, safety and environmental management The process of determining and applying appropriate standards and methods to minimise the likelihood of accidents, injuries or environmental damage both during the project and during the operation of its **deliverables**.

Hierarchical coding structure A coding system that can be represented as a multi-level tree structure in which every code except those at the top of the tree has a parent code.

Hierarchy of networks* Range of networks (**network diagrams**) at different levels of detail, from summary down to working levels, showing the relationships between those networks.

High-level requirements A high-level statement of the need that a project has to satisfy.

Histogram A graphic display of planned and/or actual resource usage over a period of time. It is in the form of a vertical **bar chart**, the height of each bar representing the quantity of resource usage in a given time unit. Bars may be single, multiple or show stacked resources.

Holiday An otherwise valid working day that has been designated as exempt from work.

Human resource management (HRM) The understanding and application of the policy and procedures that directly affect the people working in the **project team** and **working group**.

Hypercritical activities Activities on the **critical path** with **negative float**.

Idea development Develop evaluated opportunities to understand their benefits and costs.

Idea evaluation Rank the identified opportunities according to their appropriateness.

Impact The assessment of the effect on an objective of a risk occurring.

Impact analysis An assessment of the merits of pursuing a particular course of action or of the potential impact of a requested change.

Implementation (phase) Implementation is the third phase of the **project life cycle** where the **project management plan** (PMP) is executed, monitored and controlled. During this phase the design is finalised and used to build the **deliverables**.

Imposed date* A point in time determined by external circumstances.

Imposed finish A finish date imposed on an activity by external circumstances or constraints.

Imposed start A start date imposed on an activity by external circumstances or constraints.

Incentive A contribution to motivation (usually in the form of financial or other reward).

Incurred costs* The sum of actual and committed costs, whether invoiced/paid or not, at a specified time.

Indirect cost* Costs associated with a project that cannot be directly attributed to an activity or group of activities. Resources expended that are not directly identified to any specific contract, project, product or service, such as overheads and general administration.

Influence diagram A pictorial representation of the logic and sequence with which a set of variables have an effect on one another.

Information management The collection, storage, dissemination, archiving and appropriate destruction of project information.

Initiation The process of committing the organisation to begin a project. The beginning of a project at which point certain management activities are required to ensure that the project is established with clear reference terms and adequate management structure.

In progress activity An activity that has been started, but not yet completed.

Integrated baseline review (IDR) A review held following the establishment of the initial **baseline**.

Integration The process of bringing people, activities and other things together to perform effectively.

Intellectual property rights (IPR) The rights associated with intangible property that is the result of creativity.

Interdependencies An aspect of programme and portfolio management. The management of dependencies between projects, and projects and business-as-usual activities.

Interface management The management of the relationships between the work of different departments or organisations on a project or between the project and external organisations.

Interface management plan A plan identifying the interfaces internal and external to the projects and showing how they are to be managed.

Internal environment The environment in which the project must be undertaken that is internal to the organization carrying out the project.

Internal rate of return (IRR)* A discount rate at which the **net present value** of a future cash flow is zero. Note: IRR is a special case of the **discounted cash flow** procedures.

Interrelationship Used to describe the relationship between activities that need to be managed by a team or by a single person.

Investment The outlay of money or time usually for income, profit, or other benefit, such as the capital outlay for a project.

Investment appraisal The appraisal of the value of a project.

Invitation to tender (ITT) An invitation to a supplier to tender or bid for the supply of goods or services.

Island of stability A review point at the end of a programme **tranche** when progress is reviewed and the next tranche is planned.

Issue A threat to the project objectives that cannot be resolved by the **project manager**.

Issue log A log of all **issues** raised during a project or programme, showing details of each issue, its evaluation, what decisions were made and its current status.

Issue management The process by which concerns that threaten the **project objectives** and cannot be resolved by the **project manager** can be identified and addressed to remove the threats that they pose.

Issue register *See* **issue log**.

Joint venture (JV) A joint ownership of a firm by two or more persons or other firms, or a partnership between two or more companies mutually engaged in a particular venture such as a major project.

Just in time (JIT) A philosophy in which goods, services or actions are provided on demand as needed and without waiting, queuing or storage.

Key events Major events, the achievement of which is deemed to be critical to the execution of the project.

Key events schedule *See* **master schedule**.

Key milestone A **milestone**, the achievement of which is considered to be critical to the success of the project.

Key performance indicators (KPI) Measures of success that can be used throughout the project to ensure that it is progressing towards a successful conclusion.

Ladder* A device for representing a set of overlapping activities in a **network diagram**. The start and finish of each succeeding activity are linked to the start and finish of the preceding activity only by lead and lag activities, which consume only time.

Lag* In a **network diagram**, the minimum necessary lapse of time between the finish of one activity and the finish of an overlapping activity. The delay incurred between two specified activities.

Latest finish date The latest possible date by which an activity has to finish within the logical activity and imposed constraints of the network, without affecting the total project duration.

Latest start date The latest possible date by which an activity has to start within the logical and imposed constraints of the network, without affecting the total project duration.

Law of the land A slang term for existing laws.

Lead* In a **network diagram**, the minimum necessary lapse of time between the start of one activity and the start of an overlapping activity.

Leadership The ability to establish vision and direction, to influence and align others towards a common purpose, and to empower and inspire people to achieve project success. It enables the project to proceed in an environment of change and uncertainty.

Lean Lean (construction, engineering, manufacturing) is concerned with identifying the underlying principles by which environments can become more responsive, flexible, productive, reliable and cost effective.

Learning and development The continual improvement of competencies in the organisation. The identification and application of learning within projects develops the organisation's capability to undertake current and future projects.

Legal awareness An understanding of the relevant legal duties, rights and processes that should be applied to projects.

Legal duties The statutory laws that need to be followed and adhered to by all those involved in the project.

Lessons learned The identification of activities associated with the project that went well, those that could have been better, to recommend improvements applied in the future and to future projects.

Letter of intent A letter indicating an intent to sign a contract, usually so that work can commence prior to signing that contract.

Levelling *See* **resource levelling**.

Level one plan The master plan for the project. Level two and level three plans are given in successively more detail.

Liabilities Amounts owed under obligations for goods and services received and other assets aquired; includes accruals of amounts earned but not yet due and progress payments due on contract.

Life Cycle *See* **project life cycles.**

Life cycle cost The cumulative cost of a project over its whole **life cycle**.

Linked bar chart A **bar chart** that explicitly shows the dependency links between activities.

Liquidated damages The liability in a contract to pay a specified sum for a breach of contract such as late delivery of goods or services.

Litigation Any lawsuit or other reason to resort to court to determine a legal question or matter.

Logic *See* **network logic**.

Logical dependency A logical dependency is based on the dependency between two project activities or between a project activity and a **milestone**.

Logic diagram *See* **network diagram.**

Make or buy decision The decision to make a deliverable internally or to buy a finished deliverable from a supplier, for example, develop a software application in-house or purchase an existing application.

Management by exception A term used to describe management of problem or critical areas only.

Management development All aspects of staff planning, recruitment, development, training and assessment.

Management reserve* A central **contingency** pool. The sum of money held as an overall contingency to cover the cost impact of some unexpected event occurring.

Marketing Marketing involves anticipating the demands of users, and identifying and satisfying their needs by providing the right project at the right time, cost and quality.

Master network* A network showing the complete project, from which more detailed networks are derived.

Master schedule A high-level summary **project schedule** that identifies major activities and **milestones**.

Material Property that may be incorporated into or attached to an end item to be delivered under a contract or may be consumed or expended in the performance of a contract.

Material take-off A list of materials required to build an item that is derived from a drawing.

Matrix organisation (structure) An organisational structure where the **project manager** and the **functional managers** share responsibility for assigning priorities and for directing the work. Individuals stay in their functional departments while performing work on one or more projects.

Maturity The sophistication and experience of an organisation in managing projects.

Mechanical completion The point at which a facility has been fully installed and individual components have been inspected and tested using safe techniques and inert materials. Ready to start **pre-commissioning** or **commissioning**.

Mediation An attempt to settle a legal dispute through active participation of a third party (mediator) who works to find points of agreement and make those in conflict agree on a fair result.

Method A method provides a consistent framework within which project management is performed.

Methods and procedures The standard practices to be used for managing projects throughout a **life cycle**.

Method statement A plan detailing how a piece of work is to be carried out.

Milestone* A key event. An event selected for its importance in the project.

Milestone plan A plan containing milestones that highlight key points of the project.

Milestone schedule A schedule that identifies the major **milestones**. *See* **master schedule**.

Mission statement A brief summary, of approximately one or two sentences, that sums up the background, purpose and benefits of the project.

Mobilisation The bringing together of project personnel and securing of equipment and facilities.

Model A way of looking at reality, usually for the purpose of abstracting and simplifying it, to make it understandable in a particular context. Models may be either **physical** or **virtual**.

Modelling The process of creating and using a device that duplicates the physical or operational aspects of a deliverable.

Monitoring The recording, analysing and reporting of project **performance** as compared to the plan in order to identify and report deviations.

Monte Carlo simulation A technique used to estimate the likely range of outcomes from a complex process by simulating the process under randomly selected conditions a large number of times.

Near-critical activity An activity with low **total float** that may become critical under adverse conditions.

Need, problem or opportunity The underlying reason for undertaking a project. Without a definable need, problem or opportunity a project should not go ahead.

Negative (total) float* The time by which the duration of an activity or path has to be reduced in order to permit a limiting imposed date to be achieved.

Negotiated contract cost The estimated cost negotiated in a **cost plus fixed fee contract** or the negotiated contract target cost in either a fixed price incentive

144

contract or a **cost plus incentive fee contract**. *See* **contract target cost**.

Negotiation A search for agreement, seeking acceptance, consensus and alignment of views. Negotiation in a project can take place on an informal basis throughout the **project life cycle**, or on a formal basis such as during **procurement**, and between signatories to a contract.

Net present value* (NPV) The aggregate of future net cash flows discounted back to a common base date, usually the present.

Network analysis* A method used for calculating a project's critical path and activity times and **floats**. *See* **critical path analysis, project network techniques**.

Network diagram A pictorial presentation of project data in which the project logic is the main determinant of the placements of the activities in the drawing. Frequently called a flowchart, PERT chart, logic drawing, activity network or logic diagram.

Network logic The collection of activity dependencies that show logical relationships between the various activities and make up a project network.

Network path *See* **path**.

Nodes* The points in a network at which arrows start and finish.

Non-recurring costs Expenditures against specific activities that are expected to occur only once on a given project.

Non-splittable activity* An activity that, once started, has to be completed to plan without interruption.

Not earlier than A restriction on an activity that indicates that it may not start or end earlier than a specified date.

Not later than A restriction on an activity that indicates that it may not start or end later than a specified date.

Objectives Predetermined results towards which effort is directed.

Operational life As part of an extended life cycle, the operational life is part of the operations phase. It is when the deliverables are operated and maintained.

Operations phase The period during which the completed **deliverable** is used and maintained in service for its intended purpose.

Opportunity A positive risk; a risk that if it occurs will have a beneficial effect on the project. A positive aspect of project uncertainty, it may also help to negate threats.

Order of magnitude estimate An estimate carried out to give a very approximate indication of likely **outturn costs**.

Organisation A single corporate entity that is undertaking a project or providing services to a project.

Organisational breakdown structure (OBS)* A hierarchical way in which the organisation may be divided into management levels and groups, for planning and control purposes.

Organisational roles The roles performed by individuals or groups in a project. Both roles and responsibilities within projects must be defined to address the transient and unique nature of projects, and to ensure that clear accountabilities can be assigned.

Organisation chart A graphic display of reporting relationships that provides a general framework of the organisation.

Organisation design The design of the most appropriate organisation for a project.

Organisation structure The organisational environment within which the project takes place. It defines the reporting and decision-making hierarchy of an organisation and how project management operates within it.

Original budget The initial budget established at or near the time a contract was signed or a project authorised, based on the negotiated contract cost or management's authorisation.

Original duration The duration of activities or groups of activities as recorded in the **baseline schedule**.

Other direct costs (ODC) A group of accounting elements that can be isolated to specific activities, other than labour and material. Included in ODC are such items as travel, computer time and services.

Outcome The result of a project, the result of a deliberation concerning part of a project or an individual issue.

Out-of-sequence progress Progress that has been reported even though activities that have been deemed predecessors in project logic have not been completed.

Outputs Deliverables that are the result of a process. *See* **deliverables.**

Outsourcing* The contracting-out, or buying in of facilities or work (as opposed to using in-house resources).

Outturn cost The expected final cost of a project.

Overhead Costs incurred in the operation of a business that cannot be directly related to the individual products or services being produced. *See* **indirect cost.**

Overrun Costs incurred in excess of the contract target costs on an incentive type contract or of the estimated costs on a fixed fee contract. An overrun is that value of costs needed to complete a project, over that value originally authorised by management.

Owner The person or organisation for which the project is ultimately undertaken and who will own, operate and benefit from the facility in the long term.

Parallel activities Two or more activities than can be done at the same time.

Parametric estimating An estimating technique that uses a statistical relationship between historic data and other variables (for example square metreage in construction, lines of code in software development) to calculate an estimate.

Pareto diagram A **histogram** ordered by frequency of occurrence that shows how many results were generated by each identified cause.

Partnering An arrangement between two or more organisations to manage a contract between them cooperatively, as distinct from a legally established partnership. *See* **alliancing.**

Path* An activity or unbroken sequence of activities in a **network diagram**.

Payback An investment appraisal technique.

Percent complete A measure of the completion status of a partially completed activity. It may be aggregated to sections of a project or the whole project.

Performance The term used to describe the quality of the delivery and the deliverables (outputs) of the project.

Performance appraisal A review of the performance of individual people and teams on the project.

Performance management Techniques used in the management of individual and team performance. Performance management is also a term used in **earned value management** which is itself a performance management technique when applied to project performance.

Performance measurement techniques Performance measurement techniques are the methods used to estimate **earned value**. Different methods are appropriate to different **work packages**, either due to the nature of the work or due to the planned duration of the work package.

Performance specification* A statement of the totality of needs expressed by the benefits, features, characteristics, process conditions, boundaries and constraints that together define the expected performance of a **deliverable**.

Phase (of a project)* Part of a project during which a set of related and interlinked activities are performed to attain a designated objective. One of a series of distinct steps in carrying out a project that together constitute the **project life cycle**.

Phase reviews A review that takes place at the end of a life cycle phase. *See* **gate review**.

Physical models A representation of the three-dimensional, solid aspects of a deliverable which can be used to display its features or potentially test aspects it.

Physical percent complete The percentage of the work content of an activity that has been achieved.

Physical performance Actual performance of work on a project that can be measured; for example, the number of drawings produced or lines of code written.

Pilot A form of testing a new development and its implementation prior to committing to its full release.

Plan A plan is an intended future course of action. *See* **project management plan**.

Planned activity An activity not yet started.

Planned cost* The estimated cost of achieving a specified objective. *See* **budgeted cost of work scheduled**.

Planning The process of identifying the means, resources and actions necessary to accomplish an objective.

Portfolio A grouping of an organisation's projects, programmes and related business-as-usual activities taking into account **resource constraints**. Portfolios can be managed at an organisational, programme or functional level.

Portfolio management The selection and management of all of an organisation's projects, programmes and related operational activities taking into account **resource constraints**.

Portfolio prioritisation process The evaluation and prioritisation of projects within a portfolio to enable the more important projects and programmes to access the required resources and to move forward in accordance with their plans.

Post-project review Undertaken after the project **deliverables** have been handed over and before final **closeout**, this review is intended to produce lessons learnt that will enable continuous improvement.

PRAM Pram is an abbreviation of the APM Risk Management SIG's publication *Project Risk Analysis and Management Guide*.

Precedence diagram method One of the two methods of representing project as networks, in which the activities are represented by nodes and the relationships between them by arrows.

Precedence network* A multiple dependency network. An **activity-on-node** network in which a sequence arrow represents one of four forms of precedence relationship, depending on the positioning of the head and the tail of the sequence arrow. The relationships are:

finish to start
• start of activity depends on finish of preceding activity, either immediately or after a lapse of time;

finish to finish
• finish of activity depends on finish of preceding activity, either immediately or after a lapse of time;

start to start
• start of activity depends on start of preceding activity, either immediately or after a lapse of time;

start to finish
• finish of activity depends on start of preceding activity, either immediately or after a lapse of time.

Pre-commissioning The work that is carried out prior to **commissioning** in order to demonstrate that commissioning may be safely undertaken.

Predecessor An activity that must be completed (or be partially completed) before a specified activity can begin.

Predecessor activity In the **precedence diagram** method this is an activity that logically precedes the current activity.

Prime or lead contractor A main supplier who has a contract for much or all of the work on a contract. The prime contractor is responsible for managing projects that involve a number of sub-system contracts. It is responsible for coordinating the activities of subcontractors, integrating their **deliverables** and managing risks to meet the client's requirements.

PRINCE2 A project management method created for government projects. It is an acronym standing for **PR**ojects **IN** **C**ontrolled **E**nvironments (second version). It is intended to be generic.

Private finance initiative (PFI) In PFI, the public and private sectors enter into a contract which shares between them the risk of undertaking an investment project, typically to provide a major capital asset for the public services such as a school or a hospital and related services such as repairs and maintenance.

Probabilistic network A network containing alternative paths with which probabilities are associated.

Probability The likelihood of a risk occurring.

Problem In project management terms these are problems which are concerns that the project manager has to deal with on a day-to-day basis.

Procedures Procedures cover individual aspects of project management practice and form an integral part of a method.

Procedures manual A book of reference describing standard project procedures.

Process* A set of interrelated resources and activities that transform inputs into outputs.

Procurement The process by which the resources (goods and services) required by a project are acquired. It includes development of the procurement strategy, preparation of contracts, selection and acquisition of suppliers, and management of the contracts.

Procurement strategy A procurement strategy sets out how to acquire and manage resources (goods and services) required by a project.

Product *See* **deliverable**. (Note that in the PRINCE2 method product is used synonymously with deliverable).

Product breakdown structure (PBS) A hierarchy of deliverables that are required to be produced on the project. This forms the base document from which the execution strategy and product-based **work breakdown structure** may be derived. It provides a guide for **configuration control** documentation.

Product description The description of the purpose, form and components of a product. It should always be used as a basis for acceptance of the product by the customer.

Product flow diagram This diagram represents how the products are produced by identifying their derivation and the dependencies between them. It is similar to a **network diagram** but uses products rather than activities.

Productivity factor The ratio of earned hours against expended hours.

Professional development *See* **continuing professional development**.

Professionalism and ethics This relates to proper conduct. Professionalism is demonstrable awareness and applica-tion of qualities and competencies covering knowledge, appropriate skills and behaviours. Ethics covers the conduct and moral principles recognised as appropriate within the project management profession.

Profile of expenditure A project's budget is phased over time to give a profile of expenditure. This will allow a cash flow forecast for the project to be developed and a **drawdown** of funds to be agreed with the organisation.

Program evaluation and review technique (PERT) PERT is a project management technique for determining how much time a project needs before it is completed.

Programme A group of related projects, which may include related business-as-usual activities, that together achieve a beneficial change of a strategic nature for an organisation.

Programme benefits review A review to assess if targets have been reached and to measure the performance levels in the resulting business operations.

Programme brief A description of the capability that the organisation seeks from changes to its business and/or its operations. Delivery of this capability is the end goal of the **programme**.

Programme director The senior manager with the responsibility for the overall success of the **programme**.

Programme directorate A committee that directs the **programme** when circumstances arise where there is no individual to direct the programme.

Programme management The coordinated management of related projects, which may include related business-as-usual activities, that together achieve a beneficial change of a strategic nature for an organisation.

Programme management office The office responsible for the business and technical management of a specific **programme**.

Programme manager The individual with responsibility for managing a **programme**.

Programme mandate What the **programme** is intended to deliver in terms of new services and/or operational capability.

Programme support office A group that gives administrative support to the **programme** manager and the programme executive.

Progress The partial completion of a project, or a measure of the same.

Progress payments Payments made to a contractor during the life of a fixed-price type contract, on the basis of some agreed-to formula, for example **budget cost of work performed** or simply costs incurred.

Progress report A regular report to senior personnel, sponsors or stakeholders summarising the progress of a project including key events, **milestones**, costs and other issues.

Project A unique, transient endeavour undertaken to achieve a desired outcome.

Project appraisal The discipline of calculating the viability of a project. May be conducted at any time throughout the project.

Project assurance Independent monitoring and reporting of the project's performance and **deliverables**.

Project base date* *See* **base date**.

Project board *See* **steering group**.

Project brief* *See* **brief**.

Project budget *See* **budget**.

Project calendar *See* **calendars**.

Project champion* *See* **champion**.

Project charter *See* **charter**.

Project closure* *See* **closure**.

Project context The environment within which a project is undertaken. Projects do not exist in a vacuum and an appreciation of the context within which the project is being performed will assist those involved in project management to deliver a project.

Project coordination* *See* **coordination**.

Project culture *See* **culture**.

Project director The manager of a very large project that demands senior level responsibility or the person at the board level in an organisation who has the overall responsibility for project management.

Project environment *See* **environment**.

Project evaluation review A documented review of the project's performance, produced at predefined points in the **project life cycle**.

Project excellence model The basis of this model is the European Foundation for Quality Management **(EFQM) Excellence Model**. In 1997 the German Project Management Association developed the Project Excellence Model and used it as an evaluation tool to judge the annual German Project Management Awards.

Project file A file containing the overall plans of a project and any other important documents.

Project financing and funding The means by which the capital to undertake a project is initially secured and then made available at the appropriate time. Projects may be financed externally, funded internally or a combination of both.

Project initiation *See* **initiation**.

Project initiation document (PID) A document approved by the project board at project **initiation** that defines the terms of reference for the project. This document is similar and in some cases the same as the **project management plan** (PMP).

Project life cycles All projects follow a life cycle and life cycles will differ across industries and business sectors. A life cycle allows the project to be considered as a sequence of distinct phases that provide the structure and approach for progressively delivering the required outputs.

Project life cycle cost* *See* **life cycle cost**.

Project log* A project diary. A chronological record of significant occurrences throughout the project.

Project management The process by which projects are defined, planned, monitored, controlled and delivered so that agreed benefits are realised.

Project Management Body of Knowledge *See* **Body of Knowledge**.

Project management information system (PMIS) The systems, activities and data that allow information flow in a project, frequently computerised, but not always.

Project management maturity A model that describes a number of evolutionary levels in which an organisation's project management processes can be assessed, from *ad hoc* use of processes to continual improvement of its processes.

Project management plan (PMP) A plan that brings together all the plans for a project. The purpose of the PMP is to document the outcome of the planning process and to provide the reference document for managing the project. The project management plan is owned by the **project manager**.

Project management processes The generic processes that need to apply to each phase of the project life cycle. These may be described as a starting or initiating process, a defining and planning process, a monitoring and controlling process, and a learning or closing process.

Project management software Computer application software designed to help with planning and controlling projects.

Project management team Members of the **project team** who are directly involved in its management.

Project manager* The individual responsible and accountable for the successful delivery of the project.

Project mandate The initial terms of reference for the project – as defined in PRINCE2.

Project master schedule *See* **master schedule**.

Project network* A representation of activities and/or events with their interrelationships and dependencies.

Project objectives Those things that are to be achieved by the project, which usually include technical, time, cost and quality objectives but may include other items to meet **stakeholder** needs.

Project office This serves the organisation's project management needs. A project office can range from simple support functions for the **project manager** to responsibility for linking corporate strategy to project execution.

Project organisation (structure) The project organisation structure provides the maximum authority to the project manager. It provides integration of functional capabilities within projects. However, this leads to duplication of facilities, and less efficient use of resources.

Project plan *See* **project management plan**.

Project planning The development and maintenance of a project plan.

Project portfolio *See* **portfolio**.

Project procedures manual *See* **procedures manual**.

Project progress report* *See* **progress report**.

Project quality management The discipline that is applied to ensure that both the outputs of the project and the processes by which the outputs are delivered meet the required needs of **stakeholders**. Quality is broadly defined as fitness for purpose or more narrowly as the degree of **conformance** of the outputs and process.

Project review calendar* A calendar of **project evaluation review** dates, meetings and issues of reports set against project week numbers or dates.

Project risk The exposure of **stakeholders** to the consequences of **variation** in outcome.

Project risk management A structured process that allows individual **risk events** and overall **project risk** to be understood and managed proactively, optimising project success by mini-

mising threats and maximising opportunities.

Project roles and responsibilities The roles and responsibilities of those involved in the project; for example, the sponsor and project manager.

Project schedule* The timetable for a project. It shows how project activities and **milestones** are planned over a period of time. It is often shown as a milestone chart, Gantt or other **bar chart**, or as a tabular listing of dates.

Project scope management *See* **scope management**.

Project sponsor *See* **sponsor**.

Project sponsorship An active senior management role, responsible for identifying the business need, problem or opportunity. The sponsor ensures the project remains a viable proposition and that benefits are realised, resolving any issues outside the control of the **project manager**.

Project start-up The creation of the **project team** and making it effective.

Project status report A report on the status of accomplishments and any **variances** to spending and schedule plans.

Project steering group *See* **steering group**.

Project strategy A comprehensive definition of how a project will be developed and managed.

Project success The satisfaction of **stakeholder** needs measured by the **success criteria** as identified and agreed at the start of the project.

Project success criteria *See* **success criteria**.

Project support experts Individuals with expertise in particular aspects of project support such as scheduling, budgeting and cost management or reporting.

Project support office   *See* **project office**.

Project team   A set of individuals, groups and/or organisations responsible to the **project manager** for working towards a common purpose.

Project variance   Changes to cost or schedule that are within the current work plan or **scope**.

Public private partnership (PPP)   Public private partnerships (PPPs) are a generic term for the relationships formed between the private sector and public bodies often with the aim of introducing private sector resources and/or expertise in order to help provide and deliver public sector assets and services. The term PPP is used to describe a wide variety of working arrangements from loose, informal and strategic partnerships to design build finance and operate (DBFO) type service contracts and formal joint venture companies. The private finance initiative (PFI) is a form of PPP.

Public relations (PR)   An activity meant to improve the project organisation's environment in order to improve project performance and reception.

Punch list   A list of outstanding activities to be completed prior to final acceptance of the **deliverables**.

Qualitative risk analysis   A generic term for subjective methods of assessing risks that cannot be identified accurately.

Quality   The fitness for purpose or the degree of **conformance** of the outputs of the process.

Quality assurance (QA)   The process of evaluating overall project perfor-

mance on a regular basis to provide confidence that the project will satisfy the relevant quality standards.

Quality assurance plan   A plan that guarantees a quality approach and conformance to all customer requirements for all activities in a project.

Quality audit   An official examination to determine whether practices conform to specified standards or a critical analysis of whether a **deliverable** meets **quality criteria**.

Quality control (QC)   The process of monitoring specific project results to determine if they comply with relevant standards and identifying ways to eliminate causes of unsatisfactory performance.

Quality criteria   The characteristics of a product that determine whether it meets certain requirements.

Quality guide   The quality guide describes quality and **configuration management** procedures and is aimed at people directly involved with **quality reviews**, configuration management and technical exceptions.

Quality management system   The complete set of quality standards, procedures and responsibilities for a site or organisation.

Quality plan (for a project)*   That part of the project plan that concerns **quality management** and **quality assurance** strategies (see also ISO 10006).

Quality planning   The process of determining which quality standards are necessary and how to apply them.

Quality review   A review of a product against an established set of **quality criteria**.

Quantitative risk analysis   The estimation of numerical values of the probability and impact of risks on a project usually using actual or estimated values, known relationships between values, modelling, arithmetical and/or statistical techniques.

Rapid application development (RAD) A method of minimising the time necessary to complete development projects.

Reactive risk response An action or set of actions to be taken after a **risk event** has occurred.

Recurring costs Expenditures against specific activities that would occur on a repetitive basis. Examples are hire of computer equipment and tool maintenance.

Reduce A response to a **threat** that reduces its probability, impact or both on the project.

Regulatory A restriction due to the need to conform to a regulation or rule designed to control or govern conduct.

Reimbursement Method by which a contractor will be paid for the work they have undertaken.

Relationship A logical connection between two activities.

Remaining duration The time needed to complete the remainder of an activity or project.

Replanning Actions performed for any remaining effort within project **scope**.

Replenishable resource A resource that when absent or used up fresh supplies of which can be obtained. Raw materials and money are common examples. *See* **consumable resource**.

Reporting Reporting takes information and presents it in an appropriate format which includes the formal communication of project information to **stakeholders**.

Reports The presentation of information in an appropriate format. Alternatively a written record or summary, a detailed account or statement or a verbal account.

Request for change (RFC) A proposal for a change to the project.

Request for proposal (RFP) A bid document used to request proposals from prospective sellers of products or services.

Request for quotation (RFQ) Equivalent to a request for proposal but with more specific application areas.

Requirements A statement of the need that a project has to satisfy. It should be comprehensive, clear, well structured, traceable and testable.

Requirements definition* Statement of the needs that a project has to satisfy.

Requirements management The process of capturing, analysing and testing the documented statements of **stakeholder** and user wants and needs.

Reserve Similar to a contingency, a reserve is the planned allotment of time and cost or other resources for unforeseeable elements with a project.

Residual value The written-down value of a capital item at the end of the period, used in the **business case** to assess the financial integrity of the **programme** or project.

Resource aggregation* A summation of the requirements for each resource, and for each time period.

Resource allocation* The process by which resources are mapped against activities which are often shown as aggregated resource histograms against a timescale.

Resource availability The level of availability of a resource, which may vary over time.

Resource calendar A calendar that defines the working and non-working patterns for specific resources.

Resource constraint* A limitation due to the availability of a resource.

Resource-driven activity durations Activity durations that are driven by the need for scarce resources.

Resource histogram A view of project data in which resource requirements, usage and availability are shown using vertical bars against a horizontal timescale.

Resource level A specified level of resource units required by an activity per time unit.

Resource levelling Resource levelling can be applied to projects when there are **resource constraints**. Resource levelling forces the amount of work scheduled not to exceed the limits of resources available. This results in either activity durations being extended or entire activities being delayed to periods when resources are available. This often results in a longer project duration. It is also known as resource limited scheduling.

Resource limited scheduling *See* **resource levelling**.

Resource loading The amount of resources of each kind devoted to a specific activity in a particular time period.

Resource management A process that identifies and assigns resources to activities so that the project is undertaken using appropriate levels of resources and within an acceptable duration.

Resource optimisation A term for **resource levelling** and **resource smoothing**.

Resource plan A part of the **project management plan** that states how the project will be resource loaded and what supporting services, infrastructure and third party services are required.

Resource planning A process that evaluates what resources are needed to complete a project and determines the quantity needed.

Resource pool The available resources to a project. Alternatively, a group of people who can generally do the same work, so they can be chosen randomly for assignment to a project.

Resource requirement The requirement for a particular resource by a particular activity.

Resources Resources are all those items required to undertake a project and include people, finance and materials.

Resource scheduling A process that ensures that resources are available when needed and where possible are not underutilised.

Resource smoothing* A process applied to projects to ensure that resources are used as efficiently as possible. It involves utilising **float** within the project or increasing or decreasing the resources required for specific activities, such that any peaks and troughs of resource usage are smoothed out. This does not affect the project duration. It is also known as time limited scheduling.

Responsibility assignment matrix (RAM) A diagram or chart showing assigned responsibilities for elements of work. It is created by combining the **work breakdown structure** with the **organisational breakdown structure**.

Responsibility matrix *See* **responsibility assignment matrix**.

Responsible organisation A defined unit within the organisation structure that is assigned responsibility for accomplishing specific activities, or cost accounts.

Retention A part of payment withheld until the project is completed in order to ensure satisfactory performance or completion of contract terms.

Re-usable resource A resource that when no longer needed becomes available for other uses. Accommodation, machines, test equipment and people are re-usable.

Revenue cost* Expenditure charged to the profit and loss account as incurred or accrued due.

Reviews Project reviews take place throughout the project life cycle to check the likely or actual achievement of the objectives specified in the project management plan.

Re-work Repeating work already completed in producing a deliverable in order to remove defects and meet acceptance criteria.

Right first time Completing a deliverable which, on first testing, meets the agreed acceptance criteria with no defects and no re-work required.

Risk* *See* **project risk** and **risk event**.

Risk analysis* An assessment and synthesis of the risks affecting a project to gain an understanding of their individual significance and their combined impact on the project's objectives.

Risk assessment The process of quantifying the likelihood of risks occurring and assessing their likely impact on the project.

Risk avoidance *See* **avoid** (a threat).

Risk breakdown structure (RBS) A hierarchical breakdown of the risks on a project.

Risk evaluation* A process used to determine risk management priorities.

Risk event An uncertain event or set of circumstances that should it or they occur would have an effect on the achievement of one or more of the **project objectives**.

Risk exposure The degree to which a risk taker could be affected by an adverse outcome.

Risk identification* The process of identifying project risks.

Risk log A document that provides identification, estimation, impact evaluation and countermeasures for all risks to the project. It is normally maintained throughout the life of the project.

Risk management *See* **project risk management**.

Risk management maturity A measure of the extent to which a project or organisation formally applies effective risk management to support decision-making and the treatment of risk.

Risk management plan A document defining how risk management is to be implemented in the context of the particular project concerned.

Risk manager The person who is put in charge of matters connected with risk, or certain aspects of risk, on a project.

Risk monitoring   The process of observing the state of identified risks (also referred to as risk tracking).

Risk owner   The person who has responsibility for dealing with a particular risk on a project and for identifying and managing responses.

Risk prioritising   Ordering of risks according first to their risk value, and then by which risks need to be considered for **risk reduction**, risk avoidance and **risk transfer**.

Risk ranking   The allocation of a classification to the probability and impact of a risk.

Risk reduction   Action taken to reduce the likelihood and impact of a risk.

Risk register*   A body of information listing all the risks identified for the project, explaining the nature of each risk and recording information relevant to its assessment, possible impact and management.

Risk response   An action or set of actions to reduce the probability or impact of a threat or to increase the probability or impact of an opportunity.

Risk response planning   The planning of responses to risks.

Risk transfer   A contractual arrangement between two parties for delivery and acceptance of a product where the liability for the costs of a risk is transferred from one party to the other.

Rolling wave planning   The process whereby only the current phase of a project is planned in detail, future phases being planned in outline only. Each phase produces the detailed plan for the next phase.

Roll out   The process of delivering a number of nearly identical products to a number of users, usually after the product has been tested and shown to meet requirements.

Safety plan   The standards and methods that minimise to an acceptable level the likelihood of accident or damage to people or equipment.

Sales   A marketing technique used to promote a project.

Sanction   Authorisation for the project or part of a project to proceed.

Schedule   A schedule is the timetable for a project. It shows how project activities and **milestones** are planned over a period of time. It is often shown as a milestone chart, Gantt or other **bar chart**, or as a tabular listing of dates.

Schedule dates   Start and finish dates calculated with regard to resource or external constraints as well as project **logic**.

Scheduled finish   The earliest date on which an activity can finish, having regard to resource or external constraints as well as project **logic**.

Scheduled start   The earliest date on which an activity can start, having regard to resource or external constraints as well as project **logic**.

Schedule performance index (SPI)   A term used in **earned value management**. It is the ratio of work accomplished versus work planned, for a specified time period. The SPI is an efficiency rating for work accomplishment, comparing work achieved to what should have been achieved at any point in time.

Schedule variance (cost)   A term used in **earned value management**. The difference between the budgeted cost of work performed (or **earned value**) and the budgeted cost of work scheduled at any point in time.

Scheduling Scheduling is the process used to determine the overall project duration. This includes identification of activities and their logical dependencies, and estimating activity durations, taking into account requirements and availability of resources.

Scope The scope is the sum of work content of a project.

Scope change Any change in a project **scope** that requires a change in the project's cost or schedule.

Scope creep The term sometimes given to the continual extension of the **scope** of some projects.

Scope management The process by which the **deliverables** and the work to produce these are identified and defined. Identification and definition of the **scope** must describe what the project will include and what it will not include, i.e. what is in and out of scope.

Scope of work A description of the work to be accomplished or resources to be supplied.

Scope verification A process that ensures that all identified project **deliverables** have been completed satisfactorily.

Scope statement A documented description of the project that identifies the project boundaries, its output, approach and content. It is used to provide a documented basis to help make future project decisions and to confirm or develop a common understanding of the project's **scope** by **stakeholders**.

S-curve A graphic display of cumulative costs, labour hours or other quantities, plotted against time. This curve tends to be flat at the beginning and end and steep in the middle, reflecting the lower expenditure of resources at the beginnings and ends of projects. It is usual to plot planned, actual and predicted values on the same chart.

Secondary risk The risk that may occur as a result of invoking a **risk response** or fallback plan.

Sensitivity analysis An investigation of the effect on the outcome of changing parameters or data in procedures or models.

Sequence Sequence is the order in which activities will occur with respect to one another.

Share A response to an **opportunity** that increases its probability, impact or both on the project by sharing the risk with a third party.

Simulation A process whereby some dynamic aspect of a system is replicated without using the real system, often using computerised techniques.

Six sigma Six sigma is a quality management programme to achieve 'six sigma' levels of quality. It was pioneered by Motorola in the mid-1980s.

Slack Slack is an alternative term for **float**. *See* **free float** and **total float**.

Slip chart A pictorial representation of the predicted completion dates of **milestones** (also referred to as a trend chart).

Slippage The amount of **float** time used up by the current activity due to a delayed start or increased duration.

Snagging The process of identifying minor small deficiencies that have to be rectified before acceptance of the work on a project or contract.

Social capital   The pattern and intensity of networks among people and the shared values which arise from those networks.

Sole source   The only source known to be able to supply particular equipment or services, or undertake a particular contract. It may be a source specified by the client for reasons not necessarily connected to the project.

Solicitation   The process by which bids or tenders are obtained for the provision of goods or services to the project.

Source selection   Choosing from potential contractors.

Spiral model   A management model used particularly for development projects.

Splittable activity*   An activity that can be interrupted in order to allow its resources to be transferred temporarily to another activity.

Sponsor   The individual or body for whom the project is undertaken and who is the primary risk taker. The sponsor owns the **business case** and is ultimately responsible for the project and for delivering the benefits.

Stage   A subdivision of the **life cycle** phase into a natural subsection with well-defined **deliverables**.

Stage payment*   A payment made part way through a project at some predetermined **milestone**.

Stakeholder   The organisations or people who have an interest or role in the project or are impacted by the project.

Stakeholder analysis   The identification of stakeholder groups, their interest levels and ability to influence the project or **programme**.

Stakeholder grid   A matrix used as part of a stakeholder analysis to identify the relative importance of stakeholders to a project; for example, by considering their relative power.

Stakeholder identification   The process of identifying stakeholders in a project.

Stakeholder management   The systematic identification, analysis and planning of actions to communicate with, negotiate with and influence **stakeholders**.

Starting activity   A starting activity has no predecessors. It does not have to wait for any other activity to start.

Start-to-start lag   Start-to-start lag is the minimum amount of time that must pass between the start of one activity and the start of its successor(s).

Start-up   The formal process of making a new **project team** effective *or* the commissioning of a completed facility.

Start-up meeting   The initial meeting with the **project team** at the start of a project or phase of a project.

Statement of scope   *See* **scope statement.**

Statement of work* (SOW)   A document stating the requirements for a given project activity.

Status report   A description of where the project currently stands, usually in the form of a written report, issued to both the **project team** and other responsible people on a regular basis, stating the status of an activity, **work package** or whole project. It may be a formal report on the input, issues and actions resulting from a status meeting.

Statute law   Statute is the written law consisting of Acts of Parliament (including those enacted under European directives), and the rules, regulations and orders made under the powers conferred by those Acts.

Statutory approval   An approval that is required by law.

Statutory obligations   Relevant legal obligations.

Steering group   A group, usually comprising the **sponsor**, senior managers and sometimes key **stakeholders**, whose remit is to set the strategic direction of a project. It gives guidance to the sponsor and **project manager**. Often referred to as the project board.

Strategy   The high-level plan that will enable the project to reach a successful conclusion. It describes how the project is to be executed. This is the long-term plan.

Subcontract   A contractual document that legally transfers the responsibility and effort of providing goods, services, data or other hardware from one firm to another.

Subcontractor   An organisation that supplies goods or services to a supplier.

Subject matter experts   Users with subject matter knowledge and expertise who may contribute to defining requirements and acceptance criteria.

Subproject   A group of activities represented as a single activity in a higher level of the same project.

Success criteria   The qualitative or quantitative measures by which the success of the project is judged.

Success factors   Factors that when present in the project **environment** are most conducive to the achievement of a successful project. The success factors that if absent would cause the project to fail are sometimes termed critical success factors (CSFs).

Successor   A successor is an activity whose start or finish depends on the start or finish of a predecessor activity.

Sunk costs   Costs that are unavoidable, even if the project were to be terminated.

Super-critical activity   An activity that is behind schedule is considered to be super-critical if it has been delayed to a point where its **float** is calculated to be a negative value.

Supplier   A supplier is a contractor, consultant or any organisation that supplies resources to the project.

Supply chain management   The management of the chain of organisations through which goods pass on their way from raw materials to the ultimate purchaser.

Surety   An individual or organisation that has agreed to be legally liable for the debt, default or failure of a principal to satisfy a contractual obligation.

System   The complete technical output of the project including technical products.

Systems analysis   The analysis of a complex process or operation in order to improve its efficiency.

Systems engineering   A systematic approach to realising a project that takes account of all related systems and subsystems.

Systems management   Management that includes the prime activities of systems analysis, systems design and engineering, and systems development.

Talent management The development of project talented people in the organisation each of whom is capable of filling a number of roles.

Target completion date The date planned to complete an activity or project.

Target start date The date planned to start work on an activity or the project.

Task The smallest indivisible part of an activity when it is broken down to a level best understood and performed by a specific person or organisation.

Team A team is made up of two or more people working interdependently towards a common goal and a shared reward.

Team building The ability to gather the right people to join a **project team** and get them working together for the benefit of a project.

Team development The process of developing skills, as a group and individually, that enhance project performance.

Team leader The person responsible for leading a team.

Team member A person who is accountable to and has work assigned to them by the project manager to be performed either by themselves or by others in a working group.

Teamwork The process whereby people work collaboratively towards a common goal as distinct from other ways that individuals can work within a group.

Technology management The management of the relationship between available and emerging technologies, the organisation and the project. It also includes management of the enabling technologies used to deliver the project, technologies used to manage the project and the technology of the project **deliverables**.

Tender A document proposing to meet a specification in a certain way and at a stated price (or on a particular financial basis), an offer of price and conditions under which a supplier is willing to undertake work for the client. *See* **bid**.

Tender document The document issued to prospective suppliers when inviting bids or quotations for supply of goods or services.

Tendering The process of preparing and submitting a tender, quotation or bid.

Tender list A list of approved suppliers to whom a specific enquiry may be sent.

Termination (phase) The disposal of project **deliverables** at the end of their life.

Terms and conditions All the clauses in a contract.

Terms of reference A specification of a team member's responsibilities and authorities within the project.

Testing The process of determining how aspects of a **deliverable** perform when subjected to specified conditions.

Theory of constraints A theory expounded by Goldratt, which lead to the **critical chain** schedule management technique.

Threat A negative risk; a risk that if it occurs will have a detrimental effect on the project.

Three-point estimate An estimate in which the most likely mid-range value, an optimistic value and a pessimistic, worst case value are given.

Time analysis The process of calculating the early and late dates for each activity on a project, based on the duration of the activities and the logical relations between them.

Timeboxing The production of project deliverables in circumstances where time and resources including funding are fixed and the requirements are prioritised and vary depending on what can be achieved in the timebox.

Time limited scheduling* *See* resource smoothing.

Time now* A specified date from which the forward analysis is deemed to commence. The date to which current progress is reported. Sometimes referred to as the status date because all progress information entered for a project should be correct as of this date.

Time recording The recording of **effort** expended on each activity in order to update a project plan.

Time sheet A means of recording the actual **effort** expended against project and non-project activities.

Time variance The scheduled time for the work to be completed less the actual time.

Top down cost estimating The total project cost is estimated based on historical costs and other project variables and then subdivided down to individual activities.

Total float* Time by which an activity may be delayed or extended without affecting the total project duration or violating a target finish date.

Total quality management (TQM) A strategic, integrated management system for customer satisfaction that guides all employees in every aspect of their work.

Traffic light reports A type of progress report that explains the current status of the programme or project in the form of a traffic light colour, for example red = problems, amber = some concerns, green = no problems.

Tranche A group of projects that represent the delivery of all or a recognisable part of a new capability. It is used to assist the management and control of a programme.

Transfer A response to a **threat** that reduces its probability, impact or both on the project by transferring the risk to a third party.

Trend chart (*See* **slip chart**.)

Trends A general tendency observed on a project.

Turnaround report A report created especially for the various managers responsible to enter their progress status against a list of activities that are scheduled to be in progress during a particular time window.

Turnkey contract A comprehensive contract in which the contractor is responsible for the complete supply of a facility, usually with responsibility for **fitness for purpose**, training operators, **pre-commissioning** and **commissioning**. It usually has a fixed completion date, a fixed price and guaranteed performance levels.

Uncertain event *See* **risk event**.

Uncertainty A state of incomplete knowledge about a proposition. Usually associated with risks, both threats and opportunities.

Unlimited schedule* An infinite schedule, a schedule produced without resource constraint.

User acceptance test A formal test or series of tests to demonstrate the acceptability of a product to the user.

User requirements The requirements governing the project's **deliverables** or products as expressed by the user. What the user needs expressed in user terminology.

User requirements statement A document that defines the user's needs in user terminology from the user's perspective.

Users The group of people who are intended to benefit from the project or operate the **deliverables**.

Validate Testing that the deliverable meets the requirements.

Validation The process of providing evidence that a **deliverable** meets the needs of the user.

Valuation A calculation of the amount of payment due under the terms of a contract. Often undertaken at stages in large contracts and at completion.

Value A standard, principle or quality considered worthwhile or desirable. The size of a benefit associated with a requirement. In **value management** terms value is defined as the ratio of 'satisfaction of needs' over 'use of resources'.

Value engineering Concerned with optimising the conceptual, technical and operational aspects of a project's **deliverables**, value engineering utilises

a series of proven techniques during the **implementation** phase of a project.

Value management A structured approach to defining what value means to the organisation and the project. It is a framework that allows needs, problems or opportunities to be defined and then enables review of whether the initial **project objectives** can be improved to determine the optimal approach and solution.

Variance A discrepancy between the actual and planned performance on a project, either in terms of schedule or cost. (Mathematical definition – the mean square difference between the value of all the observed variables and the mean (average) of all the variables – a measure of the spread and grouping of the distribution of a variable.)

Variance at completion The difference between **budget at completion** and **estimate at completion**.

Variation A change in **scope** or timing of work that a supplier is obliged to do under a contract.

Variation order The document authorising an approved technical change or variation.

Vendor A company or person contractually committed to provide goods (either direct or through a supplier).

Verification Proof of compliance with specified requirements. Verification may be determined by test, analysis, inspection or demonstration.

Verify Testing that the deliverable meets the specification and designs.

Version control The recording and management of the **configuration** of different versions of the project's products.

Virtual models A visual representation of a deliverable which can be used to test its operational performance.

Vision statement An outward-facing description of the new capabilities resulting from a project or **programme** delivery.

Warranty A promise given by a contractor to the client or owner regarding the nature, usefulness or condition of the supplies or services delivered under the contract.

Waterfall model A management model used particularly for IT development projects.

What-if assessment The process of evaluating alternative strategies.

What-if simulation* Changing the value of the parameters of the project network to study its behaviour under various conditions of its operation.

Work The total number of hours, people or **effort** required to complete an activity.

Work breakdown code A code that represents the 'family tree' of an element in a work breakdown structure.

Work breakdown structure* (WBS) A way in which a project may be divided by level into discrete groups for programming, cost planning and control purposes. The WBS is a tool for defining the hierarchical breakdown of work required to deliver the products of a project. Major categories are broken down into smaller components. These are sub-divided until the lowest required level of detail is established. The lowest units of the WBS are generally **work packages**. In some instances work packages are further divided into activities that become the activities in a project. The WBS defines the total work to be undertaken on the project and provides a structure for all project control systems.

Working group A group of two or more people to which work is delegated to individuals and the inter-relationships between activities is managed through a single person who may be a member of the project team.

Work load Work load is the amount of work units assigned to a resource over a period of time.

Work package* A group of related activities that are defined at the same level within a **work breakdown structure**.

Work package manager A person with responsibility for leading and managing a part of a project to achieve specific aims that have been agreed with the **project manager**.

Work units Work units provide the measurement units for resources. For example people as a resource can be measured by the number of hours they work.

Yield The return on an investment.

Zero defects A measure of the quality of a deliverable where the deliverable is defect-free.

Zero float Zero float is a condition where there is no excess time between activities. An activity with zero float is considered a critical activity.

Project management acronyms

The following list details acronyms commonly used in project management across all sectors.

Where an acronym has more than one commonly used meaning, each project management-related meaning is given as a separate entry.

AC	Actual cost
ACWP	Actual cost of work performed
ACWS	Actual cost of work scheduled
ADM	Arrow diagram method
ADR	Alternative dispute resolution
ALAP	As late as possible
ALARP	As low as reasonably practicable
AOA	Activity-on-arrow
AON	Activity-on-node
APM	Association for Project Management
APMP	APM qualification at IPMA level D
ARR	Annual rate of return
ASAP	As soon as possible
B2B	Business-to-business
B2C	Business-to-consumer
BAC	Budget at completion
BCM	Business change manager
BCWP	Budgeted cost of work performed
BCWS	Budgeted cost of work scheduled
BoK	Body of knowledge
BOM	Bill of materials
BOOT	Build-own-operate-transfer
BOQ	Bill of quantities
BSI	British Standards Institution
CA	Configuration audit
CA	Control account
CAD	Computer aided design
CAM	Computer aided manufacturing
CAM	Cost account manager
CAPEX	Capital expenditure
CAPM	Certificate in Applied Project Management (PMI)
CB	Configuration board
CBS	Cost breakdown structure

CCB	Change control board
CCB	Configuration control board
CDR	Critical design review
CI	Configuration item
CM	Configuration management
CPA	Critical path analysis
CPD	Continuing professional development
CPI	Cost performance index
CPM	Certificated Project Manager (APM) – maps to IPMA Level B
CPM	Critical path method
CMM	Capability maturity model
CR	Change request
CRD	Client requirements document
CSA	Configuration status accounting
C/SCSC	Cost/schedule control systems criteria
CSF	Critical success factor
C/SPCS	Cost/schedule planning and control specification
CTC	Contract target cost
CTR	Cost–time resource
CV	Cost variance
DCF	Discounted cash flow
DCP	Detailed cost plan
DRACAS	Defect reporting and corrective action
DSDM	Dynamic systems development method
DSM	Design structure matrix
EAC	Estimate at completion
ECC	Estimated cost to complete
ECR	Engineering change request
EF	Early finish
EFQM	European Foundation for Quality Management
EFT	Earliest finish time
EMS	Environmental management system
EMV	Expected monetary value
EPC	Engineer, procure and construct
EPCC	Engineer, procure, construct and commission
EPIC	Engineer, procure, install and construct
EPMO	Enterprise project management office
ERM	Enterprise resource management
ES	Early start
ESA	End stage assessment
EST	Earliest start time
ETC	Estimate to completion

EU	European Union
EV	Earned value
EV	Expected value
EVA	Earned value analysis
EVM	Earned value management
EVMS	Earned value management system
FAST	Functional analysis and system technique
FAT	Factory acceptance test
FBOOT	Finance, build, own, operate, transfer
FCC	Forecast cost at completion
FEED	Front end engineering design
FF	Finish to finish
FF	Free float
FFP	Fit for purpose
FMEA	Failure mode and effect analysis
FMECA	Failure modes, effects and criticality analysis
FS	Finish to start
FTE	Full time equivalent
GERT	Graphical evaluation and review technique
GoPM	Governance of project management
HAZCON	Hazardous condition
HAZOP	Hazard and operability
HRM	Human resource management
HSE	Health and Safety Executive
HSE	Health, safety and environment
IBR	Integrated baseline review
IC	APM Introductory Certificate Qualification
ID	Identification
IFB	Invitation for bidding
IPMA	International Project Management Association
IPR	Intellectual property rights
IPT	Integrated project team
IRR	Internal rate of return
IS	Information systems
ISEB	Information Systems Examination Board
ISO	International Standards Organization
IST	Integrated system testing
IT	Information technology
ITT	Invitation to tender
JIT	Just in time
JV	Joint venture
KISS	Keep it simple

KM	Knowledge management
KPI	Key performance indicator
KRA	Key result area
LD	Liquidated damages
LFD	Late finish date
LOB	Line of balance
LOE	Level of effort
LOI	Letter of intent
LSD	Late start date
MIS	Management information system
MOC	Management of change
MoR™	Management of risk (OGC)
MPA	Major Projects Association
MR	Management reserve
MS	Milestone
MSP	Managing Successful Programmes (OGC)
MTO	Material take-off
NPV	Net present value
OBO	Operated by others
OBS	Organisational breakdown structure
OD	Original duration
ODC	Other direct costs
OGC	Office of Government Commerce
OPM™	Organisational Project Maturity Model
OR	Operations/operational research
PBS	Product breakdown structure
PBR	Programme benefits review
PC	Planned cost
PDM	Precedence diagramming method
PDN	Project deviation notice
PDR	Preliminary design review
PDU	Professional development unit
PEP	Project execution plan
PERT	Program evaluation and review technique
PESTLE	Political, economic, sociological, technical, legal, environmental
PF	Productivity factor
PFI	Private finance initiative
PID	Project initiation document
PIG	Probability-impact grid
PIM	Probability-impact matrix
PIR	Post implementation review

PM	Project manager
PMB	Performance measurement baseline
PM BoK®	A Guide to the Project Management Body of Knowledge (PMI)
PMCDF	Project Manager Competency Development Framework (PMI)
PMI	Project Management Institute
PMIS	Project management information system
PMM	Project management maturity
PMMM	Project Management Maturity Model (OGC)
PMO	Project management office
PMP	Project management plan
PMP®	Project Management Professional (PMI qualification)
PMS	Project master schedule
PPP	Public private partnership
PPR	Post-project review
PQ	APM Practioner Qualification-maps to IPMA Level C
PR	Public relations
PRAM	Project Risk Analysis and Management Guide
PRD	Project requirements document
PRINCE2	Projects in controlled environments
PROMPT	An early management methodology on which PRINCE was originally based
PSO	Project or programme support office
PV	Planned value
QA	Quality assurance
QC	Quality control
QMS	Quality management system
RACI	Responsible for action, accountable (yes no decisions), consult before (2 way), inform after (1 way)
R&D	Research and development
RAD	Rapid applications development
RAG	Red, amber, green
RAM	Responsibility assignment matrix
RAMP	Risk Analysis and Management for Projects
RBS	Risk breakdown structure
RCA	Root cause analysis
RFC	Request for change
RFI	Request for information
RFP	Request for proposal
RFQ	Request for quotation
RMP	Risk management plan

Project management acronyms

ROI	Return on investment
SCERT	Synergistic contingency evaluation and response/review technique
SD	System dynamics
SE	Systems engineering
SF	Start to finish
SHAMPU	Shape, harness and manage project uncertainty
SMART	Specific, measurable, achievable, realistic, time-framed
SOR	Schedule of rates
SOR	Statement of requirements
SOW	Statement of work
SPI	Schedule performance index
SS	Start to start
SSADM	Structured systems analysis and design methodology
SV	Schedule variance
SWOT	Strengths, weaknesses, opportunities, threats
TF	Total float
TLC	Through life cost
TOR	Terms of reference
TQM	Total quality management
TSO	The Stationery Office
UAT	User acceptance test
VM	Value management
VOWD	Value of work done
WBS	Work breakdown structure
WP	Work package

INDEX

accept (risk; threat or opportunity) 26, 125
acceptance 88, 125
   certificates 88
   of change 86
   of tender 74
acceptance criteria 24, 52, 54, 58, 87, 88, 94, 125
   modelling and testing and 62
   project quality management and 28
   scope management and 34
accrual 40, 125
activity 30, *34n*, 36, 37, 38, 44, 56, 86, 94, 104, 125
activity-on-arrow (network) *36n*, 125
activity-on-node (network) 36, 125
actual cost 40, 45, 125
actual expenditure 40, 126
adjudication 77, 126
agile development 54, 126
alliancing 75, 110, 126, *see also* partnering
alternative dispute resolution (ADR) 77, 126
arbitration 77, 126
assumptions 126
   business case and 68
   project management plan and 24
   project risk management and 26
assurance 126
   modelling and testing and 62
   of project management processes 14
   role of project assurance 95
   see also quality assurance (QA)
audit 46, 90, 126
   configuration 64, 131
   internal 90
   quality 28, 153
authorisation points 99, 126
avoid (threat) 26, 126

bar chart *see* Gantt chart
baseline 25, 35, 37, 42, 44, 52, 64, 84, 127
baseline plan 44, 45, 127
behavioural characteristics 114–115, 127
benchmarking 29, 127
benefits management 6, 18, 19, 127, *see also* project success and benefits management
benefits realisation review *80*, 91, 127
benefits 2, 6, 8, 12, 18, 52, 58, 81, 90, 127
   business case and 68
   change control and 42
   role of sponsor 12, 86, 89, 94
   value engineering and 61
   value management and 22
benefits realisation 12, 127
   business case and 68
   role of sponsor 18
bid 74, 127, *see also* tendering
body of knowledge 118, 127
bond 72, 77, 128
bottleneck (capacity) 8, 39, 128
bottom up (analytical) estimating 56, 128
breaches of contract 76, 128
budget 24, 40, 41, 44, 52, 56, 62, 72, 86, 90, 128
budgeting and cost management 24, 40–41, 72, 128
   earned value management and 44
buffer 37, 128
build, own, operate and transfer (BOOT) 72, 128
build stage 86, 128
business case 2, 24, 68–69, 129
   and benefits 6, 18
   contents of 68
   and cost 40
   and financing 72
   governance of project management and 99
   and life cycle *80*, 82, 84, 86
   project reviews and 90
   and scope 34
   role of sponsor 12, 86, 94
business objectives 12, 23, 129
business risk assessment 26, 129
business-as-usual 2, 6, 7, 8, 42, 47, 68, 88, 129
business-to-business (B2B) 75, 129
business-to-consumer (B2C) 75, 129

capability 81, 89, 94, 129
capability maturity models 3, 29, 129
capital 72, 129
career development 112, 116
cash flow 8, 72, 129
   discounted 69, 82, 135
   forecast 40, 129
central repository 46, 129
change 7, 24, 35, 37, 39, 41, 42, 43, 44, 46, 52, 53, 60, 64, 76, 81, 86, 93, 130
   management 2, 3, 6, 12, 130
change control 18, 25, 37, 39, 41, 42–43, 44, 52, 64, 86, 130
   configuration management and 43, 64
change freeze 43, 130

change log 42, 130
change register *see* change log
change request 42, 57, 130
charter 104, 130
claims 76, 77, 130
client 118, 130
client brief 54, 130
closeout 18, 51, 64, 80, 81, 87, 90, 104, 130, *see
    also* handover and closeout phase
coaching 14, 116
commitment 40, 74, 130
common law 76, 131
communication 30, 34, 54, 70, 84, 93, 96,
    102–103, 108, 131
    information management and reporting
        and 46
    non-verbal 102
    project management plan and 25
    stakeholder management and 21
    teamwork and 104
    verbal 102
communication plan 70, 84, 103, 131
    and information management 46, 47
    stakeholder management and 21
community of practice 15, 116, 131
comparative (analogous) estimating 56, 131
concept (phase) 18, 52, 56, 68, 72, 80, 82–83, 84,
    131
concurrent engineering 36, 131
configuration 25, 43, 64, 131
    audit 64, 131
    control 64, 131
    identification 64, 131
    item 64, 131
    management planning 64
    manager 95
    status accounting 64, 132
configuration management 28, 53, 64–65, 86,
    96, 131
    change control and 43, 64
    version control 64, 163
conflict 39, 108, 109
    organisation structure and 93
    of interest 118
    resources 6
conflict management 108–109, 132
conformance 28, 52, 64, 84
consideration 74, 76, 132
constraints 3, 8, 40, 70, 110, 132
    business case and 68
    project management plan and 24
    resource 8, 38, 155
    time 37
context *see* project context
contingency 26, 37, 40, 56, 132

continuing professional development (CPD)
    117, 132
continuous improvement 28, 90, 96, 132
contracts 74, 75, 76, 86, 88, 110, 132
    breaches of 76, 128
    conditions of 76
    parallel 74
    project context and 10
    sequence of 74
    sub 74
    termination of 77
corporate governance 9, 26, 98, *see also*
        governance of project management
cost 2, 6, 18
    actual 40, 125
    business case and 68
    change control and 42
    constraints *3*
    development and 54
    earned value management and 44
    estimate of 40, 56
    and life cycle 84, 86
    manager 95
    outturn 40, 146
    project financing and funding and 72
    project quality management and 28
    value engineering and 60
cost breakdown structure (CBS) 34, 35, 40, 133
cost management *see* budgeting and cost
        management
cost-reimbursement payment method 74, 133
critical chain 37, 134
critical path 36, 134
critical success factors (CSF) *18n, see also*
        success criteria and success factors

data 14, 44, 46, 56
decision trees 26, 134
definition (phase) 52, *80*, 81, 82, 84–85, 134
deliverables 2, 4, 10, 12, 18, 135
    acceptance criteria of 24, 62, 87, 88
    configuration management and 64
    ethical use of 118
    and life cycle 81, 86, 87, 88, 90
    operation of 30
    output *3*, 146
    and project assurance 95
    project management plan and 24
    project quality management and 28
    scope management and 34
    technology of 58
    testing of 62
    value engineering and 60
    value management and 23
    see also product

dependencies 135
   business case and 68
   project management plan and 24
   see also interdependencies
dependency 36, 135
design 86
   alternative 54, 84
   detailed 60, 135
   documentation 54
   stage 86, 135
deterministic estimate 36, 56, 135
development 54–55, 61, 135
deviations 45, 72, 86, 135
direct costs 44, 135
disclosure 99
discounted cash flow (DCF) 69, 82, 135
disposal 30, 81
dispute 76, 77, 112, 135
   resolution 74, 135
do-nothing option 68, 82, 135
drawdown 40, 72, 135
duration 45, 136
   activity 36, 37, 38, 125
   project 36, 38
duty of care 31, 136
dynamic systems development method
      (DSDM) 54, 136

earned value 44, 45, 136
earned value management (EVM) 35, 37, 40,
      44–45, 86, 136
e-commerce 75, 136
EFQM excellence model 28, 136, *see also*
     project excellence model
enhance (opportunity) 26, 136
enterprise project management office (EPMO) 15
environment 3, 70, 106, 114, 116, 136
   business 6
   external 10, 86, 137
   internal 10, 141
   operational 54, 87, 88
   organisational 92
   project context and 10
   project management plan and 25
   team 2, 104
environmental impact 30
environmental legislation 30
escalation 137
   of conflict 109
   of issues 48
   of risks 26, 86
estimate 56, 57, 137
   activity duration 36
   cost 40, 68
   level of detail 84

single-point/deterministic 36, 56, 135
   three-point 36, 56, 162
estimating 40, 56–57, 137
   bottom-up (analytical) 56, 128
   comparative (analogous) 56, 131
   funnel *56n*
   and life cycle 81
   parametric 56, 146
   scope management and 34
exception management 14, 137
exception report 46, 137
expenditure 137
   actual 40, 126
   cumulative 84
   profile of 40, 44, 149
exploit (opportunity) 26, 137
extended life cycle *see* project life cycle
external environment *see* environment
external suppliers 84, 137

fast-tracking 36, 138
feasibility 80, 82, 138
financing
   seed corn 72
   see also project financing and funding
financial appraisal 8, 138
   concept and 82
fitness for purpose 28, 52, 62, 84, 94, 138
fixed price payment method 74, 138
float 36, 38, 138
   free *36n*, 138
   total *36n*, 162
forecast 44, 138
   costs 40, 138
   out-turn costs 40, 138
form of contract 74, 138
function 22, 23, 139
functional analysis 60, 61, 139
functional analysis and system technique
     (FAST) 22, *60*, 139
functional departments 92, 139
functional organisation 92, 139

Gantt charts 36, 37, 139
gate 68, 81, *81n*, 82, 84, 86, 87
   review 41, *80*, 90, 139
goals 12, 19, 112, 114, 139
gold plating 28, 139
governance 25, 75
   corporate 9, 26, 98
governance of project management 98–99, 139
guarantees 77, 139

handover 18, 24, 34, 59, 64, 80, 87, 93, 140, *see*
    also handover and closeout phase

handover and closeout (phase) *80*, 88–89, 90,
    104, 140
health and safety 30, 112, 140
    plan 84, 140
    risk assessment 30, 140
    risk management 31
heath, safety and environmental management
        30–31, 140
    issues 25
    regulations 30
high-performing team 104
human resource management (HRM)
        112–113, 140

idea development 61, 140
idea evaluation 61, 140
implementation (phase) 54, 60, *80*, 81, 84,
        86–87, 140
indirect costs 44, 141
industrial relations 76
influence diagrams 26, 141
influencing 9, 13, 70, 106,
information management and reporting
        46–47, 58, 141
    collection 46
    storage 46
    dissemination 46
    archiving 46, 89
    destruction 46
initiation 6, *24n*, 141
    of risk management 26
integrated baseline review (IBR) 44, 141
intellectual property rights (IPR) 74, 141
interdependencies 6, 8, 141, *see also*
        dependencies
internal environment *see* environment
internal rate of return (IRR) 69, 82, 141
interrelationship 104, 141
investment 68, 72, 90, 141
investment appraisal 40, 68, 69, 141
issue 6, 48, 49, 86, 141
    ageing of 48
    escalation 49, 99
    project management plan and 25
    resolution of 48
issue log *42n*, 48, 142
issue management 48–49, 142
    programme management and 7
    project sponsorship and 12
issue register *see* issue log

key performance indicators (KPIs) 18, 19, 24, 142

law
    English *76n*
    EU 76
    common 76, 131
    of the land 76, 142
    Scottish *76n*
    statute 76, 160
leadership 12, 104, 106–107, 142
lean 28, 142
learning and development 116–117, 142
legal awareness 76–77, 142
legal duties 76, 143
legislation *see* law
lessons learned 14, 28, 54, 116, 143
    leadership and 106
    project reviews and 90
liabilities 76, 143
life cycle
    cost *60*, 143
    see also project life cycle
liquidated damages 76, 143
litigation 77, 143
logic 36, 37, 143
logical dependency 36, 143

make or buy decision 74, 143
management
    accounting 72
    by exception 14, 137
    information 45
marketing 70, 71, 143
    strategy 70
    see also marketing and sales
marketing and sales 70–71
master schedule 36, 143
matrix organisation 93, 144
mediation 77, 144
mentoring 14, 116
methods 10, 14, 22, 30, 96, 97, 99
    of conflict management 108
    of estimating 56
    of reimbursement 74
    of scheduling 36144
    see also methods and procedures
methods and procedures 96–97, 144
milestone 24, 36, 37, 144
models
    EFQM excellence model 28, 136
    maturity 3, 28
    physical 62, 147
    virtual 62, 164
    waterfall 54,164
    see also capability maturity models
modelling and testing 54, 56, 62–63, 84, 144
monitoring (and control) 23, 86, 144
    process 3, 90
    of progress 58
    of costs 40
    of project management plan 24

Monte Carlo simulation 26, 144

need, problem or opportunity 2, *3*, 12, 24, 52, 68, 79, 80, 82, 84, 144
negotiation 20, 70, 74, 77, 108, 110–111, 145
net present value (NPV) 69, 82, 145
network diagrams 36, 37, 145

objectives 145
    business (strategic) 6, 8, 12, 23, 58, 70, 82, 98, 129
    project 2, 10, 18, 19, 22, 23, 24, 26, 42, 43, 44, 48, 52, 58, 61, 62, 74, 84, 86, 90, 93, 108, 114, 151
OGC Gateway® 10, *81n*
operational life 81, 145
operational phase 59, *see also* operations phase
operations phase *80*, 81, 145
opportunity (positive risk) 26, 145
    accept 26, 125
    enhance 26, 136
    exploit 26, 137
    share 26, 158
organisational capability and maturity 10, 13, *see also* capability maturity models, EFQM excellence model, project excellence model
organisation 72, 145
    environment 86
organisational breakdown structure (OBS) 34, 35, 44, 93, 145
organisational roles 94–95
organisation structure 10, 92–93, 95, 104, 146
    functional 92, 139
    matrix 93, 144
    project 93, 152
outputs 3, 28, 80, 90, 96, 146

parametric estimating 56, 146
partnering 10, 110, 146
    and alliances 75
payback 69, 83, 146
payment methods *see* reimbursement
performance *3, see also* quality
    appraisal 89, 147
    management 40, 147
    measurement 44, 45, 147
    operational 62
    physical 44, 147
    value management and 22
PESTLE 10
phase reviews 81, 147
phase *see* project life cycle
pilot 54, 147

plan *see* project management plan
planning 30, 68, 81, 82, 147
    earned value management and 44
    for negotiation 110
    process 3, 24, 25
    quality 28
    risk responses 36
    value *60*
portfolio 8, 147
    concept and 82
    governance of project management and 98
    prioritisation process 9, 147
    project finance and funding and 72
    project office and 14
    project risk management and 26
portfolio management 6, 8–9, 147
post-project review *80*, 89, 90, 147
precedence diagram method *36n*, 148
PRAM (Project Risk Analysis and Management Guide) 27, 148
PRINCE2® 10, *24n, 42n, 48n*, 96, 148
prioritisation *see* portfolio prioritisation process
private finance initiative (PFI) 72, *80n*, 148
problem 48, 148
procedures 3, 28, 30, 42, 64, 76, 96, 97, 112, 148, *see also* methods and procedures
procurement 25, 74–75, 86, 110, 149
    ethical 75, 137
    manager 95
    strategy 74, 149
product 34, 58, 59, 149, *see also* deliverables
    life cycle *80n*
product breakdown structure (PBS) 34, 149
professionalism
    behaviour 118
    competencies 118
    conduct 118
    knowledge 118
professionalism and ethics 118–119, 149
profile of expenditure 40, 44, 149
program evaluation and review technique (PERT) 36, 149
programme 4, 6–7, 149
    concept and 82
    management of *see* programme management
    portfolio management and 8
    manager 6, 9, 150
    project financing and funding and 72
    project office and 14
    project risk management and 26
    support office *14n*, 150
programme management 4, 6–7, 9, 149
project 2, 3, 4, 150

accountant 95
  as change management 2, 3
  as part of a portfolio 8
  as part of a programme 6
  planner 95
project budget *see* budget
project charter *86n* see also charter
project context 10–11, 12, 19, 20, 70, 150
  value management and 22
project evaluation reviews *80*, 90, 116, 150
project excellence model 29, 150, *see also*
       EFQM excellence model
project financing and funding 40, 72–73, 151
project information 14, 46, 88, 99
project initiation document (PID) *24n*, 151
       see also project management plan
project life cycles 2, 9, 18, 46, 52, 70, 80–81, 96,
       99, 102, 104, 106, 110, 112, 151
  business case and 68
  concept phase 82–83, 131
  configuration management and 64
  definition phase 84–85, 134
  estimating and 56, 57
  extended life cycle 80, 137
  handover and closeout phase 88–89, 140
  implementation phase 86–87, 140
  organisation structure and 93
  project reviews and 90
  project risk management and 26
  scheduling and 37
  scope management and 34
  stakeholder management and 21
project management 2–4, 151
  behavioural characteristics and 114
  capability and maturity 3
  communication and 102
  governance of 98–99
  maturity 3, 13
  methods and procedures 96
  organisation structure 92
  portfolio management and 8
  processes 3
  as a profession 118
  programme management and *7*
  project context and 10
  project office and 14
  project sponsorship and 12
project management plan (PMP) 18, 24–25,
       151
  change control and 42
  and life cycle 80, 84, 86, 90
  procurement and 74
  scope management and 34
project manager 151
  accountability 2, 12

role of 12, 18, 24, 28, 30, 42, 48, 54, 69, 70, 72,
       76, 86, 88, 90, 92, 94, 102, 104, 106, 108,
       110, 112, 116, 118
project objectives 151
project office 9, 14–15, 151
  audits 90
  role of 14–15, 93, 94, 97
project organisation structure 93, 152
project plan 42, 62, 64, 117, 152
project quality management 28–29, 152
  configuration management and 65
  modelling and testing and 62
project reviews 40, 41, 46, 68, 79, 80, 81, 88,
       90–91
project risk 26, 27, 152
project risk management 26–27, 152
  health and safety 31
  and issue management 48
  process 26
  reporting 46
project roles and responsibilities 24, 152
  modelling and testing and 62
  organisational roles and 94
  see also project manager
  see also project office
  see also senior management
  see also sponsor/sponsorship
  see also steering group
project sponsorship 12–13, *see also* sponsor
project success 26, 54, 152
  criteria *see* success criteria
  requirements management and 52
  see also project success and benefits
       management
project success and benefits management
       18–19
project team 3, 10, 12, 19, 54, 69, 72, 153
  change control and 42
  charter *86n*, 104
  communication and 102
  human resource management and 112
  leadership 106
  learning and development and 116
  legislation 30
  organisational roles and 94
  performance appraisal 89
  project management plan and 24
  project reviews and 90
  requirements and 53
  see also teamwork
prototyping 54
public private partnership (PPP) 72, *80n*, 153

quality 2, 6, 18, 153
  constraints *3*

change control and 42
development and 54
and life cycle 84, 86, 90
management of see project quality
    management
manager 95
project management plan and 25
resource management and 38
value engineering and 61
quality assurance (QA) 28, 62, 153
quality audits 28, 153
quality control (QC) 28, 62, 153
quality plan 65, 84, 87, 153
quality planning 28, 153
quality reviews 54, 153

reduce (threat) 26, 154
regulatory 62, 154
    bodies 20
    control 30
    requirements 10
reimbursement 154
    cost 74, 133
    fixed price 74, 138
    unit rate 74,
replanning 44, 154
replenishable resource 38, 154
reporting 154, *see also* information
    management and reporting
reports 64, 86, 154
    exception 46, 137
request for proposal (RFP) 74, 154
requirements 28, 30, 36, 52, 53, 54, 55, 56, 58,
    61, 84, 94, 154
    configuration management and 64
    corporate governance 26
    high-level 82, 84, 140
    quality 28, 30
    and testing 62
    value management and 23
requirements management 34, 52–53, 154
    analysis 52
    capture 52
    testing 52
resource allocation 38, 154
resource constraints 8, 38, 155
resource levelling 38, 155
resource management 38–39, 155
resource pool 8, 155
resource smoothing 38, 155
resource scheduling 38, 155
resources 2, 6, 8, 155
    prioritisation of 9
    budgeting and cost management and 40
    change control and 42

governance of project management and 99
and life cycle 81, 82, 84, 86, 90
manager 95
organisation structure and 92
organisational roles and 94
procurement of 74
project management plan and 24
project office and 14
quality management and 28
scheduling and 36
value management and 22
value engineering and 61
responsibility assignment matrix (RAM) 34,
    93, 155
re-usable resource 38, 156
reviews 156
    independent 28
    lessons learned 54, 116
    project 40, 41, 46, 68, 79, 80, 81, 88, 90–91
    risk 26
re-work 28, 156
right first time 28, 156
risk 6, 7, 8, 12, 26, 27, 40, 54, 62
    business case and 68
    escalation 26, 99
    estimating and 56
    governance of project management and 99
    identification/identify 26, 156
    and life cycle 81, 82, 84, 86
    project management plan and 25
    response 57, 157
    response planning 26, 157
    safety assessment 30
    see also project risk and risk event
risk analysis 26, 156
    qualitative (techniques) 26, 153
    quantitative 26, 153
risk event 26, 156
risk exposure 26, 156
risk management
    plan 84, 156
    see also project risk management
roles and responsibilities *see* project roles and
    responsibilities

safety management *see* health and safety and
    health, safety and environmental
    management
sales 70, 71, 157 *see also* marketing and sales
sanction 82, 84, 157
schedule 19, 36, 37, 39, 40, 44, 56, 58, 76, 90, 157
    master 36, 143
    target 68
scheduling 34, 36–37, 158
    resource 38

scope 2, 18, 34, 35, 158
  business case and 68
  change control and 42
  and contracts 76
  and cost 40
  development and 54
  earned value management and 44
  and life cycle 84, 86
  project management plan and 24
  of project risk management process 26
  project quality management and 28
scope creep 35, 158
scope management 25, 34–35, 158
senior management 19
  and project reviews 90
  role of 6, 9, 12, 14, 82
share (opportunity) 26, 158
slack *see* float
six sigma 28, 158
social capital 112, 159
solicitation 74, 159
solution 22, 23, 53, 81
  alternative 60, 68
  change control 61
  high-level 54
  optimal 54, 55
  preferred 52, 54, 68, 81, 82, 84
  proposed 54
  technical 60
sponsor 2, 8, 10, 12, 13, 159
  business case and 68
  change control and 42
  ethical requirements 118
  issue management and 48
  and life cycle 81, 82, 84, 86, 88, 89, 91
  governance of project management and 99
  project financing and funding and 72
  project management plan and 24
  project office and 14
  project success 18, 152
  role of 18, 35, 37, 70
  steering group 94
stakeholder analysis 20, 21, 159
stakeholder grid **21**, 159
stakeholder management 20–21, 159
  communication and 103
  issue management and 48
stakeholders 20, 21, 159
  identification 20, 159
  change control and 42
  communication and 102
  development and 54, 55
  information management and reporting
    and 46
  leadership and 106

and life cycle 82, 84, 86
  governance of project management and 98
  marketing and sales and 70
  methods and procedures and 96
  organisational roles and 94
  project context and 10
  project management plan and 24
  project quality management and 28
  project sponsorship and 13
  project success and 18
  requirements management and 52
  value management and 22
start-up meeting 86, 159
statement of scope 34, 159
statute law 76, 160
statutory obligations 47, 160
steering group 110, 160
  alternative names *12n, 94n*
  chair of 12
  role of 48, 94, 95
strategy 70, 160
  business/organisation/corporate 6, 8, 14,
    23, 58, 82, 99
  project 24, 34, 70, 81, 93, 152
  procurement 74, 149
structured systems analysis and design
  methodology (SSADM) 54
sub-project 4, **7**, 160
subject matter experts 94, 160
success criteria 2, 18, 160
  business case and 68
  project management plan and 24
  project reviews and 90
  stakeholders and 20
  value management and 23
success factors 19, 160
supplier 72, 74, 84, 160
  acquisition of 74
  external 84, 137
  relationships 74
  role of 94
  selection of 74

tacit knowledge 116
talent management 112, 161
targets 6, 23, 56
  cost 56
  time 56
task *see* activity
team *see* project team
team member 70, 94, 104, 106, 161
teamwork 61, 104–105, 106, 161
technology management 58–59, 161
tender 74, 161

document 74, 161
tendering 161
  and bidding 74
termination phase *80*, 81, 161
terms and conditions 161
testing 28, 52, 54, 55, 62, 87, 88, 161 *see also*
    modelling and testing
threat (negative risk) 26, 161 *see also* issue
    management
  accept 26, 125
  avoid 26, 126
  reduce 26, 154
  transfer 26, 162
three-point estimate 36, 56, 162
time 2, 6, 18
  change control and 42
  constraints *3*, 37
  contracts and 76
  development and 54
  earned value management and 44
  estimating and 56
  and life cycle 84, 86
  project quality management and 28
  value engineering and 61
timeboxing 54, 162
timescales 24
total quality management (TQM) 28, 162
transfer (threat) 26, 162
trends 40, 44, 45, 162

uncertain event 26, 162
uncertainty 26, 56, 59, 62, 106, 108, 163
unit rate-based payment method 74
user 52, 54, 70, 88, 163
  role of 94

validate 20, 28, 62, 90, 163
  stakeholder analysis 20
validation 54, 55, 163
value 22, 52, 56, 60, 81, 163
  analysis 22
  earned value management and 44
  planning *60*
value engineering 23, 55, 60–61, 163
value management 22–23, 55, 96, 163
  value engineering and 60
variance 40, 44, 45, 163
verification 55, 163
verify 28, 163
version control 64, 163

what-if assessments 84, 164
work breakdown structure (WBS) 34, 35, 36,
    93, 164
  earned value management and 44
  estimating and 56
work package 34, 36, 93, 164
working group 94, 104, 112, 164
zero defects 28, 164

Mathematics with Reason

*The Emergent Approach
to Primary Maths*

2005

Edited by

Sue Atkinson

Hodder & Stoughton

A MEMBER OF THE HODDER HEADLINE GROUP

*This book is dedicated to the memory of
Yvonne Ward, Oxfordshire Adviser.*

Orders: please contact Bookpoint Ltd, 130 Milton Park, Abingdon, Oxon
OX14 4SB. Telephone: (44) 01235 827720, Fax: (44) 01235 400454.
Lines are open from 9.00 - 6.00, Monday to Saturday, with a 24 hour
message answering service. Email address: orders@bookpoint.co.uk

British Library Cataloguing in Publication Data

Mathematics with reason: The emergent approach to primary mathematics.
  I. Atkinson, Sue
  372.7

ISBN 0 340 54749 9

First published 1992
Impression number   17   16   15   14   13   12   11   10
Year   2004 2003 2002

Typeset by Taurus Graphics, Abingdon, Oxon.
Printed in Great Britain for Hodder & Stoughton Educational,
a division of Hodder Headline Plc, 338 Euston Road, London NW1 3BH
by J. W. Arrowsmith Ltd., Bristol.

Contents

About the editor
About the contributors
Foreword
Editor's Preface
Acknowledgments

SECTION A : INTRODUCTION

1   Children as mathematicians
    Sue Atkinson

2   A new approach to maths
    Sue Atkinson

3   What makes successful problem solving?
    Sue Atkinson

4   The use of standard notation
    Sue Atkinson and Shirley Clarke

5   Children's graphical representations
    Shirley Clarke

6   Children's own mathematical representations
    Sue Atkinson and Shirley Clarke

7   The power of the children's own intuitive
    methods
    Sue Atkinson

SECTION B : TEACHERS' STORIES

8   Nursery children explore maths
    Sarah Killworth, Lesley Neilson and Sue Atkinson

9   Young children's representations of number
    operations
    Sue Gifford

10 Young children plan a picnic
    Alison Base

11 Reception children write about their maths
    Sue Atkinson

12 A simple starting point
    Marion Bird

13 Explode a number (a) With 7–9 year-olds
                           Sue Atkinson
                      (b) With 5-year-olds
                           Alison Base

14 Children working with numbers – discussion
    starters
    Sue Atkinson

15 Tracey and Jason make a map
    A maths advisory support teacher

16 Children build a natural area and pond
    Sue Atkinson

17 A young teacher starts off with maths with
    reason
    Jenny, a primary teacher

18 Do they really know how to do it?
    Shirley Clarke

19   Teachers talk about schemes
     (a) Staffroom conversation
          Two middle school teachers
     (b) Teaching maths without relying on a
          scheme   *Moira Proudfoot*

20 I'll do it my way
    Sue Atkinson

21 Real 'real problem-solving'
    Owen Tregaskis

22 Does maths with reason work?
    Nick James

23 Whole-school approaches to maths with reason
    Sue Atkinson

SECTION C : PRACTICALITIES AND WAYS
FORWARD

24 Starting off
    Sue Atkinson

25 How can I organise myself?
    Sue Atkinson

26 How do I develop my confidence?
    Sue Atkinson

27 Asking ourselves questions
    Marion Bird

28 Conclusions

    Reflection sheet

    Resources List

    References

About the editor

SUE ATKINSON is a primary teacher, primary maths consultant, and tutor for the Open University. She is engaged in research in primary maths curriculum development and has recently become a part-time lecturer at Westminster College, Oxford.

About the contributors

ALISON BASE was, at the time of writing, a teacher at Dr. South's Primary School, Islip, Oxfordshire. She is now deputy head at Garsington Primary, Oxfordshire and was a member of the PrIME team.

MARION BIRD is senior lecturer in maths education at West Sussex Institute of Education. She has taught across the age range of 5–18 years and has written widely on maths education.

SHIRLEY CLARKE works at the Institute of Education as inset coordinator for assessment. She was formerly a primary teacher and primary maths consultant in the Inner London Education Authority. She has worked extensively in a range of primary classrooms.

SUE GIFFORD is senior lecturer in maths education at the Roehampton Institute, London, and has worked in a variety of London Schools as a teacher and maths consultant.

NICK JAMES is involved in running in-service maths education for teachers in South Africa. He was formerly a teacher and maths advisory teacher, then lecturer in maths education at the Open University.

SARAH KILLWORTH was, at the time of writing, nursery teacher at New Hinksey First School, where she worked with nursery nurse, Elizabeth Stone. She is now headteacher at Headington Nursery School, Oxford.

LESLEY NEILSON is the nursery teacher at West Oxford Primary School where she works with nursery nurses Carol Adams, Lin Byrne and Janet Hemming.

MOIRA PROUDFOOT is a headteacher in Oxfordshire with a full-time teaching commitment. She was a member of the Oxfordshire PrIME team.

OWEN TREGASKIS is a teacher who worked with primary aged children for 20 years. For the last 8 years he has also worked with students in training and teachers on in-service courses at Cheltenham and Gloucester College of Higher Education. His main interest is in the development of children's mathematical thinking.

Foreword

Mathematics with Reason is a book which is firmly based in the classroom, and which has much to offer to every primary teacher who is concerned to improve the teaching of mathematics.

The core of the book is the section on 'Teachers' Stories'. By story and anecdote we are told some of the results of traditional primary maths teaching. We hear about the children who can do the 'sums' – or who get the 'sums' wrong – but who cannot apply the 'sums' to the simplest real-life problem. We hear about children who 'can't do maths' or think it is useless. We hear about the common errors that are familiar to every teacher; their source is often in the learning of the arithmetical processes of 'school maths' without understanding.

We also hear from teachers who use non-traditional ways of teaching maths. They have tried allowing children to record their maths in their own way, encouraging children to invent their own methods, asking children to solve real-life problems such as running a sports day. They have encouraged children to 'do' and 'talk' maths. They have tried to link 'school maths' to the common-sense world of 'home maths'. They have constantly been surprised by children's unexpected ingenuity, resourcefulness and understanding when maths has a reason, and when it is set in a real context.

However, the authors recognise that it is not easy for a teacher to change her long-established classroom practices. The authors accept the fact that some teachers work in schools where the dominance of a published maths scheme makes it difficult for one teacher to change. They recognise that a young teacher may not have the status to change the views of a whole school staff. They recognise that parents are accustomed to traditional methods and may value these methods. They offer practical suggestions for making progress in maths teaching in all these situations.

I have three practical suggestions to make to the reader: read the book, reflect on the practice of maths teaching in your classroom, use some of the activities from the book.

Even if you already teach 'maths with reason', the book has something to offer you – perhaps an activity you have not tried before, or something that a teacher had noticed, but that you had not seen in your own class. As Marion Bird says on page 166:

There is always more for us to learn when we are dealing with young children – that's what makes it so exciting!

Hilary Shuard
July 1991

Editor's Preface

Why do people find maths so difficult? Why does it cause such panic? Why do some teachers lack confidence when teaching maths? How is it that a child can spend a term learning multiplication tables, but then be unable to see how that knowledge will help to find the cost of buying 50 cream eggs?

This book explores some of the thinking processes underlying such questions. It looks at ways of making our maths teaching more effective both at home and in school, particularly in the light of the requirements of the National Curriculum. I hope that it will be used as a resource book for dipping into, for home, classroom, and for discussion starters for in-service work.

The book has been divided into three sections: Section A, the Introduction, considers the theory; Section B includes teachers' real-life stories of how *Mathematics with Reason* works in practice; and Section C looks at the practicalities and the different ways forward.

To help those who want to follow through certain ideas, there is a heading at the start of each chapter, within Section B, indicating the themes it contains, the age group of the children etc.

Most of the work described has arisen from teaching and advisory work, and from research. Any apparent emphasis on subtraction and place value is because these became a focus of my own research, and does not indicate any belief in their particular importance. The rest of the work has arisen from discussions with groups of teachers and parents, from in-service days, and from various primary teachers' support groups.

Throughout this book we have referred to he and she, but both of these terms should be taken to apply to both sexes. We have tried to avoid the clumsy wording of 'he/she', 'him/her', 'himself/herself' etc.

Acknowledgments

The author and publishers would like to thank Joy Dunn for providing the cartoons on section pages 55 and 150. Hodder & Stoughton have made every effort to trace copyright holders for all previously published copyright material, and believes it has done so, but if copyright holders wish to contact Hodder & Stoughton they should do so at the publishers address.

Sue Gifford wishes to acknowledge the help of Shirley Clarke, Valerie Heal, Christine Pugh and Razia Begum for chapter 9.

I am grateful to the teachers and parents from in-service days, the support groups I run for primary teachers, and the many other people who have contributed to this book. I especially want to thank Shirley Clarke for her advice on the typescript – and hours on the telephone! Nick James, John Mason, Owen Tregaskis, Martin Hughes, Tina Bruce, David Fielker, Gillian Johnson, Pam Atkins, Jan Tugwood, Joy Dunn and Chris Laybourn have all helped at various stages, though I take responsibility for the final product. Several other colleagues have contributed to the book, but prefer not to be named. Thanks also to my colleagues in the Oxfordshire PrIME team, to Adrian Townsend for his support and encouragement, to David Atkinson for his help and advice, and to Wilma Rawson for that wonderful moment in my classroom when the initial idea for this book was born. Also to Kathy Havekin of Hodder and Stoughton who has been a marvellous editor. Most of all I am grateful to all the children, teachers and parents with whom I have worked in the classroom, including those from: Drayton Primary School, Oxfordshire, especially Marian Whiting and Pauline Higgs; New Hinksey First School, Oxford, especially Jackie Nauman, Margaret Tatton, Jean King, and Adrian Townsend; West Oxford Primary School, Oxford, especially Bobbie Jones and Jack Smellie; Brington Primary School, Huntingdon; Grendon County Combined School, Buckinghamshire; Weald Middle School, Harrow, Middlesex. They have been a constant source of delight and inspiration.

Sue Atkinson
January 1991

Section A Introduction

— 1 — Children as mathematicians
Sue Atkinson

THEMES: background theory; links with apprenticeship reading and developmental writing; the term 'maths with reason'; why maths is treated differently

A significant feature of current primary education is the growing trend towards building on the skills developed from the children's home-learning which they bring with them to school. This is reflected in the way the National Curriculum non-statutory guidance in both English and maths advocates an emphasis on the children's own methods.

One of the assumptions of this book is that educational practice which starts from where children are, (what they are thinking and the skills they already possess etc.) will be the most effective means of teaching new concepts, mathematical or otherwise. This practice will build on children's intuitive beliefs, strengths, and their 'home' or 'informal' language. This kind of educational practice will, we argue, enable children to progress more rapidly through the levels and attainment targets of the National Curriculum.

Whereas earlier educational psychologists, following Piaget, argued that children have severe developmental limitations in the their understanding (and in some senses of course that cannot be disputed), working with children can take on a whole new perspective if one builds on the modern theories of child development. These focus on the *meaning* and the *strengths* that the children already have.

The work of Margaret Donaldson (1978), Martin Hughes (1986), Vygotski (1983), and others, shows how much children are capable of. If we can negotiate shared meanings and strive to unlock children's attempts to communicate with us, (rather than interpret what they do exclusively in adult terms), we become aware of their enormous potential. There is considerable evidence (Wells and Nicholls, 1985; Donaldson *et al* 1983, and others) that by involving children actively in the processes of their own education, enabling them to search for personal meaning in what they *can* do, we deepen their understanding and open new doors in their learning.

Developmental writing

This attempt to build on what children already know underlies the emphasis on 'developmental' writing described in the work of Marie Clay (1975); Donald Graves (1983); the SCDC National Writing Project; and Nigel Hall (1989). This change in emphasis has borne fruit. In classrooms where developmental writing is encouraged, children write much more and much earlier in their school life and, it would seem, with much more meaning, involvement, enjoyment and artistic expression than was previously thought possible (Nigel Hall, 1989).

The aims of the National Writing Project include: valuing children's own work; making use of all the real writing opportunities that exist (such as thank you letters, notes, diaries etc.); providing a variety of pens, paper, and other writing equipment; providing a role model, by the teacher writing for herself; valuing writing by 'publishing' it, so viewing children as writers; and ensuring that the purposes of the writing is clear to the child.

The apprenticeship approach to reading

Similar thinking underlies the 'apprenticeship approach' to reading developed by Liz Waterland in her book *Read With Me*(1985). The adult provides the role model, reading *with* the child, as well as the child spending time in the classroom reading her own book. The literature available to the children is 'real' in the sense that they are encouraged to 'read' books which are published because of their literary merit, and not, for example, because of their 'structured' vocabulary or phonics.

In schools where delightful picture books lure children into the world of story and dominate the reading corner, reading is much more important *to the children*. It becomes more fun and the focus of much of the classroom activity. Books have a meaning that children can identify with – there is a reason for reading.

A balanced approach

Of course, many teachers believe that there is no one correct way to teach reading and writing. They still keep the more structured 'reading books' for use with children who need support. In writing, most teachers would want to give children as many different experiences as possible to encourage different sorts of writing. Teachers continue writing for children, as they have done for years, providing children with a model to copy.

In any 'new' thinking, teachers select ways to teach their class from ideas around them, but they are often caught between conflicting claims of researchers. Some would argue, for example, that the developmental approach to language is not working and that standards are falling, whereas others are convinced of its effectiveness. Somewhere down the middle is the teacher trying to teach her children in the most effective way.

Why treat maths differently from language?

In primary schools where there is ample evidence of 'good practice' in language work, why is it that maths is so often the poor relation – often a solitary activity, based on a closely followed scheme, workbook, or an ancient set of workcards? A group of teachers gave the following reasons for treating maths differently.

- Teachers perceive themselves as poor mathematicians.

- Teachers lack confidence and therefore over-rely on a maths scheme for security.

- School policy requires a scheme to be followed.

- To cover the requirements of the National Curriculum children need to be 'pushed on' and a scheme achieves that.

- Parents have been taught by teachers that maths is rows of 'sums' all ticked (in red!).

- Teachers are willing to try out new ideas but continue to believe that 'real' maths comes out of a text book.

- Use of a text book can control children very effectively and in a class of thirty, when the teacher is working with four children, the need to get twenty-six occupied means that the maths scheme often saves the day.

- Teachers and children have a very limited view of what maths is.

- Children are viewed as having potential for language activities, i.e. they come to school with abilities that are nurtured and developed. By the age of five, children have about half of the adult spoken vocabulary, but almost no maths *of the type that is normally measured and regarded as 'school' maths.*

- Children are viewed as empty vessels when it comes to understanding maths concepts. Teachers see their role as emptying the jug of knowledge about maths into the children.

- The maths in construction, design, science, technology, PE, printing, cooking, woodwork, the home corner, etc., is not recognised as such and so is not developed in any depth as a significant and meaningful mathematical activity.

- Maths *is* different! Much of it is abstract, and this sets it apart from many other aspects of the curriculum.

A 'developmental' or 'apprenticeship' approach to maths?

Is there a developmental approach to the learning of maths corresponding to that in language? It seems much harder to find developmental maths in primary classrooms than developmental language teaching. But we hope to show in this book that such an approach to maths is not only possible but effective. We have tried to answer the following questions:

- What would developmental maths mean in theory, and in the practice of implementing the National Curriculum?

- What can we translate from the apprenticeship approach to language into the maths curriculum?

- What is needed by teachers to help them allow children develop the intuitive mathematical skills and concepts that they already have?

Releasing potential

This book is about releasing potential – both the children's and the teacher's. It is about encouraging teachers (however nervous they are about teaching maths) to experiment, to view maths from a different standpoint, to take a step back and let the children try to do it their way – a way that shows there is a reason for maths.

So we argue that there can be a developmental approach to maths though we recognise that more research is needed. We also believe that many of the aims of the National Writing Project apply equally in the context of maths. The contributors to this book are *not* advocating one correct way to teach maths. We argue for a balanced approach to maths teaching, incorporating the very best of current good primary practice, and relating this to the requirements of the National Curriculum.

Despite the differences between language and maths, we will show that there are considerable similarities in the thinking processes involved. So for teachers who are confident in language teaching, much of the way they teach language can be directly applicable to the teaching of maths. The 'apprenticeship' approach to maths, for example, would involve the teacher doing some of her own maths – organising timetables, lists, charts, etc. – in the classroom, where she can share her work with the children. She will also join in with the children's work, so that adult and child are learners together.

What shall we call this approach to maths?

We face a difficulty in deciding what this approach to maths should be called.

- *Practical maths* This does not say enough. Just because children are using apparatus, does not necessarily mean that the activity is meaningful and relevant to them.

- *Emergent maths* A good term, implying children emerging as mathematicians. We maintain in this book that children come to school mathematically able – it is 'school maths' that can breed the panic. However, the term 'emergent' may have taken on a special meaning in writing terms, so 'emergent maths' does not quite express what we mean.

- *Developmental maths* This is also a good term, but has the problem that it could give the impression that mathematical understanding *always* goes through certain stages, This may be true, but more research is needed on this.

- *Constructivist maths* This is another good term. Constructivists believe that children must have the opportunity to construct meaning for themselves. However, it could give the impression (*a*) that children must, therefore, construct *all* meaning for themselves – which is not what we mean. The parent and teacher play a vital role in that construction – the role of the sensitive intervener who often supplies language and gently guides the child towards expressing the concept in a meaningful (but not necessarily conventional) way; or (*b*) that maths is rather like the progressivism of the 1960s and 1970s when teachers were led to believe that the teacher just stood back and let it all happen.

- *Intelligent maths* (Richard Skemp) Yes, this conveys much of what we mean. Intelligent learning is understood and therefore remembered. It has meaning for the child. But we also want to convey some sense of the emergence of children as mathematicians, implying a developmental process.

As a result, we have chosen the term 'maths with reason' as a summary term which seems to convey what is most helpful in these other terms.

What is 'maths with reason'?

Maths with reason rests on exactly the same philosophy of child development and classroom practice as developmental writing and apprenticeship reading. What we mean will emerge throughout the book where it will be seen that maths with reason includes the following features:

- It is maths which starts from the secure 'home learning' established in the child before she comes to school.

- It is maths based on understanding.

- It is a balanced approach using both traditional and new methods.

- It builds on the child's 'home' language and gradually, and with great care, introduces the more formal and special language of maths.

- It has as its overall aim 'to develop a positive attitude to maths and an awareness of its power to communicate and explain.'

- It puts great emphasis on the child's own methods for calculating and solving problems and rejects the previous practice of heavy emphasis on standard written algorithms.

- Maths is regarded as a powerful tool for interpreting the world and therefore should ideally be rooted in real experience across the whole curriculum. Maths with reason becomes a part of the classroom dialogue; a way of explaining the world of the child with all its mysteries and wonder.

- Maths with reason is rooted in *action*– learning through *doing*. So schemes of work (the translating of policies into actual classroom practice) always start with *activity*.

- Maths with reason puts less emphasis on representing numbers on paper as 'sums' and more emphasis on developing *mental images* in the child, and it is through language and emphasis on the inter-relationship of language and action that these mental images are used as a bridge towards the mastery of the codes of maths – its specialised symbols and meanings.

- The main tool for child and teacher to employ in the mastery of maths concepts is *language*, not pencil and paper exercises from text books. The child is encouraged to *talk* about what she is doing and the teacher's craft is to bring all her knowledge and skill into play to make her intervention appropriate.

- Errors are accepted as an essential part of the learning process. They enable teachers to assess what meaning the child is making of the activity and often become a starting point for discussion. The child, freed from the fear of criticism, will more readily experiment with ideas and mathematical language. He will think aloud, and in so doing will release enormous creative potential into the group.

- Teachers and parents work on the maths *they* are doing *with* the child. Mathematical activities like cooking, shopping, gardening, the family budget, estimating how much food is needed for the meal, are all shared with the child. In classrooms, teachers make their problems explicit to the children e.g. how shall we organise our assembly?

- Maths is brought out of the child's everyday situations, e.g. playing ludo or chess, sharing biscuits, deciding what is fair, whose turn it is on the computer and how many more days to go until someone's birthday.

- So, maths with reason emphasises the thinking processes of maths, and these are made explicit in the conversations between adult and child. The focus is on the children doing their own thinking – which is valued by the teacher – not on the children trying to work out what is in the teacher's mind.

In other words, maths with reason is consistent with other 'good practice' in primary education. We believe that it leads to higher attainment in maths in National Curriculum terms, and helps children to become mathematicians.

Martin Hughes (1986) made clear that a crucial element in maths teaching is that children come to school with considerable mathematical abilities. In the next chapter we outline his work which underpins the rest of the book.

— 2 — A new approach to maths
Sue Atkinson

THEMES: the work of Martin Hughes; background theory; the problem of children's poor maths attainment; children's own methods and symbols; the challenge to teachers and parents

One of the key recent books about maths education is *Children and Number* by Martin Hughes. His research indicates possible ways of improving children's' performance in maths – an area of great concern to teachers and parents. This chapter only presents Hughes' main findings as they relate to maths with reason, and readers are strongly encouraged to read *Children and Number* for themselves.

What is the problem?

Many surveys show that children can lack basic mathematical understanding in practical situations. Hughes looks at this problem in relation to number with some surprising conclusions.

The standard of maths seems poor in many children.

Hughes finds that young children do, in fact, have considerable mathematical language and understanding before they come to school. We will call this their 'home' or 'informal' language and understanding, because it uses the everyday informal language of the home and the child's familiar world.

One of Hughes' main points is that the more formal language of school maths (both as spoken at school and in written standard symbols, e.g. 2 + 2 = 4) is very different from this informal 'home' language. *It may be that the gap between these two languages holds the key to why so many children perform so poorly in maths tests.*

This is obviously a vitally important piece of research for parents and teachers because it involves both the home and the school, and one of Hughes' conclusions is that parents and teachers should try to work more closely together.

Central to Hughes' argument is the belief that the ability to solve problems is at the heart of maths. This is a major theme in the Cockroft Report (DES, 1982 para.249) and in the National Curriculum. In other words, teachers should be aiming to teach not only concepts and skills, but also how to apply concepts in practical situations as it is here that children seem to fail in tests.

Hughes set out to answer why it is that surveys point out the shortcomings in children's understanding of practical applications of maths, and why this kind of mathematical understanding, (often called problem solving) is so difficult for so many children.

Piaget in proportion

Piaget's work has been, and still is, of enormous significance in influencing ideas about how children learn. His theories rest on the idea of discrete stages of cognitive development in the child, i.e. separate stages that the child has to go through. Piaget was led to conclude, for example, that children under seven years of age are incapable of logical thought and are able only to see things from their own perspective.

Hughes argues that there is evidence to suggest that this view of young children – as very limited and illogical thinkers – is not correct. He suggests, as do other psychologists, that these apparent limitations to children's thinking can be partially explained because Piaget set up such unreal research situations, and used such complex language that the children simply did not understand the context and the meaning of the task that Piaget was setting them. In other words, the thinking required for the task was what Margaret Donaldson, in *Children's Minds*, calls 'disembedded thinking'.

If, however, children are set tasks similar to those used by Piaget, but in a context familiar and meaningful to the child (a task with 'human sense'), it can be shown that children understand far more than Piaget suggests. As well as his own work on this point (McGarrigle, Grieve and Hughes, 1978), Hughes cites the work of Donaldson (1978) and Gelman and Gillistel, (1978). The importance of this for teachers is the change in emphasis. Piaget focused on what children *do not* know whereas Hughes focuses on what they *do* know. This has important consequences for what we teach, and how we teach it.

Hughes proposes an approach to maths based on these new ideas of how children seem to learn and it is this new approach which underlies *Maths with Reason*.

What do children know before they come to school?

Hughes found that children know a great deal about number before they come to school. He found that even three-year-olds can carry out simple addition and subtraction provided the problems were presented in a context which made 'human sense' to them, and provided also that the numbers were kept small. Hughes describes a number of games that he devised to play with children in which he explored this pre-school ability. One of these games, the tins game, is described a little later on. These games can provide an interesting starting point for parents and nursery reception teachers.

A paradox

Having found that many children know a great deal about number before they come to school and that they seem at this stage to display a surprising range of mathematical abilities, Hughes focuses on an intriguing problem: '. . . we have something of a paradox: young children appear to start school with more mathematical knowledge than has hitherto been thought. In that case, why should they experience such difficulty with school mathematics?' (Hughes 1986b, p. 36).

School maths language is like a foreign language to the children and often fails to integrate with their already accomplished mathematical 'home' language.

The language of school maths

Children's impressive array of mathematical abilities does not always seem to carry over into the classroom because of their difficulties of learning '. . . to translate between their concrete understanding of number and the written symbolism of arithmetic.' (Hughes 1986b, p. 53). So, although children arrive at school often able to perform calculations such as 'what is two bricks and one more brick?', most teachers of small children wisely hesitate about using the written formal code 2 + 1 = ?. Likewise a child who is asked 'How many is three and one more?', might say 'One more what?' because it makes no 'human sense'. But, ask the same child 'How many is three bricks and one brick?' and he will answer 'four' because he can understand the problem as it refers to bricks.

This difficulty in translating the concrete understanding of number into school maths language is delightfully illustrated in the following conversation between Martin Hughes and Patrick (aged four years, one month).

MH: How many is two and one more?
Patrick: Four.
MH: Well, how many is two *lollipops* and one more?
Patrick: Three.
MH: How many is two *elephants* and one more?
Patrick: Three.
MH: How many is two *Giraffes* and one more?
Patrick: Three.
HM: So how many is two and one more?
Patrick: (*Looking Hughes straight in the eye*) Six.

(Hughes, 1986a, and Hughes, 1986b p. 47.)

The problem with school maths language is that it is often about nothing in particular i.e. 'What is two and one more?' – 'One more what?'; it is new to the children; it is difficult because it involves unfamiliar concepts; and, it uses words children already know in special ways such as 'and' (meaning 'add'), 'take away' (Chinese ?) and 'makes'.

So, if the maths itself is not presented in a way that is meaningful to children, if it fails to make 'human sense', and if unfamiliar language is used, problems will almost inevitably arise.

Children's own methods

Using fingers for counting

Hughes recommends that some difficulties could perhaps be prevented if children were encouraged to use their own methods from the start.

For many children, counting on fingers is their favourite 'own method'. Many parents and teachers try to discourage children using fingers for calculating, but Hughes points out how important their use is for children.

The gap

What seems to happen with many children is that they develop a completely separate way of thinking about the maths they do at school, because it fails to integrate with their accomplished informal 'home' mathematical language.

One feature of this gap is the way that children are often observed to be splitting thinking and understanding from calculations they perform. Both teachers and parents frequently see this happening when children do a calculation and come up with an answer that a moment's thought would show to be ridiculous. An example of this splitting of reason from calculating could be where ten-year-old children calculate how many 52-seater coaches would be needed to get everyone to the seaside. If, for example, 234 people were going, it would not be uncommon to get a response based on correct arithmetic (234 divided by 52), but devoid of reason – 'we need four-and-a-half coaches.'

How do we close the gap?

'Helping children to make these links is probably the single most important task in early mathematics education' (Martin Hughes)

Hughes suggests that we may be able to help children to make the crucial links between their own personal and meaningful maths with which they come to school, and the more formal and complex language of school maths, in very practical ways.

1 We could emphasise and encourage the use of the children's own methods of calculation.
2 Linked with this, we could encourage the children's own invented symbols that have meaning for them.
3 Teachers could find out all they can about the children's mathematical background from the parents, e.g. Do they like numbers and counting? Do they play mathematical games at home – dice or cards? Do they use a calculator or computer? Do they like and seem to understand activities that have a maths content, such as cooking, shopping, woodwork or using construction toys like Lego and Meccano?

4 We could set maths tasks in meaningful contexts, to allow for the children to make 'human sense' of the task and to allow them to be able to translate the unfamiliar maths language into their own individual understandings of maths.

Invented symbols

One of the most interesting aspects of Hughes' work is the invented symbolism which he found to be present in the young children he worked with.

The tins game
Hughes put out four identical tins with lids, each containing a different number of bricks, usually one, two and three bricks with one empty tin. He shuffled the tins around and asked each child individually to find, say, the tin with three bricks. Of course, this was guess work because all the tins looked the same. Once the children grasped the game, Hughes put labels on the tin, gave each child a pen and asked them to put something on the paper to show how many bricks were in the tin. The tins were shuffled after each child had written on the labels and Hughes then asked them to find, say, the tin with three bricks in. This time the children had their own invented symbols to help them. It turned out that their own representations were clearly meaningful to them and many children were able to identify correctly the number of bricks in the tins. (See Fig 2.1a and 2.1b).

Figure 2.1a Representations of 1, 2, 3 and 0 bricks by Anna (4 yrs)

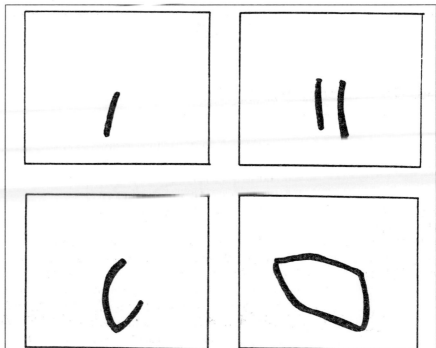

Figure 2.1b Representations of 1, 2, 3 and 0 bricks by Paul (3 yrs 8ths)

This tins game produced children's invented ways of recording numbers and some of the children's ideas are reproduced here. Again, readers are recommended to refer to Hughes' book, *Children and Number*, for greater detail.

There were various sorts of responses from the children when they were asked to 'put something on the paper'. Some children produced what can only be called 'scribble'. This doesn't, of course, mean that the scribble didn't have some meaning to the child, for as with early writing, it may well be that children have to go through this stage. Children are learning that print conveys meaning. Their 'scribble' is an attempt to say something in print and teachers are well aware of the confidence with which children 'read' these early attempts. Other children produced work that Hughes was able to analyse – shown below.

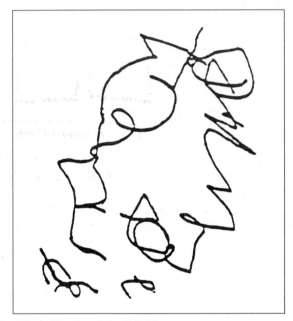

Alison (4yrs 2 mths) : 2 bricks

Leanne (4 yrs 3 mths) : 5 bricks

Halla (3 yrs 6 mths) : 1 brick

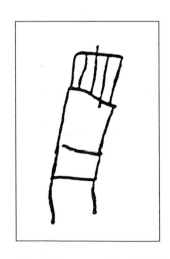

Figure 2.2 Examples of idiosyncractic responses

Nicola (4 yrs 4 mths) : 5 bricks

Analysing children's work

Hughes put the children's work into four groups, and readers may like to relate these types of responses to those found in the National Writing Project. He put the 'scribble', together with other representations where the children's meaning was not clear to him, in a group called 'idiosyncratic responses' (see Figure 2.2).

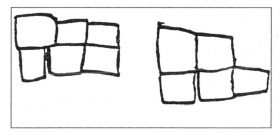

Daniel (5 yrs 11 mths) : freehand drawing representing 6 bricks and 5 bricks

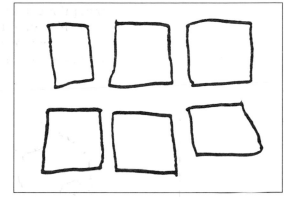

Fig 2.3 Examples of pictographic responses

Rachel (4 yrs) draws round bricks

Other children produced work that was grouped as 'pictographic responses' because it showed some semblance to a picture of what was in front of them (see Figure 2.3).

'Iconic responses' were those that, like the pictographic responses, showed a one-to-one correspondence with the bricks (i.e. an attempt at the right number of bricks), but where the children made some mark rather than a picture – so for three bricks they did three tallies or three houses (see Figure 2.4).

Fig 2.4 Examples of iconic response

Mutale (4 yrs 3 mths) : 5 bricks

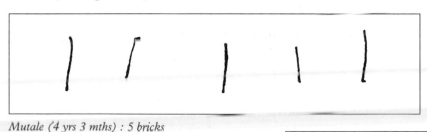

Emma(5 yrs 2 mths) : 6 bricks

Pamela(5 yrs 1 mth) : 3 bricks

'Symbolic responses' were those where some sort of conventional symbol was used (see Figure 2.5).

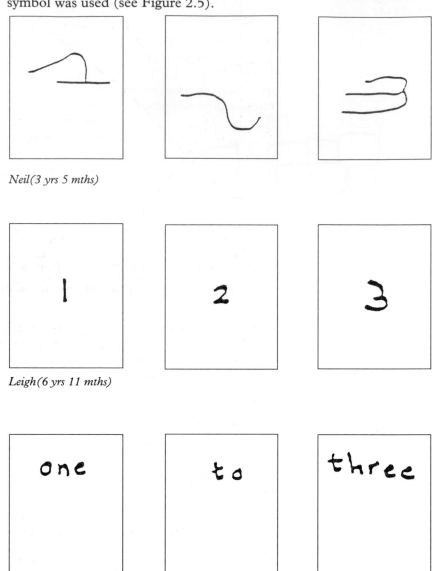

Neil (3 yrs 5 mths)

Leigh (6 yrs 11 mths)

Figure 2.5 Examples of symbolic responses (all representing 1, 2 and 3 bricks)

Kashif (7 yrs 4 mths)

From the diagram (Figure 2.6) it can be seen that it was not until children were about seven years old that conventional symbols became the most common response – a fact which surprises many adults.

Hughes notes several interesting points about these invented symbols, but just two will be mentioned here:

1   Children attached great meaning to their own symbols and they were able to interpret them up to a week later.

2   Very few of the children used conventional symbols, even children who were familiar with conventional number symbols.

Figure 2.6 Type of response: variation with age

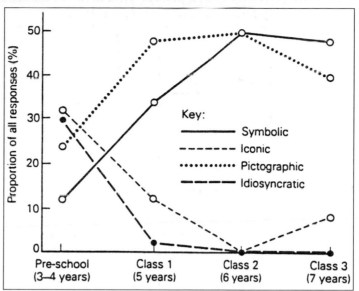

For teachers and parents the importance of invented symbols would seem to be:

- that it could show the apparent irrelevance of conventional symbols for very young children – which may reflect a similar irrelevance of, say, the traditional way of writing fractions, for an eight-year-old; and
- that it shows a clear link with early writing.

What conclusions can be drawn?

Hughes' work as it relates to maths with reason can be summarised as showing the following:

- Young children start school with their own understanding of maths and with a surprising range of mathematical abilities.

- These abilities are clear when children operate in concrete situations that make 'human sense' to them.

- When children are at school they often fail at mathematical problems where knowledge has to be applied.

- Maths should therefore have a purpose and meaning and make 'human sense' to the child.

- A gap seems to develop between the child's own informal and concrete understanding of maths and the language of maths as it is used in schools.

- Helping children to make the links between home and school maths is a <u>vital and important task for teachers and parents</u> in <u>the maths education of children</u>.

Challenges facing parents and teachers

While Hughes recognises that there is much more to be discovered about the ways children learn maths, the implications of his work for parents and teachers include the following:

- We need to redefine the aims and objectives of early maths education, giving the links *between* the concrete and the formal more emphasis.

- Parents and teachers need to work together to relate the child's 'home' mathematical background to the school's approach. For a more detailed account of this see p. 161.

- We need to build on the mathematical strategies which the child already possesses at the start of school, e.g. using fingers or counting up and down the number sequence. These are the maths strategies that are *meaningful* to young children.

- 'Obviously, we want children to move on eventually to new and more powerful strategies, but if these are forced upon children regardless of their own methods *they will not only fail to understand the new ones, but will feel ashamed and defensive about their own.*' (Hughes, 1986b, p. 177 – editor's emphasis).

- We must respect children's own invented symbolism. 'As with children's informal methods of calculation, their own invented symbolism must be given much greater prominence in the classroom.' (Hughes, 1986b p. 177).

- '. . . indeed, it turns out that *children's own inventive notations are likely to be far more appropriate in these early stages than the conventional symbolism of arithmetic . . .* Yet children are rarely encouraged to use these methods in school.' (Hughes, 1986b, p. 170 editor's emphasis)

- 'Whatever the source of children's translation difficulties might be, their consequences are undoubtedly profound. If children do not readily and fluently translate between different representations of mathematical problems, then a dangerous gap will develop. At best, this may simply mean that they will carry out their formal procedures competently but automatically, and with little understanding of their rationale or possible application. This would seem an accurate description of the way many children – and adults – perform arithmetic today. A much more damaging consequence is that their formal procedures will become faulty. Without any concrete underpinning, isolated mistakes can become habitual errors, and a *bizarre written arithmetic can easily result.*' (Hughes 1986b p. 171 – editor's emphasis).

- We should attempt to explain to the children the history and purpose of conventional symbolism. As Laurie Buxton (1982) says, 'The answer is not to avoid mathematical symbols in a child's earlier experience. Rather one should capitalise on situations where the children feel a need for symbols.' (It is interesting to relate this point to some of the aims and objectives of the National Writing Project; see p. 73.)

- We should take particular care when using symbols. In some maths schemes, non-standard symbolism (such as arrows) can be used to the point of confusion.

- We should always try to put maths into a context that children understand. For example, rather than using 'sums' out of context, we could try to set maths in 'real' or practical situations. Examples of teachers doing this can be found in Chapters 10, 16, 17, and 21.

- We should not be afraid of explicit teaching.

- We should recognise the value of computers and calculators. Teachers using LOGO find many benefits reaching right across the curriculum, but for the purposes of this book, the important points are that it stimulates mathematical discussion and thought, it improves language, communication and group cooperation generally, it engages the children's interest and develops concentration, and because of its problem–solving nature, it tends to integrate 'home' and 'school' maths, and gives a sense of purpose to the maths.

This chapter highlights the importance of building on children's strengths and making the appropriate links between 'home' and school maths. Teachers must make maths have meaning and a sense of purpose for the children – in other words, to give maths a reason.

The next five chapters give a practical focus of some of these theoretical themes.

We want to thank Martin Hughes and Basil Blackwell, publishers, for permission to reproduce diagrams and to quote from *Children and Number*.

—3— What makes successful problem–solving?
Sue Atkinson

THEMES: background theory; low achievement in maths; the problem with problems; classroom organisation; effective maths teaching

A strange anomaly seems to emerge in maths lessons. On the one hand, we see children who are quite competent at computational skills go to pieces and are unable to manage when confronted with a page of problems, and on the other hand, we have frequently shown that 'problem–solving' is a major way in which children learn. What is going on here? Are 'problems' contexts in which children perform poorly or well? Why should it be that children *learn* best in problem situations, yet continue to *function* best when only straightforward and simple calculations are involved? The following examples may prove interesting:

Martin Hughes quotes this very illuminating example from Hart (1981) in which children aged eleven to thirteen were asked:

'The Green family have to drive 261 miles to get from London to Leeds. After driving 87 miles, they stop for lunch. How do you work out how far they still have to drive?

$$87 \times 3 \quad 261 + 87 \quad 87 + 261 \quad 261 - 87$$

$$261 \times 87 \quad 261 - 87 \quad 87 - 261 \quad 87 + 174$$

Despite the fact that the children only needed to select the calculation required, only 60 per cent of twelve-year-olds selected the correct answer (261 - 87).

Adults have problems too

It is not just children who have this problem. A BBC survey (1990) of 1000 people aged between twenty-one and sixty found that:

- More than one in ten adults could not cope with calculating how much a dozen 30p chocolate bars would cost and how much change they would get from £10.

- Forty per cent could not divide a £30.35 restaurant bill between five people.

- Nearly half could not work out 15 per cent VAT on £80.

The people were allowed to use calculators, the tests were done at home, and the tests were disguised and made as friendly as possible so that people would be at ease.

Elizabeth tries to do some problems

Here is the sort of example that teachers encounter frequently. Elizabeth, a bright child of ten, was working on subtraction in a scheme. She successfully completed three pages of straight 'sums'. She then turned over to a double page of similar sums, but embedded in words – what the scheme called a 'problems' page. Elizabeth could not cope with this and said that she did not know what to do. The teacher knew that Elizabeth approached other problem–solving situations positively and successfully, so what was so difficult to her about this page of written problems? It was not simply a matter of reading the problems, as she was a fluent reader. The teacher sat with Elizabeth and, taking the problems one at a time, tried to explore what the real meanings of the problems were – trying to get Elizabeth to see the 'human sense' in them. Eventually Elizabeth saw the meaning of each problem and worked it out correctly in her head. But then she asked, 'How do I write that down?' She seemed unable to relate what she could now see as the answer, to the conventional form of a standard algorithm. Elizabeth is by no means alone, and many teachers find this inconsistency in children's computational skills and applications required by 'problems'.

It would appear that Elizabeth needed both to have the problem explained in a context which was meaningful to her and, having got the right answers mentally, she still, despite being in the top maths group, needed these related to standard conventional ways of writing sums down.

Here, then, is a clue to understanding our anomaly. As Margaret Donaldson points out, (and we stress elsewhere in this book), a crucial factor in successful mathematics is the *context* in which the problem is set. This must be *clear and meaningful* and make 'human sense' to the child. This isn't always the case with scheme 'problems' pages. Not only do children not care how much the wood cost Mr Smith when he was making his garage, but not many of them can find the situation meaningful.

What might contribute to this 'problem with problems'?

'Problems' in books can cause reading difficulties for some children, but it is often more complex than this, because they can also cause difficulties for good readers as well. Perhaps it is the language of 'problems'. There is clearly a huge difference between children saying 'How much squash do you think we'll need for the party?' and the grand text book language of 'Thirty-two children decide to have a party. Each child will drink 230 ml of squash and . . . ' etc.

Children see text book 'problems' as 'word sums' and perceive them as being harder than straightforward calculations. Children seem to operate in 'school maths mode' when they see maths written down, and this is characterised by:

- leaving behind informal, secure, intuitive methods;

- the use of taught school methods for calculations (standard written algorithms) – if they can be remembered;

- an apparent inability to continue to ask if the answer is reasonable; and

- the willingness to believe that *it need have no meaning!*

Adult   Why did you put a little 'one' under the line?
Barry   That's what Mrs Smith does.
(aged 8)

Ben, aged 9, calculating 27 + 3 wrote: 27
                               +3
                               57

but mentally he worked it out to be 30.

Adult   So which is right?
Ben   They both are.
Adult   Can you explain that to me?
Ben   Well, sometimes that happens when you write it down.

How can we teach maths more effectively?

- We need to ensure that problems are set in meaningful contexts.
- Writing maths down (hence the need to use symbols), tends to make children and adults operate in 'school maths mode'.
- Symbols can be very powerful – but they cause their own difficulties.
- Written maths often causes people to abandon their more secure informal methods.
- Written maths often causes people to forget how to perform calculations.

So how can we make the best of problem pages in schemes and other resource books? Basically, we should aim to:

- give the children plenty of time;

- let them work in groups so that they can discuss;

- give the problem verbally where possible;

- make sure the children feel the problem is real enough to be worth solving!

- make sure the problems are interesting;

- explain that learning to think problems through and find a solution is an important part of the National Curriculum, and it is an important 'life skill' which children will need as adults; and

- ensure that, particularly for under-sevens, the problem makes 'human sense'.

—4— The use of standard notation
Sue Atkinson and Shirley Clarke

> THEMES: *when and how to introduce standard notation; children's own methods and symbols; successive shorthanding; discussion starters*

The following sections have been produced by groups of teachers. They are provided here as a basis for discussion for groups of parents and teachers.

What is standard notation?

Figure 4.1 shows a collection of all the maths symbols we could think of.

The advantages of symbols

- Symbols are part of the universal language of maths.
- They are time-saving.
- Using symbols correctly can give children a great sense of achievement.
- Getting children to use them impresses the parents!

The disadvantages of symbols

- They do tend to restrict children's methods.
- You need a good memory to remember them and to use them confidently.
- You also need to understand (*a*) the symbol; (*b*) the process; (*c*) its application.
- They can tend to give a sense of failure if they are not understood.
- They are too abstract for young children.
- Copied symbols from books can mislead parents over what their children can understand.

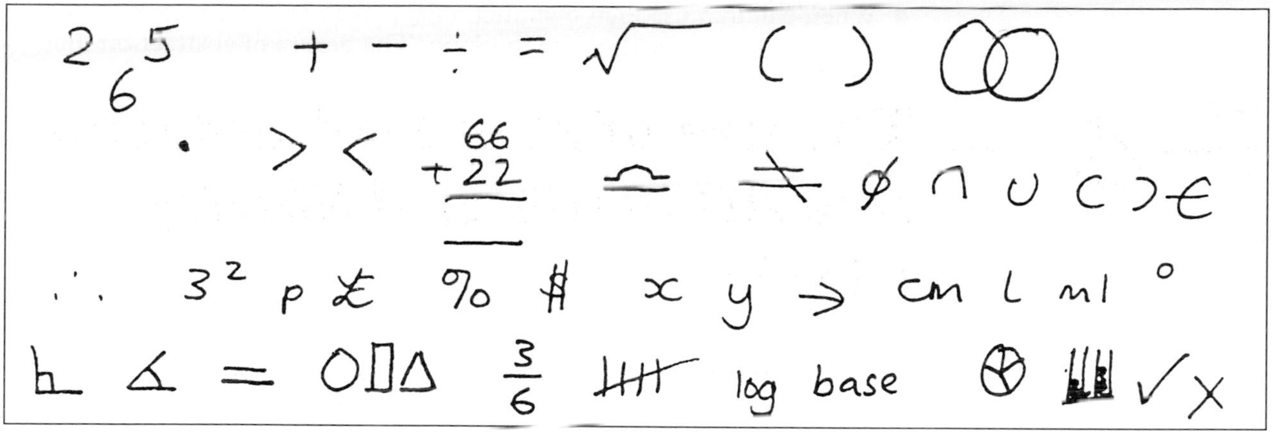

Figure 4.1 Standard notation

Reasons for not using standard notation

- It may be the wrong moment for certain children. They may not be ready for anything other than their own methods which have meaning for them.

- They may not understand the need for any kind of quick shorthand.

- Someone else's method could cause some children to devalue their own methods causing low self-esteem and lack of confidence in maths.

- Standard teacher–taught methods can give an impression that it is the teacher who holds all the right answers and the power. This again can lower children's confidence and willingness to think for themselves and to produce their own methods.

- Some standard forms of notation and calculation are inefficient. For example, in many maths schemes, arrows are used in so many ways that children soon become confused.

When are standard forms of notation appropriate?

- When the notation is understood.

- When the children understand the method being used.

- When the children have had opportunities to explore their own and others' methods.

- When it is the most efficient method for the children's purposes.

- When there is a 'democratic' atmosphere within the classroom.

Why is it important to find their own methods?

- They involve children in their own learning, and therefore give children confidence.

- By comparing methods, children are helped to appreciate the need for using commonly understood symbols and for making their methods quick.

- It keeps open the idea of exploring alternatives, instead of the emphasis on 'one right way'.

- When children use their own methods, it is easier for teachers to be in touch with how children are thinking. The degree of abstraction that children have reached can be observed.

- Children's own methods and symbols are used and understood in writing, so the children can readily translate this into maths. This makes maths less of a mystery.

- Focusing on children's own methods increases the likelihood of building on the children's secure 'home' knowledge (see p. 44).

The process of successive shorthanding

When children work on 'do and talk' maths, first exploring mathematical ideas through games and activities, then recording in their own way perhaps with words and drawings, they are trying to represent the pictures in their minds. These pictures will often arise from the apparatus that the children have been using. The link can then be made from these pictures to standard notation. Children readily come to appreciate the need for increased speed of recording and the need to write things down concisely.

This is illustrated by work done by some seven-to-nine-year-olds on multiplication. Children first did several 'do and talk' maths activities, putting Unifix into groups, such as 3 groups of 4. They had to describe their work to each other, 'I've got 3 groups of 4 Unifix and it makes 12 altogether, 4, 8, 12.' Then the activity was made into games with two dice. When the children were confident with this (and had stopped putting out a 3 and a 4 for 3 groups of 4), they were asked to record their work in some way. Most drew the 3 groups of 4, and others recorded in longhand, writing 'three groups of four'.

They were then asked to find quicker ways to record this.

- Some children wrote 3 g of 4 (3 groups of 4).

- Others wrote 3 l of 4 (3 lots of 4).

- One group liked to write: 3 ④.

This last example was clearly quicker than using any letters, so the teacher encouraged these children to share their method with the rest of the class.

The teacher could see a clear link from this last method, with the 4 in a circle, to the conventional writing of 3 (4). The children just had to draw two of the sides of their circle. The teacher explained to the children that if they use this bracket symbol, every mathematician in the world would understand them. The children were very impressed.

Clearly lots of children knew the 'times' sign – '×' – so this was obviously discussed in the class. These children seemed to have no problem in relating their own shorthanding to conventional notations, especially when using a calculator. After half a term's topic on multiplication they seemed secure with the concepts involved.

It had been a very slow process to start off with. Some children and parents could not see why they did not just learn tables, but by the end of the half term, it was clear that the learning which had gone on was very secure. Children were then able to learn tables quickly by heart.

When and how do I introduce standard symbols?

The problems for teachers are *when* and *how* to introduce standard notation. Clearly we want children to use conventional forms fluently and with understanding. If children are encouraged to use their own symbols from the age of five, standard symbols can also be introduced alongside the children's own, but generally, and this is true for all ages, after children have had a chance to link the meaning embedded in the maths to their own intuitive understandings and mental images.

One major way to get children to appreciate the need for quicker or standard symbols is, after giving them time to explore their own methods, to talk about these methods and compare them with the efficiency of the different ways friends have recorded.

In classroom settings where an emphasis is given to the children's own recording, activities need to be developed which expose children to the standard symbols. Two examples are given below.

1   Using calculators

It is clear working with young children who are given free access to calculators, that they readily come to understand the symbols of the four rules for themselves. However, they need help to link the standard symbols with the many words often used in the language of maths, e.g. the multiplication sign means 'times', 'lots of ', 'sets of ', and so on.

2   Activities designed to teach standard symbols

The simple activity called 'trio-tricks' (Open University Development of Mathematical Thinking) can be used by children from about the age of six. The activity is a series of cards with words like 'altogether makes', 'add', 'difference between' and the standard symbols of '+' and ' '. The children select three related numbers, e.g. 4, 5, and 9, then take it in turns to make as many sentences as they can using just these three numbers, e.g. '9 is 5 more than 4', '4 add 5 equals 9'; '4 and 5 altogether makes 9'; and '4 + 5 = 9'.

The children set out their cards, making their sentences by slotting words into homemade card 'pockets'. Blank card is provided for the children to write in any symbol or word not given.

A second set of cards and numbers relating multiplication to division, can be made for children from about the age of seven. Here the numbers would be 3, 4, and 12, and the sentences would be along the lines of: '3 sets of 4 makes 12' and so on.

Cards provided would include the standard symbols of brackets, multiplication etc., as well as words like 'lots of ', 'divided by' etc. To help children accept these symbols, they could be told the following:

33

- These are signs and symbols that the world recognises, just like the Russian, Urdu and English alphabets.

- Just as we needed to understand Kelly's shorthand:
  (d b 6, 3, 3)   meant for her 'The difference between 6 and 3 makes 3', so it must be clear what we mean, and that is why standard symbols have developed.

- These standard methods are not necessarily 'better' than the children's own, but they are used throughout the world so they are important to learn.

We would like to thank all the participating maths consultants, advisers and teachers on the course run at the Abbey Wood Maths Centre entitled 'Is there a link between developmental writing and children's recording of mathematics?'

—5— Children's graphical representations
Shirley Clarke

❙ *THEMES: children's own methods; links with children's writing*

My research with children seemed to point out four or five stages in recording information graphically:

I asked different children aged between four-and seven-years-old, at many different times, to collect information about something they were interested in. When this had been collected they had, in most cases, produced a list of some kind. My next question was always 'Can you show clearly what you have found out, so that we don't have to look all down the list?' It became evident that the children's earliest graphical representation within this context tended to be a picture of each item arranged at random on the paper, e.g., for colours of cars, they would draw the following:

Figure 5.1

If asked to show more clearly which colour was the most popular (or how to make the information even clearer) strategies adopted included (*a*) drawing the whole thing twice the size! or (*b*) drawing (if it were the red cars) the red cars bigger than the others, or maybe just one of them.

The next 'stage' in evidence was the same drawings of objects but with set rings drawn around each group, as shown on the next page (Fig 5.2):

Figure 5.2

Figure 5.3

When asked to show more clearly which group had most, the strategies adopted included (*a*) drawing a thick line around the set ring enclosing the largest group; or (*b*) using some kind of visual aid to draw attention to the largest set (e.g. sun spikes, a tick).

The next 'stage' was the absence of set rings, still drawn objects, but arranged horizontally in a vertical column, in no particular numerical order, and with no one-to-one correspondence within the vertical columns (Fig 5.3).

The next 'stages' were more predictable. The horizontal arrays in 'stacks' appear to be natural for children for a considerable time. This is interesting compared to a conventional graph or bar chart which has vertical columns. Research from the 'CAN' (Calculator Aware Number) project also produced evidence that children write their own algorithms horizontally, rather than in a 'sum' layout and appear to develop a mental model of a linear number line, if standard methods are not given. Presumably, these 'horizontal' recordings reflect the directionality of reading and writing in which children are heavily immersed during the early years. Two questions which occurred to me at the time were (a) Is it educationally appropriate to present a sum or standard algorithm to children? If not, when should they be presented? and (b) Why is the process of children finding their own methods important?

I used a specific example of work I had done with two four-year-olds to help teachers see how best to encourage children to record their findings. The problem was as follows: 'The cook is cooking eggs and chips for dinner. She can only put six things on the plate: any amount of eggs or chips, but only six altogether.' The children werc given one cardboard plate and lots of cut-out eggs and chips. After they had set up lots of combinations, I asked how we could remember all the ways to tell the cook. Figure 5.4 shows Martyn's first recording. The first plate drawn was the largest, a common start. He then realised the plates would not all fit if he carried on with that size, so they became smaller. In Figure 5.5 he decided to start again and, interestingly, started with six chips and worked round in a backwards spiral. In Figure 5.6 Martyn

Figure 5.4

Figure 5.5

Figure 5.6

spontaneously wrote the numbers underneath each plate to show the combinations. I had asked him if he could write on the paper what was on the plates, expecting him to write something simple like 'These are all the ways you can have egg and chips'. I was really surprised that he had written the numbers, and thought that this was an example of how, as teachers, we often have rather low expectations. This is one reason why I always try to ask open-ended questions. By asking Martyn to respond in this open-ended manner, he wrote the number combinations in this systematic way. Martyn's teacher was astonished, saying she did not know he could write the numbers, let alone make the addition bonds for six.

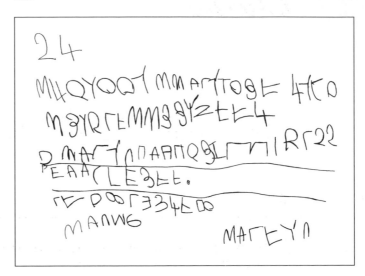

Figure 5.7

I then asked Martyn to write down everything that he did (Figure 5.7). He read this to me, and part of it was something like '4 and 2 together make 6'. You can clearly see the word 'together' towards the end of the top line. Then I asked him 'What were you actually doing?' and he wrote the bottom line 'MANW6' and read this as 'Making up numbers with 6'. This is a typical written response of a child of this age using the first letters to stand for words, but it is far from the typical sort of mathematical response we have come to expect from a four-year-old.

The addition symbol '+' is often omitted by children of all ages when left to record in their own way, as demonstrated by Hughes (1986) and by the findings of the CAN curriculum project (1991). However, the child working with Martyn did choose to use '+' when she recorded what they had done. This is included in Sue Gifford's article on p. 73, Figure 9.16.

—6— Children's own mathematical representations
Sue Atkinson & Shirley Clarke

THEMES: children's own methods and symbols; successive shorthanding; recording maths; discussion starters

Questions for teachers

Working with groups of teachers we set about asking ourselves the questions we wanted to answer.

- Are we giving the children a sufficiently good role model in maths?
- Do we share our own maths with children?
- Do we join in maths activities, doing our own recording, and not just remaining an observer?
- Could we find maths activities where a more apprenticeship approach to maths could be used?
- Do we value the children's own work?
- Do children come into recording maths at a later stage than they do in writing, or are we just not seeing children's early maths because we fail to provide the opportunity?
- Where do maths and language separate — if at all?
- Is there a 'scribble' stage in early maths as with early writing? If so, how do we enable children to experience that stage?

Implications for teachers of children's own recording

As teachers, we sometimes assume children understand more than they do, so their own recording can be helpful in telling us what they really understand. Teachers need to provide challenging activities in order to encourage children to record their work in individualised ways, and they need to balance their own input and intervention with plenty of listening and observing.

They must be ready for children to come up with ideas that they would not themselves have thought of; teachers are co-learners, not the ones with all the answers. Working as co-learner seems to prevent 'learned helplessness' becoming a feature of the class – where the children learn to let the teacher do all the thinking. The teacher must work to promote an ethos within the classroom of mutual support and trust, where everyone's efforts are valued.

Teachers' reasons why children are helped by recording maths

- To communicate information.
- To remember things, results or numbers.
- To clarify a thought process.
- Because the teacher says so.
- To gain peer group admiration.
- To help work something out.
- To play or for pleasure.
- To compare methods.

Teachers' reasons why they are helped by children recording

- To help assess the children's understanding and stage of development.
- To help know what to plan next.
- To help children solve problems for themselves.
- To encourage children to compare methods.
- To keep children quiet and occupied.
- To extend a practical activity, especially when the teacher has to move to another group.

Parents' reasons for children recording maths

- To see where the child is.
- To be able to talk to the child about what they have done.

A summary of our main findings

- Children's own symbols hold enormous meaning for them. For example, invented symbols for price labels in the class shop, introduced and interpreted by a child, can be accepted and understood by the class for several weeks.

- Martin Hughes found that few children use conventional symbols for number operations. I have found this to be true, but recently I have found that children do sometimes spontaneously use standard signs and I wonder whether this is the influence of using calculators.

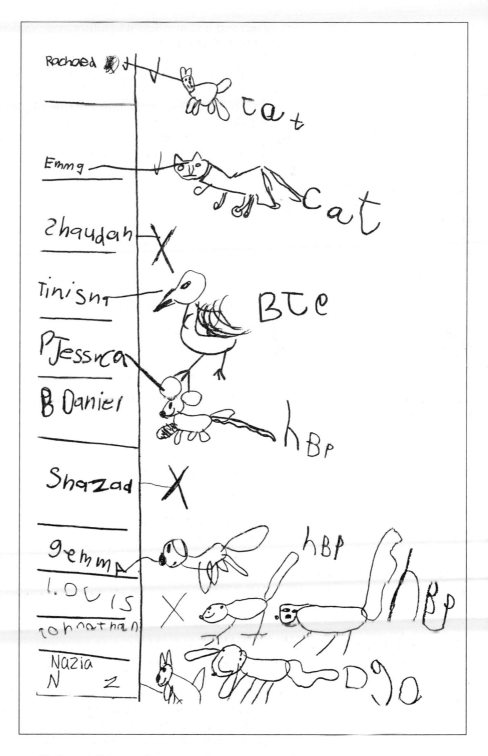

Figure 6.1

- Giving children of seven and eight years of age the time and space to develop their own symbols and shorthands for such aspects of maths, such as division and fractions, seems to reap benefits in secure learning. Most have few difficulties making the transition to

41

conventional symbols when they feel confident and secure with the concepts involved.

- The processes of successive shorthanding provide a link between the language of maths and conventional symbols.

- The calculator seems to promote rapid understanding of conventional symbols

- A survey in many classrooms reveals that teachers prefer vertical columns in bar charts, but children prefer horizontal arrays, as noted by Shirley Clarke on p. 36. Children's organisation of their work does seem to depend, though on how they start their work. Children will mostly start off working horizontally, for both charts or writing. So, if the first thing they do is to list, say, favourite types of breakfast cereal, they may do this along the bottom of their paper horizontally, therefore leaving them to record their results vertically in stacks above this. If, however, they write down the children's names first, they are often influenced by the class register format, and so produce their list vertically, thus recording their results in horizontal arrays (Figure 6.1 on the previous page).

- Many children seem to have their own clear mental images for representations of maths, e.g. a personal number line. There is clearly a great significance in this for children's own recording.

- Many teachers report that when children see a need to record for themselves, the recordings usually help the children's thinking processes. However they report some confusion in thinking when recording is for another (usually adult) reason.

There is more research needed on these and other aspects of children's own recording, but my work so far shows this whole area to be a fruitful one for trying to understand more clearly how children learn maths.

—7— The power of children's own intuitive methods
Sue Atkinson

> **| THEMES:** *maths thinking processes; children's mistakes*

I first became interested in children's own methods in maths after doing
the Open University course 'The Development of Mathematical Thinking'.
Then Martin Hughes published *Children and Number* and it seemed both
Hughes and the views expressed on the course were saying something
similar, i.e. children run into difficulties with maths, and attain at lower
levels than we might expect, because adults impose their methods of
working – standard algorithms – onto children.

Hughes suggests that children seem to develop a gap in their
understanding in maths. I visualised this as a gap between two brick walls
(see Figure 7.1). Ground level represents starting school. Children come
to school with the secure foundations of early mathematical experiences
which are part of 'home' language and learning (see Tizard and Hughes,
1984). This is part of the secure brick wall on the left. Children are
receptive to new knowledge but, because teachers often fail to relate maths
lessons to the foundation of 'home' understandings, another wall is built
quite separately. This second wall – we will call it 'school maths' – has no
secure foundation. It is based on teacher-imposed ideas and methods and,
as I will go on to illustrate, this is the mode of maths in which children
often seem to operate when in classroom settings.

Which wall am I building?

A reception class teacher making the context of the maths clear to the
children would place a brick on the first wall, on top of the secure
foundation – so 'two Unifix and two more Unifix' would make 'human
sense' to the child. However, using unrelated 'sums' with unfamiliar
symbols, like 2 + 2 = 4, then rushing on to 'tens and units' taught by a
standard teacher-imposed method, would be in great danger of building
on the unrelated and insecure second wall - where the knowledge could

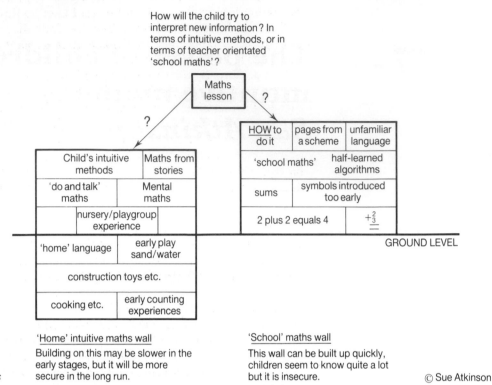

How will the child try to interpret new information? In terms of intuitive methods, or in terms of teacher orientated 'school maths'?

Maths lesson

HOW to do it	pages from a scheme	unfamiliar language
'school maths'	half-learned algorithms	
sums	symbols introduced too early	
2 plus 2 equals 4	$+\frac{2}{3}$	

Child's intuitive methods	Maths from stories
'do and talk' maths	Mental maths
nursery/playgroup experience	

GROUND LEVEL

'home' language	early play sand/water
construction toys etc.	
cooking etc.	early counting experiences

'Home' intuitive maths wall
Building on this may be slower in the early stages, but it will be more secure in the long run.

'School' maths wall
This wall can be built up quickly, children seem to know quite a lot but it is insecure.

© Sue Atkinson

Figure 7.1 The two brick walls

be worse than useless to the child, perhaps resulting in the 'bizarre written arithmetic' observed by Hughes (1986b).

The question I asked myself was that if Hughes was right, where were the children in my class putting their learning in any particular maths lesson? Was it being added to the secure wall, or was I using unfamiliar language or concepts so that it was being put, unhelpfully, on the insecure 'school maths' wall? (Hopefully, in time, the bricks from the 'school maths' wall can be built onto the secure 'home' maths wall, for eventually the meaning of '2 + 2 = 4' becomes clear, and children learn to use conventional symbols. The real power of maths comes in this ultimate combination of the power of children's own reasoning and the ability of conventional symbolism to communicate highly complex ideas).

I needed to look very closely at my own teaching, and even more at children's own methods of working. I set about keeping a diary of my work with children, and some of my results are shown in this chapter.

The classroom setting

I started a new full-time job as deputy head and maths co-ordinator in a big city first school. I was interested to discover that my six-to-nine year olds perceived 'real maths' as 'doing their scheme'. Although many of the children said that they liked 'doing sums', there was also evidence of considerable unease about maths. Comments such as 'it's hard', 'I don't understand it', and 'I'm no good at maths' were common. Maths was defined as 'doing the card' and when I tried to develop ideas or deal with difficulties, I got the reaction, 'But I've done that card'. My carefully thought out 'do and talk' maths activities, separate from the scheme, were not regarded as 'real' maths!

The scheme seemed to give some limited security to the children – and also to the teachers. Having a scheme certainly helped me to cope with those 34 six-to nine- year-olds, with their huge spread of ability! However, it was increasingly clear that the security the scheme gave was an unreal one. As I got children to talk about what they were doing, and as I probed into their understanding, it was clear that the scheme was failing. It was failing to give children confidence in what they were doing. It was failing to give them deep understanding or an adequate language of maths.

My initial questions

I wanted to tackle the problem of the children's lack of confidence and understanding. I wondered if I could focus them away from the obsession with getting the right answer and the related belief that the answer is the only important thing about maths. That is not to say that answers are not important – but I wanted to give equal weight to *how* you get the answer.

I set out to record my observations, and to look at children's own methods, taking as my base-line the fact that this class of six- to nine-year-olds had pretty negative feelings about maths and that I had taken as one of my assumptions that it was best to aim for understanding. I asked myself some questions. Was it really true that understanding was important? Would Martin Hughes' findings relate to my situation? What did the children in the class *actually do* when they engaged in mathematical activity? How is it that they pick up such a fear of maths? How do children *learn* mathematical concepts? Will letting them develop their own methods really help them to be better mathematically? My aim was to find out how they could learn maths in a more secure way.

How do children learn maths?

Filling in the dinner slip with the numbers of children having lunch, or sandwiches, or going home, was a daily task in which I involved the children. They were used to this, but totally thrown by my question 'How did you work that out, Andrew?

They found it hard at first to express their methods, but given encouragement, they would come up with explanations like the following. For example, given the problem: There are 31 children here, no-one goes home, 24 have sandwiches, so how many have school lunch? the children might suggest:

24 count on to 31 (usually using fingers);
31 count back to 24;
31 round down to 30, 4 from 10 is 16, add 1 makes 7;
30 to 25 is 5, so 30 to 24 is 6, so 31 to 24 is 7.

There was great surprise that there were so many ways to do it and the children gradually gained confidence in talking through what they were thinking.

One day, early in the school year, there were 30 children present with 25 having sandwiches. Several children said that they 'just knew' that left five to have dinner. This was something new. They really did not need to have a method in their heads for this as they knew their number bonds so well. Discussing this with the children, I found myself making it explicit that learning number bonds was an important aim in maths. This was received with great excitement by the children. As the weeks went by I began to see what was underlying that excitement. It was a sense of 'ownership'. I learnt that explaining *why* we were doing a particular piece of maths dramatically changed the attitude that the children had to maths.

The children appreciated being involved in why they did maths, and what it was all for. Was this something to do with Hughes' 'meaning'? It seemed that they were becoming more aware of their own mathematical thinking processes as their own methods were being emphasised and praised. They clearly found this exciting, and would frequently discuss the relative merits of different methods. The parents, too, became fascinated by the shift in emphasis in the children's perceptions of maths. Parents would tell sad stories of their own maths learning, and were delighted that their children were picking up a more positive message.

I was beginning to see that my early attempts at making children aware of their own thinking powers in maths was producing very positive results. Involving children in their own evaluations of their work seemed to have a similar encouraging effect. I obtained such dramatically positive results with my classes over three years that I have gone on exploring this issue in the past three years as a supply teacher in many different situations.

Unlocking children's own mathematical thinking

If we are teaching for attainment in National Curriculum terms, I conclude from my work over the past six years that children who are encouraged to use their own methods attain higher levels than children who are taught standard written algorithms first.

With this in mind, I will now explain how I try to get the children I meet in various supply teaching situations to unlock their mathematical thinking – to become aware of the methods that they use. In 'brick wall' terms, I am trying to create situations in which the children will develop an awareness of their own intuitive methods, and start to be able to place their school maths knowledge upon that secure wall which enables them to achieve at higher levels.

1 First I make them feel good about their own methods. 'Wow! What a good method Ross, could you explain it again?'

2 I make it explicit that *there is no 'right' way*. Everyone's method is

subject to checking of course, but if a method does not work, or a slip is made, *it does not matter at this stage – we are exploring ideas*. 'Don't worry that it didn't work out, Lee, you have some really good ideas.' (I am not saying that it is not important to get the right answer – but there is a big difference between making a 'slip' and a child being unable to see *how* to work it out. The difference needs to be made explicit. A slip can be corrected in a matter of seconds – not seeing how may take weeks of work.)

3 Minimising peer negative attitudes and derisory comments is often the hardest part. In supply teaching situations I find children very willing to offer information that they feel I should know, such as 'He won't be able to do it, Miss, he's thick', or they will roar with laughter at a child struggling to verbalise her method. How can freedom of thought survive if one is put down or laughed at?

4 Simply counting the number of different ways the group can find to work out one specific calculation encourages thinking.

5 I encourage the children to develop 'mental images' – 'pictures' in their minds. Some find this difficult, but children, and adults, *do have mental images*. Ask any group of people a complex (particularly spatial) question and you will often see them shut their eyes, or roll them up to the ceiling. Are they looking for the pictures in their mind? I think they are. Ask yourself the following question and see if you look for mental images. If you strung a cube up horizontally and dipped it into a bowl of water, it would not be hard to see that the shape at water level would be a square. However, if you strung the cube up by one of its corners and lowered it into the water, what would the shape at water level be then?

It is important to work on classroom strategies to develop children's mental pictures of maths.

A key theme to this book is the need to develop children's mental pictures of maths and I find, when working with groups in this way, that many children are able to describe their mental images.

Drawing mental images

Recently, I spent ten minutes with a group of nine- to eleven-year-olds exploring how we worked out mathematical calculations mentally and talking about pictures in our minds. Then I set the quite difficult task of asking the children to draw (or write) about their mental pictures. Here is the sequence of my work.

1 I started with an easy calculation, 13 + 13. Most children were able to explain how they did this. Many worked out 10 + 10, then 3 + 3. Some did the tens first, some did the units. Some did 13 + 10 = 23, + 3 = 26.

2 Then another similar one, 21 + 24. I made it explicit that it was *how* they did it that I was interested in and that no calling out the answer was allowed as it would disturb other people's thinking. Any method was allowed, including using fingers.

3 I then moved on to subtraction, starting again with an easy one, 27 − 4. Most counted back, some said 4 count on 3 is 7 so it is 23.

4 At this point I introduced the idea of pictures in their minds. Some children completely flipped out at this point – quite a normal reaction to a new idea. It is well worth spending time to let children talk about these ideas as this will help children who are not conscious of their own methods or images to begin to see what it is all about. Some people see a number line, some see Dienes blocks, and some see little tallies, or fingers. Whatever you see, it is OK.

5 Then I moved on to the harder subtractions which really test out children's security with their own methods. The sum 23 − 17 led to the following different methods:

Yasmeen: 23 − 10 − 7 = 6.

Kim: 17 add 6 is 23.

David: 17 count on 6 is 23 (done on his fingers and he insisted this was different from Kim's method of adding 'because it's a take away not an add').

Ross: 17 is 20 minus 3, and 3 and 3 is 6.

Alison: 20 take 10, plus 3 minus 7 makes 6.

Shakoar: 23 count back 7 is 16 minus 10 is 6.

6 This had all taken just a few minutes and I then explained that I wanted them to find a way to draw what they had in their minds – to find a way of making a picture to show what they do to work out a calculation. Of course, this is very hard for children, so talking about the pictures in their minds first is vital. Then everyone has some idea of what is expected of them. I suggest to children that if they are stuck, they could work with a favourite piece of apparatus, like Unifix or Dienes – *not* calculators yet.

It is really quite difficult to give children the security that they need to do a task like this, while encouraging them to explore their own ideas. Give them too much guidance and they will grab onto one of your ideas thinking that the task is to work out what the teacher has in her mind. Give them too little support and encouragement and they will panic and learn that maths is difficult to understand, the very opposite of your intentions.

7 Making all this a pleasurable and understandable task is vital.

Children's written work

Once the children began to write things down, 'gaps' started to appear between their own powerful mental methods and what they had become used to as 'school maths'. Some of the children's work is reproduced in Figure 7.2. Matthew, working out 16 + 17 said, using his fingers, '16 (*pointing to one finger*), 17 (*pointing to the next one so that now he had two fingers*). It's 2'.

Gordon was totally unable to put on paper what he could explain to me. This raises important points – these methods are *mental methods* and children find it hard to relate them to written methods; and representing what is in your mind on paper is hard!

Gordon said to me, working out 121 − 49, 'Well, if it was 50, and if it was 120, it would be . . . (*mumbled and counted on fingers, touching his lips as he counted*) er . . . 50, 60, 70, 80, 90, 100, 110, 120 . . . so that's 80 (*holding up 8 fingers*) but it was 121, so add 1 . . . er . . . 81, but it was 49 not 50, so it's 82.' He remained unaware of his counting error, starting at 50, not at 60, but his method was rather good, and when I asked him to work out similar calculations mentally, he used his intuitive method correctly. However, a glimpse in Gordon's maths exercise book shows me that he could not work out standard written algorithms of similar difficulty. This seems to show that children like Gordon have developed their own effective mental methods, (on the secure brick wall), but his school maths has developed in a separate compartment.

Ross attempted to work out 63 − 47 by writing it vertically as in his scheme. I had written it horizontally on the board, but nine children wrote it vertically. All nine children got it wrong, for various reasons, Ross making a common error.

Was the problem too unrelated to anything else for him to give it any meaning? Did he know a bit about the 'trick' for subtraction? I asked Ross to calculate some other similar subtractions mentally, e.g. 71 subtract 38, 94 take away 27. He got *all* of these right! Clearly there was something about writing it down that caused him problems. I asked him to talk me through what he had done in his written work. He seemed unable to see his error. I asked him how he could check to see if his answer, 24, was right. He said, 'I didn't know how to do that'. Yet, when I challenged him to prove that his mental method was right, he had no problem explaining how he had arrived at answers *and* how he could check them. These are startling anomalies.

Figure 7.2 (here and following pages.)
Matthew (9 yrs)

$16 + 17 = 2$

Gordon (9 yrs)

$121 - 49 =$

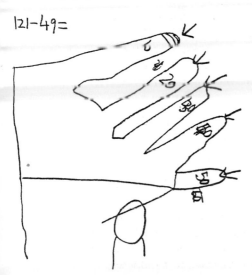

Ross (9 yrs)
Ross was able to work it out mentally, but not on paper

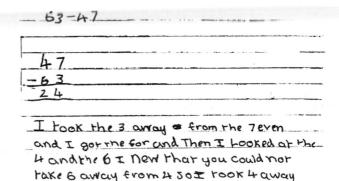

63 − 47

```
  47
 -63
  24
```

I took the 3 away from the 7 even and I got the for and Then I Looked at the 4 and the 6 I New that you could not take 6 away from 4 so I took 4 away from six

Katie's work is typical of many children. She sees it in words, not pictures. (The importance of language and the limitations of symbols are explored elsewhere in the book.) However, I would expect children like Katie eventually to find that they do have 'pictures' in their minds, and discovering these gives them enormous pleasure.

Annie had used Dienes apparatus to help her as she was stuck for almost 20 minutes on representing '23 take away 17'. Mentally she had no problem with this. She had told me she did it by adding on 6; yet she tried to show taking away 6. It is interesting that in order to represent it she came to me repeatedly to ask what to do next. It was quite hard to keep throwing the ball back in her court! She seemed to be one of those children who believe that a war of attrition can eventually get the teacher to reveal 'the answer' out of sheer frustration! Yet I was trying to give her a positive experience of maths! Was the task just too difficult for her – an example of mismatch? But her maths book showed she tackled this type of calculation regularly from the scheme.

I suggested crossing out to another child, and Annie then crossed out some of hers. I asked her if there was some way she could show what was left – the 'answer'. She couldn't. She eventually copied another child by putting a line around it. This method did not have much meaning for Annie! It is significant that when we were working verbally, all together, she was always one of the first to put up her hand.

Sally seemed to find the task of drawing her mental pictures easy and she represented her method with dots. She asked for something harder,

121 –49

go to the nearest ten (50) back that away from 1st wich eqmels 50 then ade 21 wich eqmels 71 back the 1 away and the answer is 70

Katie (9 yrs)

Annie (10 yrs)

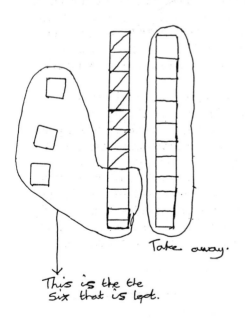

Take away.

This is the the six that is left.

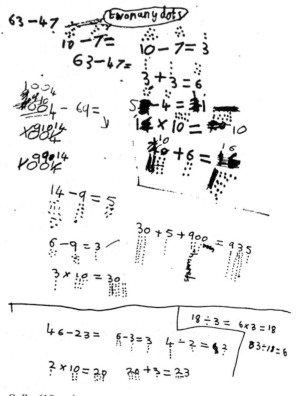

Sally (10 yrs)

50

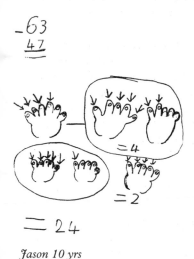

-63
47

=24

Jason 10 yrs

so I suggested that she try 1004 subtract 69. She managed this after a few false starts. I'm not sure that the dots are really one of her own informal methods. I think they may have been put in to meet my criterion of a 'picture'.

Jason insisted he had no picture in his mind (quite a common reaction in the early stages). He said he always used his fingers. Could he draw the fingers he was using, I asked? A look of relief came over his face and he sat down and spent 30 minutes counting on his fingers, drawing, rubbing out, and looking increasingly perplexed. At last he looked pleased with himself and I sat beside him. He explained his work, but unfortunately I had nothing to write on so the reasoning behind it (which sounded very plausible at the time), is lost.

It is worth pondering his drawing. *Top drawing* – is it 4 fingers take away 7 leaves 4? Or is it 7 take away 3, (which he has not included in the drawing) leaves 4. *Lower drawing* – is it 6 fingers take away 4 leaves 2? (This time working from left to right.) Whatever he meant he got it wrong, but it is very important to note that Jason did not have such problems with mental calculations of similar difficulty. Is there something about the calculation being written down?

I found that no child got 121 subtract 49 right, and wondered whether if I had written it vertically (as it was in their scheme) I would have got a different result?

Of course, some of the children were able to get the calculations correct, especially when they worked on them mentally, but there was a steep decline in correct calculations once they worked on paper. In this account I cannot adequately represent the powerful mental methods that the children shared when we worked together initially. These were often not related to these later 'pictures'. The children seemed to operate in a different mode once they had to write maths down. I call this 'school maths mode' and believe it to be the way that the insecure 'school maths' wall shows itself.

Of course, as a supply teacher I was having to pluck problems out of the air, and there were presumably difficulties for the children in understanding exactly what it was that a teacher they had known only for a few days was asking them to do. However, despite these problems, my account is presented here because I suggest that this sort of activity – making children's own methods explicit to them – is valuable and raises important issues. It helps teachers to see how their children are thinking so they can assess what each child needs next; and it helps to close up the gap that develops unhelpfully between the methods developed in school or shown to them by parents, and the intuitive methods that children have developed for themselves.

Why was so much written work wrong?

What was so remarkable in the work with the children was their enthusiasm as I praised and encouraged their mental methods and the speed with which they could mentally calculate accurately and confidently. This changed dramatically when writing down calculations of similar difficulty. These were often totally wrong, and children showed a marked resistance to applying their strong mental methods to the written work – for example their inability to check their work. This is a common reaction, but, given time and the opportunity to explore their own methods, the gap begins to close. Children begin to relate 'school maths' methods to their own methods.

Specific teaching

It also needs to be said that the importance of children's own methods does not eliminate the need to engage in specific teaching, particularly when children are experiencing difficulty. There *is* a place in maths teaching for exposition by the teacher, explaining what standard symbols, like + or - or = mean. It is a difficult aspect of our craft knowledge to know *when* and *how* to do specific teaching – and important to remember that we teachers tend to do far too much exposition!

When children seem to be struggling we apply our complex craft knowledge in exactly the same way as we do in language teaching. We do a great deal of observation, making formative assessments of what children can do and what they find difficult. We have to look back at the early ideas and concepts – the foundations of the brick wall – and ask ourselves if children are trying to build 'school maths' apart from their 'home' experiences. The activity described earlier, developing mental pictures, is one way to start to close that gap.

'Specific' teaching might be used to sort out *how* and *when* to teach standard notation and symbols; to work out what to do with children whose own methods have shortcomings, such as very slow, long-winded methods; and to help children who are persistently 'stuck' – one strategy being to let them choose someone else's method, or some piece of apparatus, and to go for understanding of just one way of doing it, repeating this until they succeed (unless there is a mismatch between the task and the child's mental abilities, when it is best to leave it and come back to it in a few months).

NB it is of course essential to involve parents with a child who is persistently stuck over the same thing, as your combined efforts will certainly be more successful than just one of you working with the child.

Conclusions

1 The main thing that I have learnt from this work is that it is important not to start with an adult-imposed method for doing a calculation, i.e. a standard written algorithm. The difficulty that many adults find with this is that it goes against everything that they can remember about

their own maths learning. We were shown *how* to subtract, *how* to do long division, *how* to operate xs and ys, and if in doubt we had little tricks like, 'turn it upside down and multiply'.

2   There is no one right way to teach anyone to do a calculation, but building the school maths onto already existing secure home knowledge seems to make sense.

3   It is a common finding in present day maths education, and implicit in the 1978 HMI report, that children who spend less time on arithmetic and more time engaging in a wider curriculum are the ones who actually achieve better. I have found this to be true over and over again with my own classes, and more recently in schools where I go on supply. It is in schools with a 'wider curriculum' and where children are allowed to develop and use their own methods, that they achieve at a far higher level in National Curriculum terms. Some possible reasons for this are given in Chapter 2, such as the need for number to have 'meaning' for children. So, if we are teaching for the highest attainment possible there are clear implications here for teaching styles.

4   It seems that children who are shown methods of how to do calculations, partially abandon their own methods (those established on the secure brick wall), but often do not fully understand the ones they are taught (part of the 'school maths' wall). In other words, when they have to calculate something in a school setting, they are often secure with *neither* method. This may be one explanation why so many errors appear in children's work when they try to write calculations down – an area in need of further research.

5   The child needs to have *his own mathematical thinking* opened up to him. The whole process must be related to some method that he already uses – to his secure 'brick wall', otherwise he is always operating on half power, on the second-hand methods of various teachers and maths schemes.

If we unlock children's own intuitive methods, (by emphasising and encouraging them), engage in specific teaching with apparatus that makes sense to them and relates to their intuitive methods, give them time to reflect, boost their self-esteem, make it a positive experience and a meaningful one, then they can operate at full power.

Doing this for a child is one of the most thrilling things in teaching! It's like that magic moment when a small child rushes up to you, her face glowing with pleasure and tells you that she can read. When those special moments come you can stand back and watch the child race off, powered with her own understanding. The success breeds more success and it is my experience that a child can go from being a poor performer to a child who can function well above the level that might be expected for her age.

That is the power of the child's intuitive methods.

Section B – Teacher's stories

This section comprises teachers' stories about their work with children. The stories are more or less arranged according to the age of the children.

$$213-$$
$$167$$

You cross out the 2 and put a 1,
then you put a little 1 next to the 1,
so that makes 11, then you cross out
the 11 and put a 10, then you put
a little 1 by the 3, and that makes 13
so you take 7 from the 13 .... er ...
or is it 13 from 7 .... er ... big from
little ... er ... bottom from top ... so
thats 7 from 13 is 6 so you put a 6
under the line and you carry a 10
... no ... you borrow a 10 ... er ... no
... the 10 is on the top line, so,
um ... maybe its not a take-
away ... it might be an
add ...

© *Joy Dunn*

—8— Nursery children explore maths
Sarah Killworth, Lesley Neilson and Sue Atkinson

Age	3–5
Situation	teachers with groups
Maths	the early language stage
Theme	classroom organisation; children's own methods and symbols; links with writing

Teachers working with children at the start of their formal education outside the home are aware of the need to provide plenty of varied experience at this crucial stage in the learning process. Children need to be involved in situations that make 'human sense' and to see meaning and purpose in their learning.

Language and activity hold the key

It cannot be emphasised enough that language development and children's activity at this stage are vital in their process of learning. The 'home' language of the children and their intuitive understandings are nurtured by sensitive adults, laying firm foundations for secure learning later on. It is also the stage when children seem to be given the most freedom in the education process – the freedom to play – to search actively for shared and personal meanings.

Of course, this is often what we might term 'structured play' because the equipment has been selected with particular learning experiences in mind. In this context the children explore, share, and use language to find their way towards the development of concepts, ideas and skills. They are constantly trying to give situations their own meaning.

Children explore

Hughes (1986) indicates that children at this stage are capable of a great deal. Sometimes adults do not see what meanings the children are giving to a situation, but by talking with them we can explore ideas together and try to see how the children are thinking. It is important to try to provide an exciting environment with plenty of opportunity to talk and explore.

Children experiment

Three children, Tracey, Jane and Gary, began with a book that showed children doing an investigation suspending magnets. The work was well under way before we noticed what the children were doing. At the start of the day we had put the magnets on the woodwork bench. We were using the bench as a conventional table, but wondered if the children perceived it as an area for construction which encouraged them in their task?

No adult was involved in the work except for discussion with the children about what they were doing, and listening to their language as they cut the string and threaded it through the chairs, working out how to suspend the magnets. One child, aged just four, 'read' the instructions to the other children from the magnet book. The activity lasted all morning and well into the afternoon. The children were willing to draw their work and write about it (Figure 8.1 on the next page) although this could not show the richness of the experience.

It is often not possible to divide up a young child's learning into the subjects of the National Curriculum but this one was very rich in mathematical language and covered a surprising number of the maths attainment targets – as well as attainment targets in English, science and technology. What was so exciting about talking to the children about what they had done, was that they had clearly been able to give the situation enormous meaning. Here was another brick placed firmly on the wall that has its foundations in early intuitive knowledge and experience.

Singing rhymes

Children as young as three join in enthusiastically with number songs like *Five little speckled frogs*. (See resource list at the back of the book for other number songs etc.) In our nursery we sing the song with five children pretending to be frogs, who, as we sing, jump into the pool one at a time. The other children hold up their five fingers, and it is clear that they are able to do the counting back one at a time accurately, matching the number of frogs to their number of fingers. We provide lots of other

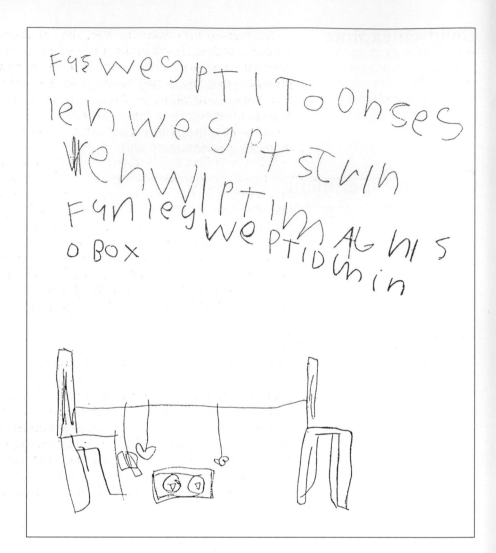

Figure 8.1 Jane
First we put two chairs
together then we put some
wool to each chair. And
then we put a few pieces of
wool hanging down and
then we put some magnets
on the pieces of wool
hanging down. Finally we
put two bits of magnets in a
box.

situations for early counting experiences, like games, a shop, and of course the Play House. We aim to give the children confidence in their mathematical abilities and, where possible, involve the parents in our work.

A place to write and draw

In Lesley's nursery, they provided the children with a variety of writing tools, paper, and an old typewriter.

Melissa, a little girl aged four years and two months, who was working with the typewriter on which the '5' key was missing said, 'Look, I can count.' She began to type, counting as she went. 'Two, three, four . . . hmm . . . '(*knowing from experience that the 5 key was missing*) 'Let's pretend this is the five'. She pressed the 6 key but said, 'Five'. Then, pressing the 7 she said 'six', and so on, continuing counting in sequence.

The atmosphere at home and school is important in creating an environment in which children can use their own symbols and ideas

She seemed fully aware of what she was doing – using 'pretend' symbols, and when she had got to the end of the row of numbers on the typewriter and pressed the zero for 9, she hesitated and said, 'It's just pretend – that one is nine really,' pointing to the correct 9 key. Then, with a great flourish of satisfaction she said 'ten,' pressing two keys, the j and x; and 'eleven' pressing the k and x. At this point her counting broke down and she said 'fifteen, sixteen' but continued to choose letter keys to represent these numbers.

What is so interesting about this is the way that Melissa knew that she was not always using the conventional symbols for numbers, but was able to use others in their place. Her willingness to pretend and her lack of fear in telling an adult what she was doing is typical of young children's ability to use symbols to fit in with their own meaning.

Providing an accepting atmosphere at both home and school would seem to be very important in giving children the chance to explore early maths ideas in contexts which they can understand. (This point about children using their own symbols is explored further on p. 64 and 80 and by Marion Bird in her book *Mathematics For Young Children*.)

Mathematical writing

Sarah and Elizabeth, in their nursery, also give children a similar space to explore writing and the use of symbols in mathematical contexts. They have a huge table with pencils, crayons and felt tips in all shapes and sizes, along with plenty of paper. Children use the materials frequently. Arabell (aged four years and eight months) wrote down her recipe for hot cross buns. (Figure 8.2). When she read this back, she had included all the ingredients, and had remembered exactly what to do.

Figure 8.2 Arabell (4 yrs 8 mths)

Lubna (aged four) sat at the table making the staff coffee list. She asked for the teachers' names, 'small please', and then wrote the names down. She went to each teacher and asked them if they wanted coffee, ticking each name, and counting them up, before drawing three cups of coffee. She then put out three teachers' cups and helped to serve it.

There was no doubt about the meaning this had for Lubna and, as the weeks went by, she became increasingly confident in writing down mathematical ideas, usually using a mixture of her own symbols and conventional ones that she had remembered, or had asked an adult to draw for her to copy.

Figure 8.3 Samuel (4yrs 5mths)

Samuel (aged four years and five months) used numbers in a very interesting manner. It was not always easy to see what Samuel meant; indeed, we sometimes concluded that he may not have attached meaning to everything that he wrote. Figure 8.3 shows a typical example of his work. Samuel was unable to explain what he was doing, but this may have been a result of the fact that he lived in Uganda until he was three, and had problems communicating in English. What is important, however, is that we allowed him the chance to explore his own meaning. (It is also important to note that a few months later, in school, Samuel coped very well with mathematical tasks, showing a particular aptitude for maths. For example, on his second try, he managed to write the numbers on a circular clock face in the correct positions – a task that can often defeat an eight-year-old.)

Making maths explicit

Placing number apparatus on the writing table can prompt children to include maths in their writing. Shelly (aged four years and three months) wrote from the right saying 'One, two, three, four'. She used the conventional symbol for one at the start but, seeming unconcerned, 'pretended' the rest (see Figure 8.4). She was able to count the Unifix correctly up to seven, which indicated that her mathematical abilities clearly went beyond her abilities to use conventional symbols accurately.

Beth (aged four years and eight months) wrote 'five fishes' in a spontaneous response to a jigsaw (figure 8.5), and Lisa (aged three years and eleven months) tried to draw her brother's birthday cake with six candles (Figure 8.6).

It was very apparent that other children liked the opportunity to practice numbers in writing situations. Nadim (aged 4 years and nine months) showed that she liked to write numbers (Figure 8.7). She used

Figure 8.4 Shelly (4yrs 3mths)

Figure 8.5 Beth (4yrs 8mths)

Figure 8.6 Lisa (3yrs 11mths)
A cake with 6 candles

Figure 8.7 Nadim (4 yrs 9 mths)

Figure 8.8 Samuel (4 yrs 5 mths)

all of these symbols conventionally and could count accurately up to eight. Samuel, mentioned earlier, showed a typical mixture of conventional, invented, and reversed symbols (Figure 8.8).

Figure 8.9 Clive (4 yrs 6 mths)
I will cut your hair this afternoon.
Come at 3 o'clock.

Figure 8.10 Gary (4 yrs 1 mth) A bill for £3

At the hairdressers

Creating a hairdressers as part of a topic about 'ourselves' led to some fascinating mathematical writing. Children were able to give their clients appointments in the large appointment book (Figure 8.9) and related appointment cards.

When the hair was washed, cut, curled and dried, clients were given a bill (Figure 8.10).

The baby shop

The children became very interested in photos of themselves as babies, so we decided to start a baby shop selling nappies, bottles, etc. Tania (aged four-and-a-half) stuck price labels on the goods (Figure 8.11), and the other children accepted her invented symbols and could remember the meanings.

Figure 8.11 Tania (4 yrs 6 mths)

2p   *4p (written as To To)*   *5p (written as To To E)*

— 9 — Young children's representations of number operations
Sue Gifford

Age	4 – 7
Situation	group with advisory teacher
Maths	calculator; number operations
Themes	children's own methods and use of invented symbols; links with writing

When do children start to use symbols to represent practical addition and subtraction situations? This was the question that arose from the work of Martin Hughes (1986b). He had found that not one of 90 'sum-fed' infants chose to use plus or minus signs to record practical addition and subtraction activities.

With the help of colleagues from the ILEA Abbey Wood Maths Centre, and from ILEA CAN project, I have collected various examples of children's own arithmetical recordings, including invented symbols. They point to the ingenuity of some children when faced with the problem of representing number operations.

Does the calculator help children to use standard symbols?

Being involved in working with six-year-olds and calculators (as part of the CAN project in ILEA), I wondered if the introduction of the calculator would help to make children more likely to use the standard symbols to record practical activities. I chose to do the 'yoghurt pots' activity with pairs of six-year-olds. Each pair had a pot with six nuts: one child had to turn over the pot, leaving some nuts out, and trapping a number under the pot for the other child to 'guess'. When they had become confident in doing this, I gave the children paper and pens and asked them, 'can you put something on paper to show all the different ways that you've found?' I assured them that they could show this in any way they liked. Initially they were unsure. Eventually they all set to work, except one child who did nothing at all, insisting he could not think of any way of recording the activity.

The children had used a variety of ways of recording, including pictorial, written and symbolic, but none had used conventional symbols. I then realised that I was unclear how to assess or interpret the children's representations. Of the two children who chose a written mode of recording, Ashley (see Figure 9.1) produced a string of letters in a 'whole sentence' format, writing across the page, and apart from using numerals, using the conventions of written language. He read his work as, 'I can make two in and four out. I can make three in and three out.'

John, in contrast (see Figure 9.2) was more economical and read his work as, 'three in and three out, four in and two out, six in and none out, one in and five out.' This seemed to indicate a move towards abstraction in the elimination of superfluous words and so I judged this to be a more 'mathematical' piece of recording.

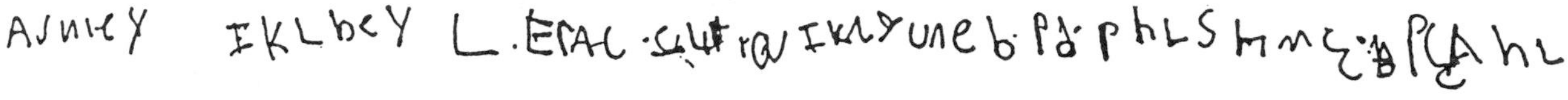

Figure 9.1 Ashley: I can make 2 in and 4 out. I can make 3 in and 3 out

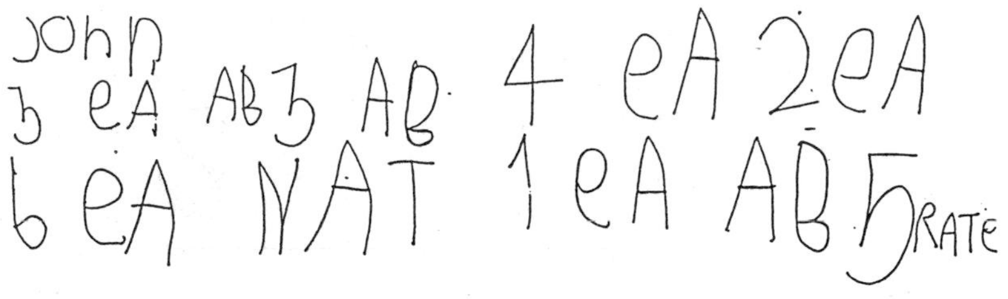

Figure 9.2 John: 3 in and 3 out, 4 in and 2 out,
6 in none out, 1 in and 5 out

Then I looked at Thu Hein's work (see Figure 9.3). She had chosen a pictorial mode for her recording. Far from abstracting key mathematical information, she had included minute details of the nuts, using the conventions of close observational drawing (encouraged by the school art policy at the time). I concluded that she may have been more interested in the nuts than my imposed request! I also realised that her perception of the task may have been quite different from mine: how was she to know why I wanted her to record? Not having any real purpose, how was she to decide that a simplified mathematical mode rather than an elaborate artistic one was called for? Perhaps she had done her best drawing to entertain me, or for me to put on the wall to show parents and visitors.

On the other hand, Thu Hein's work was arranged in a highly mathematical tabular form: there were, in effect, two columns of paired

Figure 9.3 Thu Hein

drawings showing the numbers of nuts in and out of the pot (and
showing almost all the possible combinations, with no duplicates). I
suddenly realised that, instead of a series of equations, such as 2 + 4 = 6,
which I had in mind, she had used the most effective layout for recording
number combinations. Hers was a pictorial version of a list of number
pairs. In one way, then, Thu Hein's work was an effective mathematical
representation, without being at all symbolic. (But then, by asking the
children to record number *combinations*, I had presented no real need to
represent *any operations*, symbolically or otherwise (something which I
had overlooked). Was this evidence, in National Curriculum terms, of
being able to 'record things systematically'? (See NAT 1 level 3)

Jancev was the other child who had used a pictorial mode to record,
and she had used simplified drawings of the nuts, together with numbers
(see Figure 9.4). This seemed more mathematical, as redundant details of

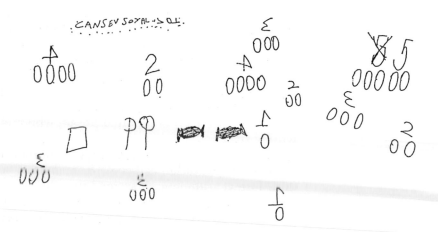

Figure 9.4 Jancev

nuts and pots had been omitted and helpful numbers added. Despite this apparent sophistication, Jancev's record is hard to comprehend. The pictures are dotted about all over the page. Although the pictures on the left, 4 and 2, or 3 and 3, may be intended as pairs, it is not possible to work out her intentions from the others. The need for pairing, or spatial organisation of some kind is evident.

Children do use symbols

One child did attempt to use symbols. Katie (see Figure 9.5) arranged numerals in a vertical column, alternating them with lines. She read her page as follows 'plus two, plus four, plus five and one, two and four' . This seemed to show that the lines were intended as plus signs. What struck me about this was that although Katie does not know the plus sign and how to use it, she does know something about the conventions of written arithmetic, namely the vertical format. The fact is that you can combine numerals with signs which are called things like 'plus'. Exceptionally, what she did, unlike all the children in Hughes' sample, is recognise an arithmetical activity and attempt to use the appropriate written conventions. The reason for this possibly lay in my role as a maths consultant, known to the children as someone who regularly came to do maths with them. My presence no doubt signalled to Katie that this was a maths activity. Hughes' presence with the children he studied would not carry the same influence, and yet he had used obviously mathematical language like 'add' and 'take away' which could well have given some children a clue. Katie's readiness to use symbols is therefore not totally explained: perhaps her experience with the calculator (slight at this stage) or the novelty of writing arithmetic had produced positive attitudes?

Later I did the same activity with a group of six- and seven-year-olds, who were more arithmetically confident and so had ten counters in their yoghurt pots. To my surprise and delight, Susan *asked* if they could have paper to keep the scores, thereby supplying the children with their own purpose for recording. I subverted this by suggesting that they also make a note of the numbers of counters involved.

None of these children used whole sentences or pictures, and all used a vertical list format. Typically, Steven used numerals and the words, 'in' and 'out' for maximum brevity (see Figure 9.6). Sarah improved on this by grouping the 'ins' and 'outs' together, and so using a listed pairs format (see Figure 9.7). Then I spotted Susan, who was recording the activity by writing standard equations (see Figure 9.8). So much for total irrelevance of the operations symbols or of the equation format to this activity!

Interestingly, Susan had come from another school where she had done formal arithmetic. It seemed that she knew and understood the conventional way of recording number bonds, and had identified this as a 'number bonds' activity. Presumably, as with Katie, she had been able to

Figure 9.5 Katie: Plus 2, plus 4, plus 5 and 1, 2 and 4

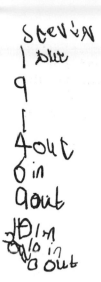

read the contextual clues (e.g. my presence) so as to select the appropriate format from her repertoire.

What happened next was intriguing: Sarah looked across at Susan's paper and copied Susan's last equation, 5 + 5 = 10. She then wrote at the top of her paper, 2 + 2 = 4. I presumed that she must have been thinking something like, 'Oh yes, it's one of those, like 2 + 2 = 4.' Perhaps she was attracted by the standard 'grown–up' style, or perhaps she liked copying Susan. Was this a link with her experience with the calculator, or another example of the fact that not all learning is acquired in school? Certainly Sarah was intrigued enough to make connections with her past experience.

In contrast to Hughes' findings, at least two or three children out of twelve were willing to use symbols to record a practical maths activity. It is hard to say why: the calculators may have had something to do with it, perhaps more through creating positive attitudes out of the novelty than through any great depth of understanding of the concepts.

Focusing on the operations

One question remained, When would the rest of the children use plus and minus signs to represent the actual operations of adding and subtracting? A practical 'function machine' box was suggested by a colleague, Val Heal (see Figure 9.9 on next page). The children have to guess the machine's function from the number of cubes going into and coming out of the box. The value of this activity lay in the focus on the operation being performed, the clear purpose for recording, a defined audience in

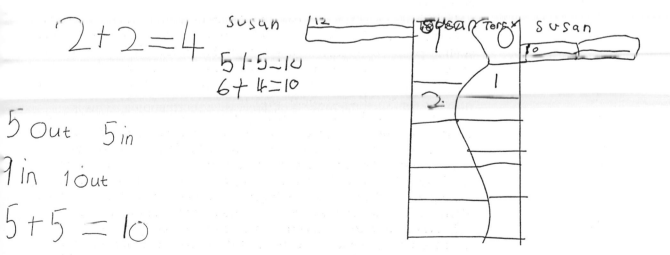

Figure 9.7 Sarah   Figure 9.8 Susan (The bit on the right is her way of keeping the score)

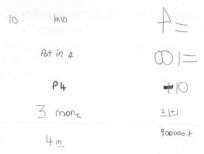

Figure 9.9 Function machine instructions

the writing of instructions for the machine operator, and a need for brevity forced by the size of the paper and the impatience of the children waiting to guess.

Initially, the children's instructions concerned the total number of cubes to be pushed out, rather than the number to be added or taken away. This difficulty in focusing on the operation rather than the total was what Hughes had also found. (I had assumed that a diet of sums had led to this, as sums usually require children to work out the total, rather than the operation. However these children were not used to sums, so I presume that operations are hard for six-year-olds to think about.)

The children then began to write statements like, 'three more' or 'put two', which they subsequently reduced to just '3m' and 'p2', thus using letters as symbols for the operations. Some children began using the equals sign, which they read as 'more' or 'plus'. (They had frequently referred to the equals key on the calculator as 'plus', perhaps because the equals key is frequently the one that produces the action, and so is more memorable.) Then one child altered the equals to plus, and after that plus and minus signs became common on the slips of paper. The signs were in various positions in relation to the numbers, to the left, right, or above.

Successive shorthanding

None of the children spontaneously saw the relevance of operations signs to this activity. With encouragement to think of 'quicker ways', however, they went through the process of 'successive shorthanding'. This is described by the Open University's course, 'Developing mathematical thinking' as the result of an approach which requires children to record activities in their own way, and by repetition of the same activity, to develop more economical forms in successive stages. Certainly the repetition of the activity gives the children time to see the redundancy of some information, to search for abbreviations, and to see the relevance of symbols, either their own, or standard forms.

Their use of symbols may have been related to experience with the calculator, or the similarity of the machine to it. As before, the children had no doubt that this was maths. Perhaps it was that in this activity, as Hughes puts it, 'symbolism serves a meaningful purpose'? Interestingly, they made no attempt to draw. Is this because, as Dufour-Janvier et. al. (1987), and others point out, language is better for capturing actions, while pictures are fine for amounts?

A meaningful context for symbols

It seems that children as young as five can find ways of representing operations. One interesting activity suggested by Hughes, which provides a meaningful context for symbols, is that of leaving a message to show how many counters have been secretly added to or removed from a box. If the others in the group know the original number in the box, the message helps them to work out how many there are in the box. Whereas Hughes suggested this as a way of introducing plus and minus symbols, Christine Pugh used it to suggest that children find their own ways of writing such messages. Jamie, aged five, devised a system for showing addition and subtraction, without the use of symbols (see Figure 9.10). He simply drew the pot, with the counters taken away shown at a distance, or the counters added shown in the pot. This record is very economical and within the familiar context, needs little or no explanation.

Another interesting example is that of Asif (see Figure 9.11), who did not so much invent symbols, as invent his own number sentence form. He was finding numbers that could be made with any combination of twos and fives, using colourfactor rods, and his teacher, Razia Begum, encouraged him to record his results in his own way with the purpose of discussing them with his teacher and classmates later. He simply wrote

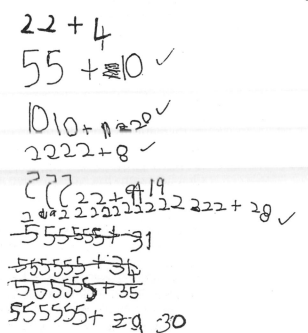

Figure 9.10 Jamie   *Figure 9.11 Asif*

down all the numbers used, then '+', then the total. He told me that he had written: 'Two, two, plus, four'. When I asked him what 'plus' meant, he explained, 'Two numbers put together,' (implying that the plus sign showed what you had to do with the whole list of numbers). He clearly understood his invented system, which was far more economical than the standard number sentence, and quite appropriate for the context. The one drawback of this system is that it does not distinguish between a single digit and a multiple digit number. However, the spacing indicates this and within the context, little confusion is likely to arise. This made me realise that a plus sign may be used by children as a separator rather than as an operator: that is, it performs a punctuation function rather than representing an abstract relationship.

Other children have tackled the problem of separating numbers in their own ways of recording and have got round it in a variety of ways. Sophie used a vertical list, under the heading of the total (see Figure 9.12). Another child wrote, 'two fours makes eight' leaving a gap between numbers as one does between words when writing and thereby making the multiplication sign redundant. Another child wrote, '11.2 is 22', which he read as, 'eleven twos is twenty-two'. Was the dot an invented symbol for multiplication, or merely keeping the numbers apart? This use of mathematical symbols to aid the layout of information underlines the lack of relevance of the operations signs to many contexts.

The invention of symbols

One situation which seems to give rise to the invention of symbols, is that of finding the difference between numbers. Perhaps this is because children are introduced to the minus sign as 'take away' and then have trouble relating it to 'how many more'? I have not found any infant age children who spontaneously represent such situations with a minus sign. I once asked two six-year-olds to show, in their own way, the game they were playing about finding the difference between two lots of counters, determined by a dice (see Figure 9.13). Tania's record is rich in mathematically superfluous detail, clearly showing her interpretation of my request as referring to the whole context. Melanie, however, homed in on the counters, indicating the difference by colouring in (as her Fletcher maths book did). When asked if she could show the difference in a quicker way, she put a line between the 7 and 8, which might be seen either as a separator, or as an invented symbol for difference, like a minus sign on its side. She read what she had done as 'the difference between 7 and 8 is 1'.

A similar symbol is used by Karen and read as 'You need four to get from 2 up to 6' (see Figure 9.14). Karen also circles the difference number: this common device clearly seems to serve a punctuating function, of emphasising the result of the calculation. Both these methods seem to fulfil admirably their purpose of providing an economical record, to be shared by people who already know the context well. Perhaps this shows one of the dangers of encouraging children to

Figure 9.12 Sophie

Melanie

Figure 9.13 Melanie and Tania

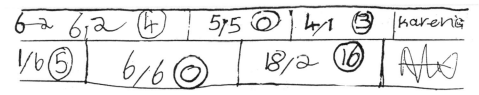

Figure 9.14 Karen

use standard symbols before they are ready. It may be that we too easily
assume that children understand the concepts behind the symbols,
whereas to children the signs are just a way of keeping numbers apart.

Other children invent forms which reflect the apparatus used in the
activity. One example of this is Koysor (see Figure 9.15 overleaf), who
was finding the difference between pairs of numbers on a number line.
She used a 'skipping rope' type representation, which seems to reflect an
idea of the distance between the numbers, especially as she then chose to
indicate the pair with the greatest difference by the longest line. This
method is highly effective for representing the idea of 'difference', and
certainly seems more helpful for young children than a minus sign.

Another example was Peter, aged six. He was playing a game of 'higher
and lower' with a dice numbered to 20 and a butter bean coloured blue
on one side. With 20 as his starting number for the activity, he threw the
dice and bean together: if he threw blue and 16 he guessed what 16
higher than 20 was. If the bean came up white, he guessed 16 lower than
20. He then checked his results on the calculator. To represent this he
used an arrow either going up or down, (interestingly, rejecting the

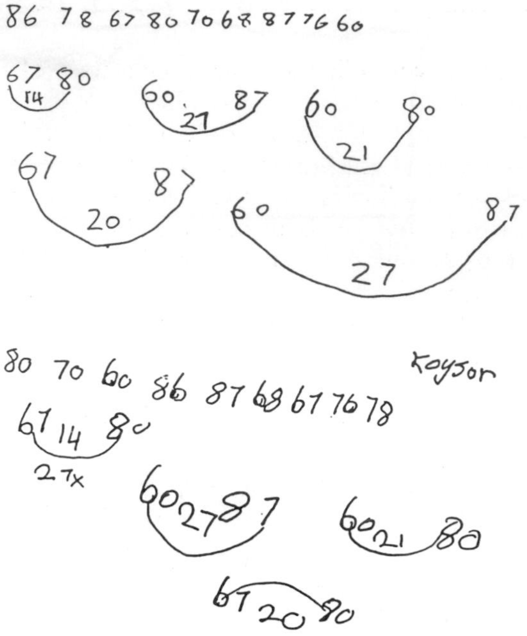

Figure 9.15 Koysor

calculator signs in favour of his own symbols). These seem to me a much more effective way of representing addition or subtraction, than the standard plus and minus symbols, which bear no relationship, visual or verbal, to the ideas that they represent, whereas the arrows reflect something of the essence of the operations. They may also reflect the language of the activity, and Peter's previous experience with a wooden number ladder.

You need to understand symbols to use a calculator

Children's difficulties with 'minus' in representing 'the difference' were underlined for me when I asked some children to select the appropriate keys on the calculator to check their results from the same practical game as Tania and Melanie played previously. Although they had been given more clues than children in the other activities, as far as having their options limited to the calculator keyboard, most children still had trouble, and started off adding the numbers. It was only by knowing the result that they were able to work out that it was the 'lowering key' they wanted, as one child put it. Those children who knew how to put two numbers into a calculator, and get a lower one on the display, could use the standard symbols to represent a practical problem. This seems to me one of the times when standard symbols are relevant and useful to young children: you need them to communicate with a calculator, if not with other people.

Eggs and chips

Finally, I would like to relate an example of a very young reception age child who demonstrated a readiness to use standard symbols in representing a practical problem. Some children were working with maths consultant Shirley Clarke on the 'school cook's problem'. This involved finding out what you could put on the children's plates if they were only allowed six things, and there were only eggs and chips. They had drawn pictures to represent the possibilities, added numbers to these, and then were asked if they wanted to write about what they had been doing. One child's writing, reproduced in Figure 9.16, seems to show an

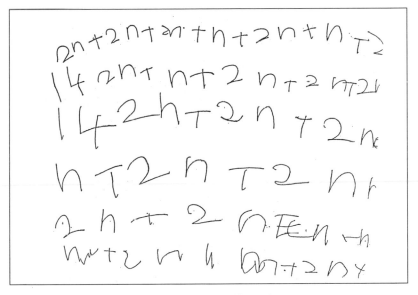

Figure 9.16 This was read by the child as 'There's 2 eggs and 4 chips and 3 eggs and 3 chips'

awareness that numerals and plus signs are appropriate in this context. This seems to indicate that some young children already know a lot about mathematical communication, the forms it takes, and the kinds of things it is used for, in much the same way as they know a lot about what writing looks like and what it is used for, before they understand it fully. And some children, given half a chance, demonstrate a readiness to try out their knowledge of mathematical conventions. Is this because they have not yet learned a fear of failure, or been shown the 'correct' way to do things?

How does maths relate to writing?

As regards this approach, I believe we can learn from current practice in teaching writing to young children, as proposed by the National Writing project (1989). This emphasises:

● writing for real purposes rather than just assessment;

- teachers responding to the content rather than the form in the first instance; and
- setting up a classroom ethos where children respond to each other's work, and discuss and compare different forms.

As with the English National Curriculum attainment targets we could put more emphasis in maths activities on selecting a style which is appropriate to the audience and purpose. It also means creating an atmosphere where, although standard forms are known from an early age, doing your own thing is doing it 'right'.

The implications of the national writing project for maths

So how does this approach fit in with mathematics teaching in the era of the National Curriculum? There are two main implications. Children using their own ways of recording maths are using notation systems that they understand and that are in their control. These systems give us valuable insights into the children's thinking and their understanding. On the other hand, children who are shown how to record may reveal only their compliance, rather than their understanding of operations and symbols. Secondly, we can use these insights to help children, and to move them on from non-standard forms whilst still maintaining understanding of what they are doing.

The non-statutory guidance emphasises the importance of children's own ways of working and recording:

'In developing skills in paper and pencil methods for calculations, pupils need to have opportunities to:

- record the results of operating with numbers in a variety of contexts and a variety of ways, e.g. recording work done with structural apparatus;

- develop informal, personal methods of recording calculations with pencil and paper;

- compare and discuss different pencil and paper approaches to calculations.' (E.34)

If children are encouraged to use their own methods, to choose from a range of forms and discuss these choices, they will be in a better position to select the right form for the context and audience, or, as the National Curriculum puts it, 'be able to record findings and present them in oral, written, or visual form as appropriate' (NAT 1 Level 4). Eventually this should make them better able at Level 10 'to use symbolisation with confidence'. Or was this what Asif and Peter, aged six, were doing?

This article first appeared in *Maths Teaching* (1990), the Journal of the Association of Teachers of Mathematics.

—10— Young children plan a picnic
Alison Base

Age	4 – 7
Situation	whole class with teacher
Maths	real problem solving
Themes	making maths meaningful; classroom organisation; teacher intervention

In this chapter, Alison, working on a course for her own professional development, had to plan some 'real problem solving'. It was rather daunting at first, but Alison's and the children's enjoyment shows up as she describes it.

I was teaching a small class in a two-class village school and had to decide on a project that would include some very basic maths, but would also provide some challenging problems for the seven-year-olds i.e. real problem solving.

Ideally, the real problem should have come from the children, but that isn't always easy – especially when you have a specific project to write up. I had some misgivings about making the decision of what we would do because the children might not have felt the problem real to them. However, I decided that a trip out for the day to a local beauty spot would appeal, and it seemed to have plenty of mathematical potential. I booked the minibus and cancelled our school meal. The children were rather anxious to hear there was no school dinner for that day, but they soon got excited about a picnic.

Though I had some ideas, I very much wanted to hand the problem over to the children. However, like most teachers, I can intervene far too much which takes the problem away from the children, but I think that you have to think out all the eventualities that might arise. It's not easy to sit back and let the children do it – especially when you first try it – as I was rapidly discovering.

First we had a brainstorming session (see Figure 10.1) with me as the scribe, writing down every idea to do with the problem. This is a way of getting the children to see the problem and to comprehend the many issues involved. As in all brainstorms, ideas flew around in all directions, with one little boy insisting that we take ice-cream! I could not just say, 'No, it will melt.'

The P.R.O.B.L.E.M.S acronym

Pose the problem – what is our problem? Can we do anything about it? (This works well as a brainstorming session where all ideas are valued and written down.)

Refining into areas for investigation – Decide what the problem is and what needs investigating (usually worked on by children dividing up into groups).

Outline the questions to ask – What do we need to find out? Will we be able to find the answers? Will the answers help us solve the problem?

Bring the data home – Collect the information needed.

Look for solutions – Can we find a clear result? Did the information answer our questions? What is the solution?

Establish recommendations – How can we fit the solution together? Who will be affected?

Make it happen – Get the solution into action. Does it work?

So what next?

Adapted from the Open University (1980) *Maths Across the Curriculum*. One of the structures for the course involves the process of solving problems, shown by the acronym. At any stage in this process it might be necessary to return to a previous stage.

Figure 10.1 The P.R.O.B.L.E.M.S acronym

Soon the children were all involved, and we sorted out the main questions, mostly about food.

- What sort of sandwich filling do we want?
- Shall we have brown bread or white?
- Shall we use butter or margarine?
- What shall we take to drink?

I divided the children up into small groups and we shared out the questions to be answered. They went off in their groups to sort out their own methods of collecting data through surveys and questions. It is important at this stage to let the children answer their questions in their own way because this is the only way that the problem will remain *their* problem.

I found it very interesting to see the different ways they tackled the questions. The children came up with far better ways of making surveys than my usual teacher approach. By allowing the children to do it their way, they learnt far more than if I had imposed a method on them. Sometimes their methods of gathering information didn't quite work out, like when one boy (aged five) copied out all the children's names on a piece of paper and went round asking whether children liked brown or white bread. He carefully ticked off each child as he asked them. When he reported back he realised that he had not actually recorded their answers!

Another boy, David, invented his own chart – a sandwich spider – writing down all the fillings his group could think of. Then each child had to tick those they liked and cross those they didn't – a very fair method. However, his 'sandwich spider' proved rather difficult to interpret; he had crosses and ticks all over the place, sometimes on top of each other. I let him go on with it for a bit because he is a very bright child, but he often has tremendous problems with presentation. In the end, when it came to analysing the results, the children could not count the ticks! The spider was a brilliant idea, but David hadn't quite carried it off. This led to some real learning for David about the importance of presentation – more meaningful than me nagging him.

Sometimes the children's methods of recording information were successful but unconventional. They attached enormous meaning to their own information gathering when it was their own way of doing it.

Once each small group had answered their questions and analysed their data, they came back to the whole class discussions and announced their results with great pride.

Some difficulties

Initially, the drinks group suffered from a common difficulty in real problem solving – dominant characters in the group making decisions on the basis of what *they* wanted. Two children carried out their drinks survey by 'looking' as if they were being fair. They wrote down a selection of drinks for their survey, but actually asked, 'You do like pineapple juice don't you?' They soon had to rethink as shouts of, 'That's not fair' went up from around the class. We talked as a group about how to make fair surveys.

Then they had another problem. Orange juice had proved the most popular, but I needed to examine the economics of providing orange juice for a whole class of children. The children in the drinks group came to see that they had still not asked themselves a basic question *How much drink do we need?'*

This sort of backtracking to basic questions happened again and again and is an important part of the learning process, especially when some answers to questions then generated new questions.

Making maths meaningful

When children are solving problems like this, they soon come to realise how mathematical ideas can help. They have a clear idea of what they are trying to do and so, when they use mathematical skills, it is in a meaningful context. For example, when the drinks group tried to solve the problem of how much drink they needed, we made a whole class decision to take two cupfuls each (more than this would mean too many loo visits!).

I intervened to tell the children that squash is sold in litres and the concentrate usually says how much squash it will make up with water. I also told them that the two adults going would be taking coffee so they were soon able to calculate that they needed thirty cupfuls of squash altogether.

Emma said to the others, 'Let's find how many cups make a litre.' Tasks were designated and the activity was done several times because they felt that 'Kate spilt too much!' They were very pleased with themselves when they were at last able to say 'Six cupfuls in the litre.' Kate and Anna then started on the next litre when Emma exclaimed, 'But we don't need to do it again!' The others looked perplexed and I had to be very encouraging to Emma at this point. I could see that she knew they did not need to repeat their investigation but she did not know how to explain it to the others.

Emma got thirty Unifix and put them into towers of six. I was not with them at this point but I could see that they were talking about it very excitedly. When they had made their discovery they rushed over to me and shouted 'We need five litres!'

The crisp group had found out the three favourite flavours by listing all the different flavours of crisps, and then doing a survey in which each child had to tick their three favourite flavours. Again, not how I would have approached it, but very fair. They could see that they would need to prevent arguments about who had which crisps at the picnic so they decided to mix them all up. Each of the three sorts came in six little bags and I had three bowls that we could take with us. The question was, how could they mix them up fairly so that no one had more of the Wotsits (the clear favourite)?

Once at the picnic I was impressed to see the very young children in this group share out the crisps into the three bowls. There was a great deal of discussion. Vicky could see she had six bags of each kind so she emptied one whole bag into one bowl, the next bag into the next bowl and the third bag into the third bowl. 'That's right,' she said, 'there's three left.' The others in her group could then see what she was doing and were quick to copy. So three five-year-olds solved their problem through division in a real and concrete way and got a great deal of satisfaction from it. Making something happen like this makes the maths very meaningful because the children know its purpose.

–11– Reception children write about their maths
Sue Atkinson

Age	5
Situation	group with class teacher
Maths	weighing
Themes	linking maths to writing; classroom organisation; children's own symbols

A reception class teacher describes how her class had a writing corner and were used to 'trying writing' in which they used their own symbols for their work. The teacher shows how she developed her own confidence in maths by using 'trying writing' to understand more of the children's mathematical thinking.

From the first day of term I found it fairly easy to get the children to write on their own, and to sit and 'read' with me. However, it was another thing to get them to think this way about maths. They were hung up on 'how do you write a five'. Of course, I had a number frieze and was actively teaching them their numbers, and intended to go on doing that, so I knew I had to relax about using a similar apprenticeship approach to maths, in the same way that I do for language.

In writing I go for confidence, for using the child's own intuitive methods, and I praise and encourage all along the line. I find it easy to make writing meaningful and of course the children enjoy it. The writing corner is well equipped and is always one of the most popular areas to work in.

I find that a great stimulus to getting children to write is to think of a very wide variety of writing situations, so cards, letters, lists, stories, rules for games, things to remember and captions for pictures are being written throughout the week. Many of these writing situations were more mathematical than I had at first realised, for example, rules for games or writing a sequence of events as when Stephen wanted to write down how to make a pop-up bird card. It seemed that if I wanted to have the same approach to maths as I do to language, I could help myself if I first concentrated on finding the maths within the work we were already doing.

The language stage

This process was much easier than I thought because as soon as I started listening to the children talking about their maths, I could see how much maths is dependent on language development. We talk of the early stages of maths learning as 'the language stage', and I realised that whatever maths they were doing (and it is important that they were actively doing something) the children found their way towards understanding it *through language*.

Integrating maths into other classroom activities

My task then, as the teacher, was to integrate maths much more into the ethos of the classroom, where children's own efforts to read and write are valued.

We set up a baker's shop and I suggested that the children should price label the things. Mary's price tags (see Figure 11.1) were accepted by the other children and I noticed that they could 'read' the prices for the whole six weeks that we had the shop. This acceptance of their own symbols for numbers seemed to be a turning point. It was clear that I had made far too clear a division between maths work and all the other work of the classroom, so I decided that it was far better for the children to do all their work in one book. This really paid off and from then on, I found that the children wrote more about their maths.

They would write about numbers, cooking, buying things at the baker's. I felt that not only was I becoming more accepting of maths being integrated into the rest of the classroom activity, but the children and parents were as well.

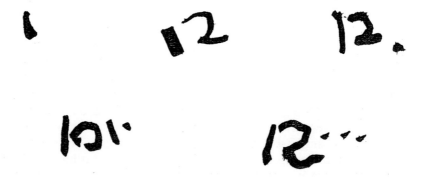

Figure 11.1 Mary's price tags for 1p 2p 3p 4p and 5p (5 yrs 1 mth)

Weighing the glo-bug

One day, Beccy was very interested in the bucket scales and she started trying to weigh her glo-bug – a toy she had brought to school. Weighing was an important feature of the shop and was a favourite activity, so I had put the scales on a table with some Unifix, conkers and bottle-tops. Beccy chose a group to work with her, and they set about weighing various objects.

I could not work with Beccy's group all the time as I was busy with reading, so after talking through with them what they had done, I suggested that they write about it so that they could read it to the others. These written records had many advantages.

1 The children enjoyed reading them to the class.

2 Several children made a display focusing on things they had weighed and made a book of their writing.

3 Writing integrated maths into the rest of the curriculum. I felt that these early maths experiences were meaningful – partly because I was giving the children *time to talk* as they wrote and drew.

4 The work was valuable for me to assess the level of individual children's understandings. For example, Katie's work (see Figure 11.2) shows no sign of any understanding that the scales balanced with the glo-bug in one side and twelve Unifix in the other. I thought when we were talking as a group that she had understood the idea of 'heavier than'. However, through her writing I could see that this was not the case. On checking this with her on her own, she was clearly vague about the whole concept of 'heavier', and what happens to the balance when you are comparing mass. The writing was giving me insight's into children's thinking that I might not otherwise have had.

Beccy's work (see Figure 11.3) showed a similar and common

Here is a glowbug
and unifix

Figure 11.2 Katie (5 yrs 1 mth) Here is a glo-bug and Unifix

Figure 11.3 Beccy (5 yrs 4 mths) The cubes are bigger than the glo-bug

misunderstanding, with 'biggest' being substituted for 'heaviest'. It was several weeks before she could grasp the idea of 'heavier' – yet in group discussion, I had missed this fact.

John and Barry, working together, showed the usual huge spread of ability I was dealing with. John merely drew the shoe, (see Figure 11.4) but Barry was totally confident about the whole task (see Figure 11.5).

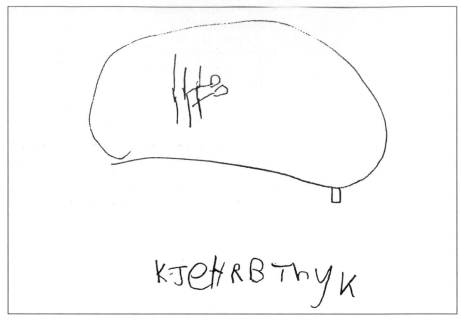

Figure 11.4 John (5 yrs 3 mths) Here is a black shoe

Figure 11.5 Barry (5yrs 2 mths) This is the scales with shoes in the scales.
Mine was heavier.

Reception class organisation

- Although I was using children's own symbols, I continued with all my usual teaching of standard symbols for numbers. This did not seem to cause any problems.

- The children used calculators and accepted their own notations alongside mine and the more angular ones of the calculator.

- Of course it is hard to measure one class against another, but I did think that this class was very alert to numbers and no one showed any sign of fear of maths.

- I used games to teach maths concepts and to teach the conventional signs for mathematical operations. (See Hughes, 1986b.)

- I felt more confident about teaching maths! I think that I am integrating it into the rest of the classroom experience.

- I started using a 'maths diary' in the children's book. I do not put an entry every day, but I get parents to help me if they have done an activity.

−12− A simple starting point
Marion Bird

Age	7 – 9
Situation	maths education lecturer with a group
Maths	a number investigation
Themes	children reflecting on their work; exploring ideas and generalising findings

Marion Bird writes about her work with a group where they explore maths from a simple starting point and look for ways of generalising their findings.

I asked the children to choose a number which was greater than 9 but less than 100. Wendy chose 52. I wrote '52' on a piece of paper in front of the group, then asked Debbie how many tens there were in it and Sally how many units there were left over. Both girls answered correctly. Then I asked the group which number we would obtain if we turned the digits '5' and '2' round the other way. Debbie said we would get 25. I asked Bora how many tens there were in 25 and Debbie how many units were left over. Both answered correctly. (I asked about the tens and units in both instances because I wanted to hint at the ideas that we could not just reverse the digits without making a big change to the actual numbers involved.)

I said that I would like each person in the group to work out what they would have left if they started with 52 and took 25 away from it. Debbie asked if they should write the sum on the pieces of paper I had given out before the start of the session, but I told the group that I did not mind how they worked out the subtraction. I waited until more than half the group were showing signs of having finished, then asked to hear the answers. Everyone who had finished had made the answer 27.

Jane had finished very early on and I took the opportunity of asking her how she had worked out the answer. She had not used paper but her description of what she had done revealed that she had managed to use the method of subtraction by decomposition in her head. She said, 'First I took 10 away from 50 and put it in the units. Then I took 5 away from that, that was 5, and added the 2, that made 7. Then I took 20 away.'

I also asked Debbie to tell us how she had worked hers out on paper. She said, 'I saw that there wasn't enough to take away 5 from the 2 so I exchanged one ten, put a circle round it . . . the 2 . . . and put a little 10 in it and then . . . I took . . . the 2 away from the 4 which was there and it added up to 27.' I realised that she had not really finished telling us about her calculation so I said, 'So the 2 from the 4 there (pointing) gives you 2 tens and the 5 from the . . .' (I hesitated here because I did not know if she had subtracted 5 from 10 or 12). She continued ' . . .10 you've got 5 left and you add it on to 2 and it makes 5. . . 6 . . . 7, so it makes 7.' She also added that she was used to doing sums like that on worksheets and that she had got the idea of them!

I then invited each of the children to choose about five numbers between 9 and 100, to 'reverse' them, that was to turn them round the other way, and to take the smaller number from the larger number in each case. Again I stressed that I did not mind how the children worked out the subtractions, but I did suggest that they made a note of their pairs of numbers this time, in case we wanted to refer back to them.

Bora immediately recorded '99 − 99 = 0' and said he thought he had better not do any more of those! I think he felt I thought he was 'cheating'. I said that I thought he had come up with an interesting finding and wondered if he could suggest other numbers which would yield 0 too. His written record of his subsequent subtractions and comment is shown in Figure 12.1. Stacey also made the same observation and her written record of her thinking can be seen in Figure 12.2.

$$99 - 99 = 0$$

$$37 - 73 = 36$$
$$15 - 51 = 36$$
$$44 - 44 = 0$$
$$88 - 88 = 0.$$
$$45 - 54 = 09$$
$$61 - 16 = 45$$
$$12 - 21 = 09$$

Thae This is the numbers
11 thur make 0 when
22 you take it away.
33
44
55
66
77
88
99

Figure 12.1 Bora

$$77 - 77 = 0$$
$$99 - 99 = 0$$
$$75 - 57 = 18$$
$$10 - 01 = 9$$
$$22 - 22 = 0$$
$$33 - 33 = 18$$
$$41 - 14 = 27$$

The one's that are the Same. If you take away them you will get nort.

Figure 12.2 Stacey

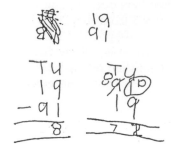

Figure 12.3 Wendy

It is also evident from these two records that Stacey made sure she ended up with the larger number first in each of her other subtractions, whereas Bora did not. I made a mental note of talking with the children about the differences in how they were writing the numbers. Some of the other children did not just write the numbers down with the smaller ones first, they actually started to work out the subtractions like that. Wendy was a case in point as can be seen from the snippet of her work shown in Figure 12.3. She commented that she was stuck because she could not take 9 from 1 in the sum:

$$\begin{array}{r} 19 \\ -91 \\ \hline 8 \end{array}$$

I asked the rest of the group what they thought was wrong, to which Ray replied that she should have 'put the 91 down first'. It was interesting to note that Ray managed to decide which of the numbers in each of his pairs would come first before writing anything down: he did not have to make any alterations as can be seen from Figure 12.4.

I had plenty of opportunity to ask the children about other points in connection with their subtractions. As an example, I noticed that Linda had written the answer to 43 - 34 as 10 so I asked her how she had worked it out. She told me how she had exchanged a ten for ten units, then written ten little strokes for those, added 3 more strokes to them, crossed off 4 of them and then counted up how many were left. When she recounted she found that there were, in fact, 9 left, not 10. She corrected her record of her work, as can be seen in Figure 12.5.

Like Linda, several other children were tallying numbers either as stroked on paper, or with their fingers, then taking numbers off. Wendy suddenly announced, though, that she had found a quick way of 'taking away little numbers'. She said, 'Well, say if you had to take away 7 from

Figure 12.4 Ray

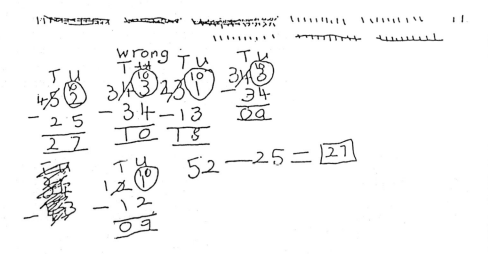

Figure 12.5 Linda

86

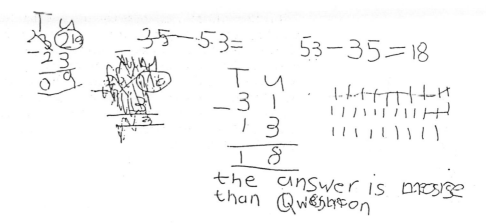

the answer is more
than Question

Figure 12.6 Jane

12, well all you have to do is go 8, 9, 10, 11, 12 and that's the answer you get.' I asked her how this was different from 'taking numbers away' and she said she was 'adding on'. Bora said that was what he was doing too and it was a lot better than Linda's idea because it was taking her (Linda) some time to write down all the little lines! Linda subsequently tried the adding on idea.

Once the children had each carried out several subtractions, I asked them to stop, to look at their answers and to jot down anything they noticed. I did not expect them to recognise the answers as being numbers from the 9 times table because I knew that they had not considered that particular table in class, but I did wonder if anyone might notice about the digits adding to 9. This, however, was not the case.

Jane said that in one of her questions the answer was more than the question (see Figure 12.6). When I asked her what she meant she said that the 18 was more than the 'taking away bit'. Linda noticed that the first subtraction we had carried out was like that too.

Debbie said that for 75 - 57, 'I found that the amount that I took away was more than . . . less than . . . the answer I got left in the units.' She showed us how the 7 in the units of 57 was one less than the 8 in the units of the 18 (Figure 12.7). Wendy said that she had an example like that too and showed us her 51 - 15 = 36 example.

Amongst other things, Joyce noticed that two of her answers were the same (see Figure 12.8). This sparked off other children looking to see if some of their answers were the same too.

They are 1 morre
Then you
took away

Figure 12.7 Debbie

two of my answers
are both 18.

Figure 12.8 Joyce

$$72 - 27 = 45$$
$$91 - 19 = 72$$
$$81 - 18 = 63$$
$$51 - 15 = 36$$
$$54 - 45 = 9$$
$$94 - 49 = 45$$
$$61 - 16 = 45$$
$$73 - 37 = 36$$
$$75 - 57 = 18$$
$$97 - 79 = 18$$
$$31 - 13 = 18$$
$$86 - 68 = 18$$
$$21 - 12 = 9$$
$$10 - 1 = 9$$
$$76 - 67 = 9$$
$$32 - 23 = 9$$

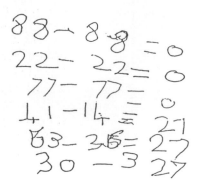

$$88 - 88 = 0$$
$$22 - 22 = 0$$
$$77 - 77 = 0$$
$$41 - 14 = 27$$
$$63 - 36 = 27$$
$$30 - 3 = 27$$

Figure 12.9 Debbie

Indeed, in response to Joyce's remark, the children became very interested in comparing their answers, so I suggested we did just that. We collected together lots of different examples as can be seen in Debbie's record of the collection (Figure 12.9). The children were excited by the fact that they kept on finding examples with the same answers. I asked if they noticed anything about the numbers but they did not. I suggested that we wrote out the numbers in order to see if this showed anything more clearly. They called out the numbers in turn, starting from 0. Soon we had in front of us

> 0   9   18   27   36   45   63   72   (Note, no 54)

Suddenly, Stacey announced that the numbers went up in 9s! We counted on 9 from 9 to 18, then from 18 to 27, from 27 to 36, from 36 to 45 and 45 . . . some of the children called out 63 before others had finished counting, and were dismayed to find the rest came to 54! Much delight followed when Wendy then found that she had a subtraction on her paper which gave an answer of 54! (see Figure 12.10). Again there was excitement when counting on 9 from 54 gave us 63 and from 63 gave us 72.

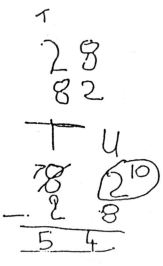

Figure 12.10 Wendy

Bora then said that we were not just adding on 9, we were sort of 'timesing by 9'. He had previously been doing work on counting sets of, say 3, with counting on in 3s. We went through the sequence of numbers to check that idea too and found that one lot of 9 gave us 9, two lots of 9 gave us 18, three lots of 9 gave us 27 and so on. Several then commented on the fact that we had found the 9 times table! Debbie also noticed how the units went down by one and the tens went up by one.

I asked the children if they had any ideas as to what we might try next. Joyce suggested picking pairs of answers and adding them up or subtracting them and seeing what we got for new answers. Stacey wanted to add up all the answers. Joyce suggested picking one number from each of the numbers in the original 'sums', but not in the answers, and adding them up. Bora suggested trying 3 digit numbers instead of 2 digit ones. The children chose one idea each and worked on it for the last quarter of an hour of the session. Examples of the written records of their ensuing work can be seen in Figures 12.11 to 12.14.

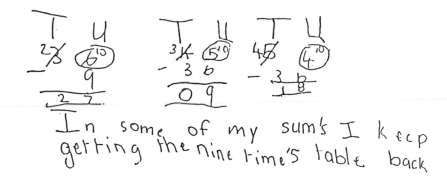

Figure 12.11 Wendy

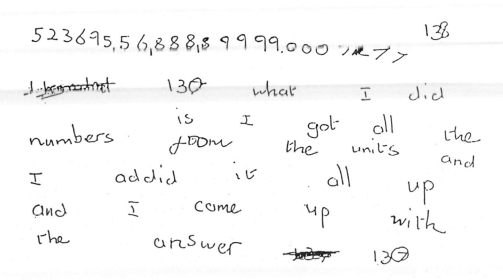

Figure 12.12 Linda

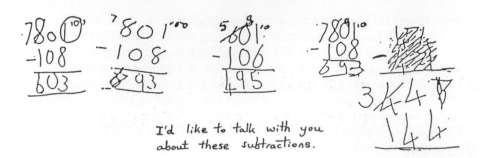

I'd like to talk with you about these subtractions.

Figure 12.13 Joyce

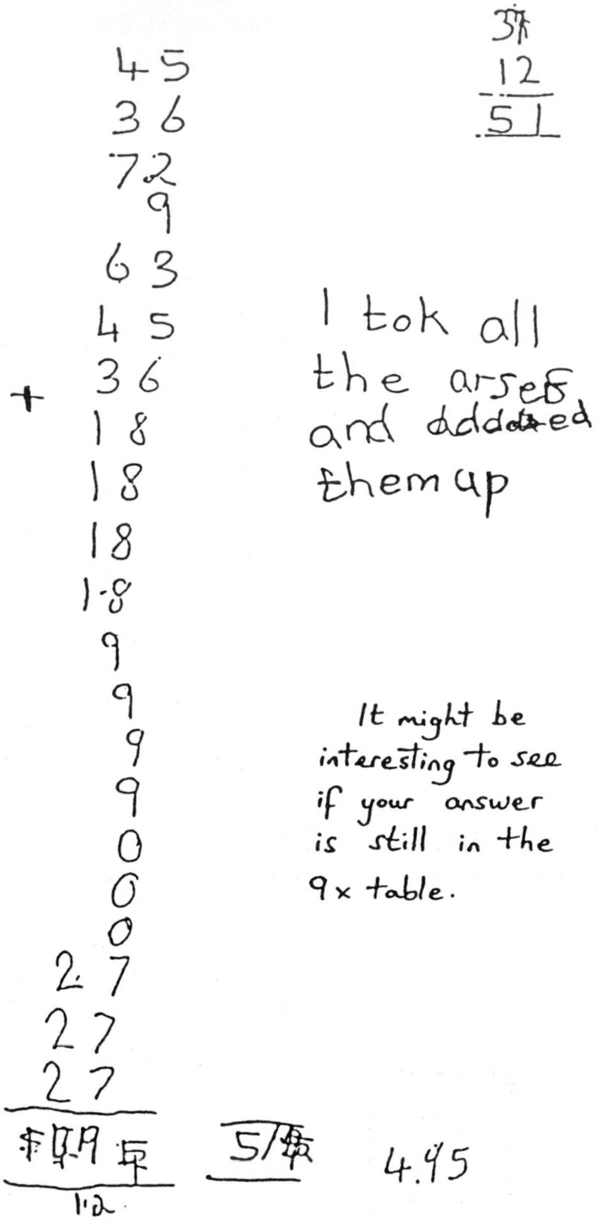

45
36
72
9
63
45
+ 36
18
18
18
1·8
9
9
9
9
0
0
0
2·7
27
27

I tok all the arseß and ddddbed them up

It might be interesting to see if your answer is still in the 9x table.

Figure 12.14 Stacey

−13− Explode a number
Sue Atkinson and Alison Base

This chapter has been split into two parts – 'A' and 'B'. Part 'A' recounts work with seven- to nine-year olds and is written by Sue Atkinson; Part 'B' recounts work with five-year olds and is written by Alison Base.

A

Age	7–9
Situation	teacher with whole class in 30-minute lesson
Maths	investigating a number
Themes	children exploring their own ideas; teacher role

'Explode a number' is a name given to an activity in which the starting point is just a number and the children are free to explore and investigate it in any way they choose. The children were working on the number '18' at the end of a week in which all them had done an activity involving counting in 3s, building up to the 3 times table.

Children work on 18

I asked the children to investigate the number 18 in any way they wished. (I suggested that the children should start without using pencil and paper.) Here are some of the results.

1 Using the large place value boards and Dienes or Unifix.

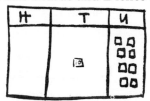

Figure 13.1 *Using Dienes*   Figure 13.2 *Using Unifix*

2 Using Unifix place value boats. We talked about the similarities and differences with this one.

Figure 13.3 Using Unifix place value boats   *Figure 13.4*

3 With weights (I've given up trying to get children to call them masses!)

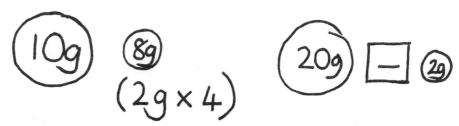

Figure 13.5

4 Unifix was used a great deal in various arrangements:

9 + 9, 14 + 4, (i.e. 14 red and 4 blue) 10 + 8 etc.

6 lots of 3, 1 set of 18, 2 lots of 9, 9 towers of 2 etc.

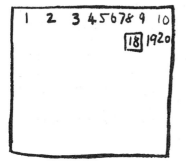

5 Using Unifix 'windows' on the 100 square.
– some put a 'window' every 18; some just marked where 18 was. Sarah had put a 'window' on every even number in yellow and on every third number in red and she said '18 is even and it's in the 3 times table. So is 12.' This led eventually to some work on prime numbers.
   Some children had designed different layouts of the 100 squares (i.e. changing from the top row always being 1 to 10 with the bottom right-hand square being 100). This led to some interesting number patterns including spirals which the children explored later on triangular and hexagonal grid paper.

Figure 13.6

6 Using the Unifix number lines.
Some children just marked 18, but Jason marked 18, then counted on 18 and marked that. He went on with the sequence, on paper, up into the thousands, developing a confidence with large numbers that others began to share.

Figure 13.7

7 A great many children counted out 18 of something. (This does tend to be what children start with, but I intervene if children go on doing it.) Marie, a very low ability child, did a hoop like this:

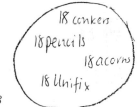

Figure 13.8

I was perplexed to know how to comment on this. I was so delighted that she had (mostly) got 18 of each item that in the end I decided that she should *check* her work but I wouldn't query her description of her work, 'I done a set of 18.' It seemed more important to boost her confidence and to let her feel success than to criticise her work.

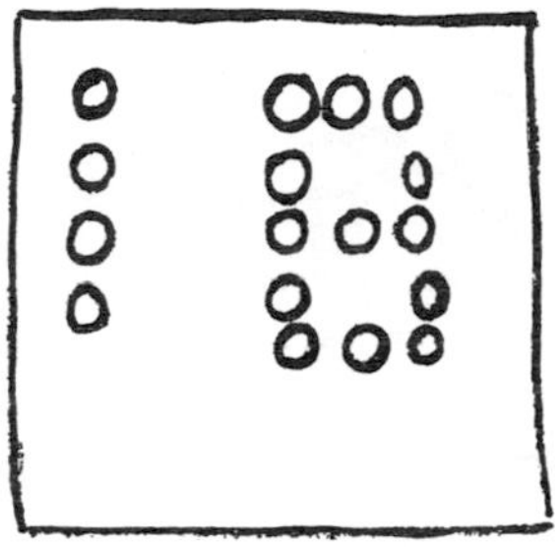

8 Pegs in pegboards are a great favourite to explore. This one used 18 pegs (see Figure 13.9).

9 Mark made an interesting one with straws. He said 'I made 9 crosses with 18 straws.' It was a moment to tell him about intersections.

Figure 13.9

Figure 13.10

10 Calculators are always used and many children bring in their own. It is difficult to see what is going on with calculators, especially when the game becomes 'Let's see who can do the biggest sum to get to 18.' The children became very confident with numbers because of their calculator work. Some could tell me they were doing 6 × 3=18 etc. and, as always, it is good to see that these children (who accept that using apparatus is a *good thing* not a babyish thing) will *check* what they are doing with Unifix, Dienes etc. I asked Ben to write down one of his 'big sums' (see Figure 13.11).

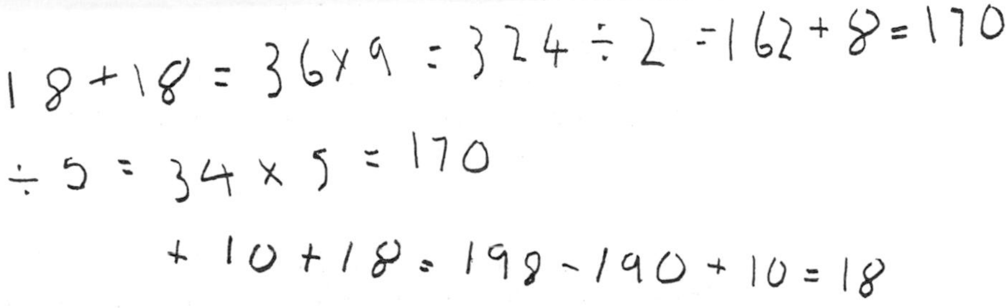

$$18+18 = 36 \times 9 = 324 \div 2 = 162 + 8 = 170$$
$$\div 5 = 34 \times 5 = 170$$
$$+ 10 + 18 = 198 - 190 + 10 = 18$$

Figure 13.11 Ben (7 yrs)

11 A ruler

Figure 13.12

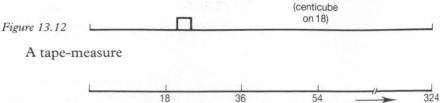

(centicube on 18)

A tape-measure

18   36   54   324

Figure 13.13

12 Interlocking cubes are always one of the most popular bits of apparatus. We constructed the 'Iron Man', made with 18 cubes (I had just finished reading the class the story).

'R' is the eighteenth letter of the alphabet and it was made with 18 cubes.

Figure 13.14 The Iron Man   *Figure 13.15 The letter 'R'*

Leon made a 'transformer' out of 18 cubes which changed from a robot to an 'attack plane'.

13 The school has hundreds of Cuisenaire rods and the children were very resourceful with them. Robert built an 18 cm high tower with them, and then another tower with 18 '10 rods'. Ryan counted out 18 'ten rods'. Shaun and he had a long discussion on whether it was 'right'. Shaun said, 'But 18 tens is 180.' Others tried variations on a theme of splitting up 18 (see Figure 13.16)

Figure 13.16

14 A bucket balance was used with 18 red Unifix balancing 18 blue Unifix. (I had been working on equations with them like this: 18 = 18

and had introduced the idea of the equals sign meaning each side 'balancing'.)

15 18 ml of water. Kelly said 'Three full medicine spoonfuls and a bit more.'

16 Barry, a nine-year-old with learning difficulties, needed a lot of help with the clock earlier in the term. He put the hands at 9:18 (almost) on his own.

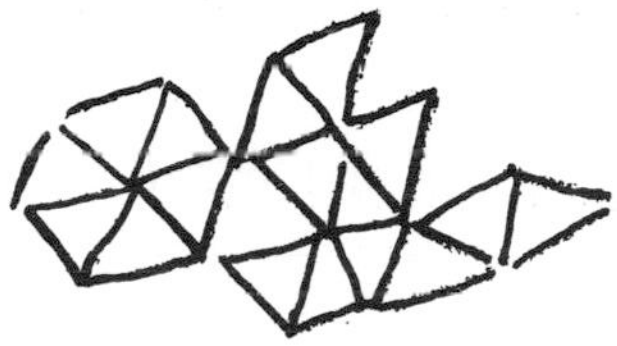

17 Children used shapes a great deal. Carol (an eight-year-old with learning difficulties) made two hexagons out of the equilateral triangles then put the other six around the edge as shown in Figure 13.17. (I introduced an investigation using triangular gridsheets the next week to lead on from this.)

Figure 13.17

I could easily have over-intervened here to tell Carol she had enough triangles to make another hexagon. I asked her to tell me what she was doing. To my surprise she said '18 makes two groups of 6 and 6 left over.' We had just done a sharing activity when a child had brought in a bag of sweets for his birthday to share with the class. I had certainly not expected Carol of all people to say that.

Other uses of shape included numerous polydron ideas. Paul made a tower out of 18 polydrons that would support 500 g.

My role

My role as the children are working is very varied and has changed as the group have got used to investigating a number in this way. I noted the following things I did as the children worked.

1 I talked with parents and encouraged them to talk with children.

2 I talked with the children about what they were doing.

3 I listened to explanations from the children – this is a time when gaps in understanding show up.

4 I encouraged children to branch out, especially children who just counted out 18 things. I used open-ended suggestions like, 'Could you try to use a piece of apparatus that you have never worked with?' Or, for children who needed much more structure, 'You haven't done anything with a calculator/balance/Dienes blocks; could you try that now?'

5 I promoted the spread of ideas. This isn't copying, it is sharing and should be encouraged as generating the right sort of enquiring ethos in the classroom.

6 I injected language into situations where children's explanations needed extending, e.g. if they put out six groups of 3 Unifix and could *only* express it as '6 lots of 3', I would ask for ideas from others. If this failed to prompt discussion, I might suggest: '6 rows of 3', '6 towers of 3', '6 sets of 3'. I would then try to get the child to make a sentence out of the ideas.

Me: Let's see if you can put that all together in a sentence. Tell me about your Unifix group here.

Child: I've got 6 sets of 3 and it makes 18 altogether and I know it's 18 because I counted in 3s – 3, 6, 9, 12, 15, 18.

7 As I moved around the room I looked for opportunities to get children to generalise about what they were doing, e.g. '6 groups of 3 and 3 groups of 6 makes the same number.'

8 I noted down on my clipboard chart significant things for some individuals to put into their maths diary and notes for my own record keeping e.g.: *Sarah* saw 6×3 same as 3×6; *Sally* used calculator confidently today.

Ending the session

I end sessions like this by giving the children two minutes to go around the class to look at the ideas of others. Then we all go around the classroom together and talk about some of the ideas. This getting together is a time for me to boost confidence, to praise and encourage. I regularly tell them what wonderful mathematicians they are.

I find this way of doing maths very exciting. Someone always comes up with something I would never think of, and everyone enjoys it. It keeps ideas ticking over and it is a good way of assessing children's difficulties and progress. This practical maths, where the children are free to create ideas for themselves, also presents a context that is *meaningful* for the children. It fulfils the conditions given by Martin Hughes, for the children to be able to integrate their accomplished informal ideas about maths with the language of 'school' maths.

B

Age	5
Situation	teacher with group
Maths	investigating the number 6
Themes	children exploring their own ideas

I first tried 'explode a number' when I was in my second year of teaching, sharing a class of 34 Year 1 and 2 children. I was really nervous about trying something different in maths, something not part of the scheme, but I thought I would give it a try.

This activity provides a good starting point for teachers exploring maths with reason. Working in this way we enable children to use and explore thier 'home' or intuitive maths, and we are creating situations in which children can explore their own methods of recording. The activity can be developed with older children too, e.g., 'How many ways can you arrange six squares (in a net) so that they make a cube?'

One afternoon, I found I was left with just ten five-year-olds, due to plenty of other helpers being to hand. I sat them on the carpet and began by reminding them of the other number work they had been doing recently. I then said, 'We're going to do some work about the number 6 today and I want you to use any of the apparatus on the carpet – shapes, beads, Unifix, pencil and paper – and see what you can show me about the number 6.'

Of course, I got lots of blank looks because it was something new. They didn't know what I meant, but they started very tentatively. I soon realised it was a mistake to have put out the paper, as one little girl went straight for it. The rest, of course, followed because it was a new situation. They all drew a number 6 and said, 'I've done it.' My heart sank, and I quickly got rid of the paper and said that we were going to 'explore the apparatus'.

Most of these children had only experienced maths as something that you do on pieces of paper so it was all very different for them. I therefore wasn't really too surprised that they were so stuck. I had to make lots of suggestions at first: 'You can make shapes with the bricks' or 'You could use the beads'. I tried to throw out ideas to reassure them and give them some ideas. Then a child made a picture of a man using six shapes. I called the others over to have a look at it, and from then on they were off.

The activity takes off

At first they just did the same – they all made a man with six shapes – but after about ten minutes I could have walked away and left them to it as they were so engrossed trying out different ideas. I stayed, though, because I wanted to observe them and to ask them questions.

They were very inventive and concentrated for the whole 50 minutes which was good considering how young they were and how hard I had been finding it to think of things that would keep them busy and interested for longer than a few minutes. I was also able to inject a lot of language and to ask probing questions.

Having done this activity, I now know to hide the pencil and paper and only bring it out when the children have explored the apparatus, so that they can record what they have done. This keeps the attention on the 'doing and talking', so they are thinking mathematically.

Children working with numbers – discussion starters
Sue Atkinson

A   Andrew

Age	4–7
Situation	individual
Maths	addition
Theme	children's errors

'Andrew (aged six) was adding two numbers and repeatedly making the same mistake when using the number line provided on the workbook page (see Figure 14.1 below).

$$4 + 2 = 5 \qquad 3 + 7 = 9 \qquad 8 + 4 = 11$$

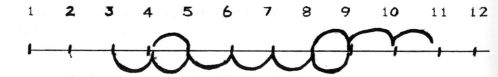

Figure 14.1

Questions for discussion

1 What do you think Andrew was doing?

2 How would you help him?

(Andrew was counting in the number he was on.)

B A bright group

Age	7–9
Situation	group with researcher
Maths	subtraction/place value
Theme	mental methods compared with written algorithms

A top maths group of eight- to nine-year-olds, described by their teacher as 'a bright lot', were asked to write down and work out, without looking at anyone else's work, '127 take away 84'.

18 children wrote: $127 - 84 = 43$ (correct answer)

1 child wrote: $127 - 84 = 53$

Out of the remaining children who chose to write it down vertically, as below, only 2 got it right – 15 got it wrong!

Errors in vertical forms included:

(1)	*(2)*	*(3)*	*(4)*
$\begin{array}{r} 127 \\ -\ 84 \\ \hline 143 \end{array}$	$\begin{array}{r} 127 \\ -\ 84 \\ \hline 163 \end{array}$	$\begin{array}{r} 127 \\ -84 \\ \hline 727 \end{array}$	$\begin{array}{r} \overset{1}{1}27 \\ 84 \\ \hline 88 \end{array}$

At story time at the end of the session, a similar problem was put to the children to work out *mentally:* $136 - 54$.

Although there are problems in assessing what individual children are actually thinking in a group session like this, it seemed that every child could work this out mentally. They had several different strategies, such as adding on, counting back, rounding up/down etc. Several used fingers and all seemed relaxed about their own method. The striking thing about this for the researcher was:

1 The enthusiasm with which the children described their own methods and the apparent ease with which they worked out this calculation with their own informal methods compared with the difficulties they seemed to encounter when writing it.

2 That even the children who got it wrong in the written form had no problem, it would seem, when it was worked out mentally.

3 The way their own teacher encouraged the children to 'do without apparatus now you are 8.'

Questions for discussion

1 Does this tell us something about writing problems vertically?

2 Did the children think that this was the *correct* way to write it?

C Julie

Age	7–9
Situation	individual
Maths	place value
Theme	children's errors

Julie's mother came to see me to tell me that Julie (aged eight) sometimes got upset in school because she kept getting her sums wrong. She wanted me to give Julie some extra lessons out of school. I had a chat with Julie who seemed an able child until we got onto the subject of maths, when she became cautious and defensive. I asked Julie what the problem was, and she said, 'I get lots of things wrong. I'm no good at adding.'

I got her to write down 26 add 32, then 327 add 143. She was able to do both of these calculations, but was quite unable to talk me through what she was doing, or why she was doing it.

(1)
```
  26
  32
 ───
  58
 ───
```

(2)
```
 327
 184
 ───
 470
 ───
   1
```

She had no explanation for why she put a 'little 1' under the line in the second sum. She just said 'That's how you do it.'

When asked to write down 43 add 8 she wrote this:

```
  43
 +8
 ───

 123
```

Me   Do you think you are right?
Julie   Don't know.
Me   How could you check?
Julie   Check?
Me   Yes. You know... 43 add 8 is 123... Are you right?
Julie   Don't know.
Me   Could you do it another way – 43 add 8?
Julie   (*Holding her head down and counting on her fingers*) It's 51.

A long conversation followed in which I tried to get Julie to decide which was right, 51 or 123. She was getting increasingly puzzled.

Julie   When you write it, it's 123, but when you do it on your fingers it's 51.
Me   So which is right?

Julie   123.

Me   Why?

Julie   Because you mustn't count on your fingers.

Questions for discussion   1 If you were Julie's mother what would you do?

2 If you were teaching Julie what would you do?

D   Ellie

Age	7–9
Situation	individual
Maths	subtraction
Theme	children's errors

Ellie (aged eight) was asked to write down a subtraction problem, 12 take away 4. She wrote: $12 \div 4 = 8$. She would regularly check with her teacher when faced with a new page of sums, and would say things like: 'Is it an add or a take away?' 'Will you show me how to do the first one?'

It was not surprising, therefore, that on most pages of her book the teacher had done two or three sums at the top first. Ellie would then do the rest, getting most of them right until the rule she was applying changed. So, for example, if part way down the page the sums changed from addition to subtraction, she would be unable to do this. She could follow a rule she was taught, but could not apply it in a new situation. She could not remember the different symbols for number operations like divide and multiply etc.

Questions for discussion   1 How would you help her?

2 What are the main problems that children face when they try to decode the use of conventional symbols?

3 Will calculators help children to understand the use of symbols more thoroughly?

E   Zoe uses symbols her own way

Age	7–11
Situation	individual in class
Maths	multiplication
Theme	children's own methods of recording and use of symbols

Zoe (aged eight) has her own way of multiplying large numbers. Figure 14.2 shows her method of splitting up the numbers, then multiplying them. She uses a conventional division sign in an unconventional way – for multiplying. Was she influenced by the use of table squares for multiplication?

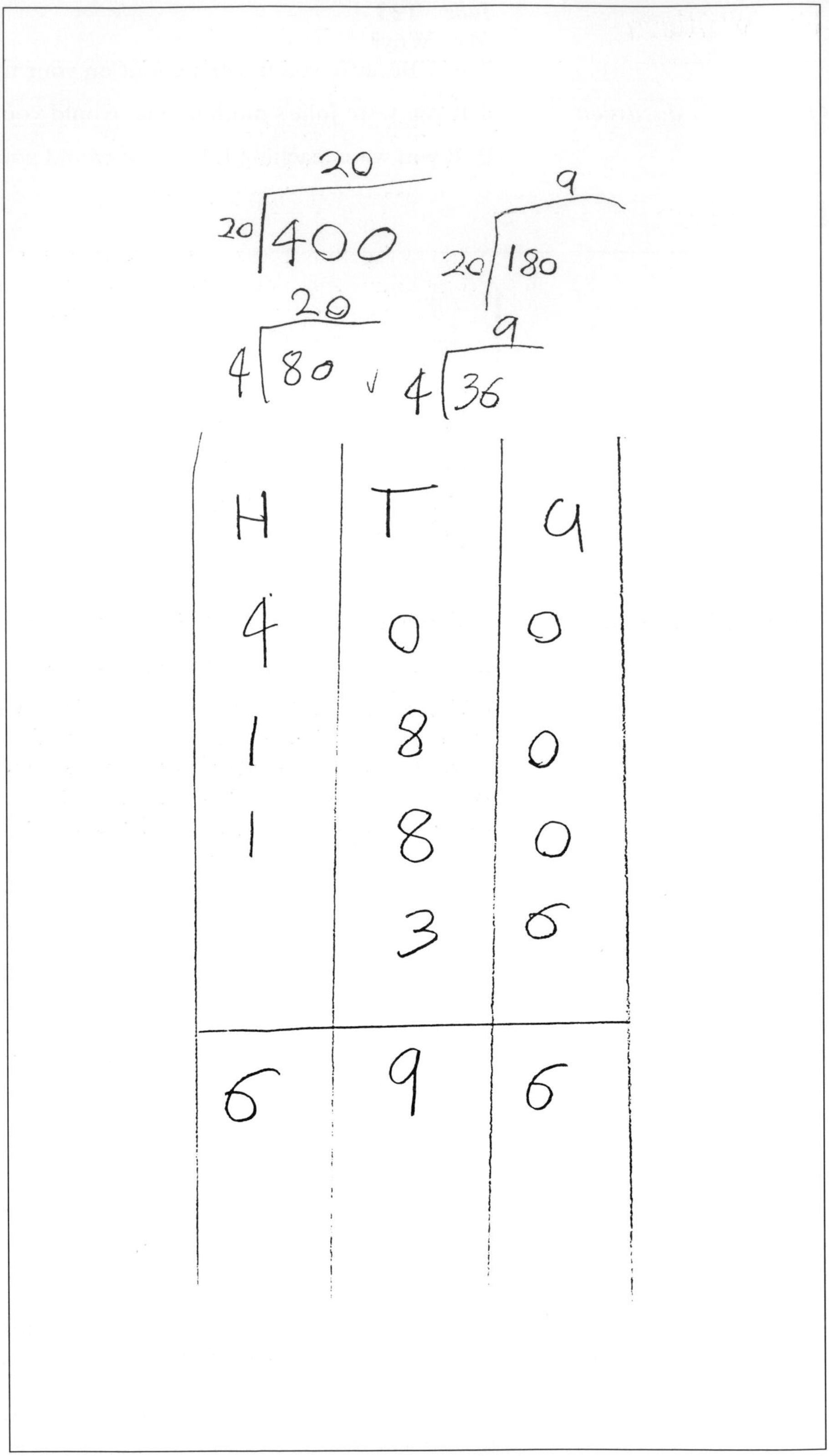

Figure 14.2 Zoe (8 yrs)

F William

Age	9–11
Situation	individual
Maths	place value
Theme	children's errors

William (aged ten) was very good at maths, but he was making a few errors in his work and it took his teacher some time to work out whether this was carelessness or due to some personal 'rule' that William was using.

(1)
```
  148
  234 +
  169
 ─────
  542
  1 1
```

(2)
```
   48 ×
    4
 ─────
  183
    2
```

Questions for discussion

1 Can you see the 'rule' William was applying?

2 How would you help William if you were his teacher?

(William's rule was that in a 'carrying' situation he always put the smaller of the two numbers in the next column. So very often this would not show up, but in (1), where the units came to 21, he incorrectly put the smaller of the two numbers, the 1, in the tens column. When he multiplied 8 by 4 in (2) he got 32, and the 2 was put in the tens column.)

−15− Tracey and Jason make a map
A maths advisory support teacher

Age	7–9
Situation	group
Maths	measurement and place value
Theme	children's errors; children's own methods of recording

I was suddenly accosted in the corridor by two children with a metre stick, a large piece of paper and a pencil each.

'What's after nine thousand, Miss, is it a million?'
'Well, not really,' I said.
'Told yer! Yer thick!'

I could see a fight brewing, so I hastily asked the children to explain to me what they were doing and I would see if I could help them. It was lunch time and the children knew this but said they wanted to finish their work. Their explanation of their task was that they were 'measuring the corridor'. I asked them to show me what they had done so far. (As this particular school seemed to have miles of corridor I wondered whether they had got the task right.)

Their drawings (see Figures 15.1, 15.2 and 15.3) were obviously clear to them, and as I was intrigued by them, I asked them to show me what they were doing. They showed me the way they had measured the corridor by putting down the metre rule, and I noted that they were not aware of the need to measure in a straight line, nor were they marking the point where the rule ended with any great accuracy. They used an adequate method, Tracey keeping her finger more or less still while she argued with Jason who was writing down the results. Tracey occasionally got up to hit Jason, then put her finger back somewhere near where it had been.

The crux of the problem as they saw it was that they had come to '9000' (Figure 15.1), so that next metre 'made it a million'. Or did it? Asking them about their recording in Figure 15.1, it seemed to me they were adding on 100 after each metre. 'It says 100 there, Miss,' pointing to the

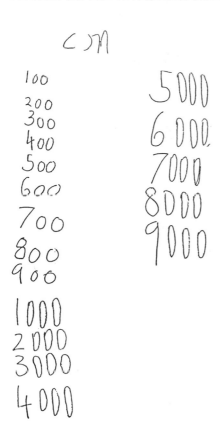

Figure 15.1 Tracy (8 yrs)
(Note this is cm for centimetres)

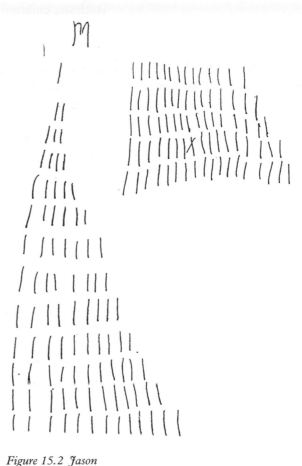

Figure 15.2 Jason
(Note this is m for metres)

Figure 15.3 Jason (9 yrs)

100 cm mark. (It transpired later in the conversation that they had not done this until they had changed who did the recording).

'So how long is this stick?' I asked, pointing to the metre rule.
'Hundred metres, Miss.'

So it seemed that they had recorded each metre as 100 metres, then at 900 metres, one more metre had been recorded as 1000, which seemed to show an inability to understand large numbers. Apart from their obvious errors of place value, they were clearly enjoying the work and it seemed to have great personal meaning for them.

'What are you going to do with your results?' I asked.
'We're going to make a map, ain't we Jason, an' we're going to get a "super-work" sticker.'

At this point a teacher appeared in the corridor and became very angry with the children. They were supposed to be outside. She took one look at their work and said, 'This is rubbish. It's not what I asked you to do at all.' Apparently they were supposed to be finding out how *wide* the corridor was.

Both the children looked upset and hurt so I cheerily told the teacher that I had been chatting to them and would try to 'sort them out'. I decided to get them to explain their recordings. Jason, who had been the first one to record the work (Figure 15.2), had 'tallied' up to 18 in a fascinating way. I asked him what he had done next. He pointed to a small corner of his paper (Figure 15.3) 'I done it quicker,' he said.

Figure 15.2, it seems, had been the start of their work, with Jason tallying each metre correctly, then realising that this was a slow method, he changed to the method shown in Figure 15.3, and tallied the odd one for 19, then wrote 20, then tallied 9 more before putting 30, and so on.

Tracey had then said that it was her turn to do the writing down, from a hundred metres, so she had done it on her paper (Figure 15.1). At this point they seemed to have stopped tallying and had recorded the next metre after 100 as '200' ('because it says 100 here, Miss,' pointing to the 100 cm). Tracey had recorded up in hundreds and they had now reached 9000, having gone from 900 to 1000, then to 2000 until they reached 9000. Their rationale for this was that they believed that 2000 was 100 more than 1000, and so on.

It was at this point that I met the children in the corridor and was faced with their question as to whether a million came next. I asked the children if I could photocopy their work, which they readily agreed to, and they were planning a way to get 'Miss' to let them finish after play.

At the end of the day I asked the teacher how they had got on. The teacher explained to me that both the children were 'stupid' and 'troublemakers' and that they were both unable to follow a task through, without fighting or causing chaos. I asked her what she thought of the work that they had done in the morning. 'Utter rubbish. I put it in the bin.'

Questions for discussion

1 What would you have done, or felt, as one of the children?

2 How would you react as a parent of one of the children?

3 What would you have done if you had been me? (A maths advisory support teacher.)

4 What would you have done as the teacher? (She was a supply teacher.)

−16− Children build a natural area and pond
Sue Atkinson

Age	7–9
Situation	whole class with teacher
Maths	real problem solving
Theme	the extensive range of maths; making maths meaningful

The school had undertaken a project to build a pond, and this was well under way when I talked with my class about what we might do for our problem solving activity. I was working on an Open University course at the time and, trying to be realistic, I decided to make the 'problem' the focus of the topic for the term. After taking a vote, 'making the natural area more interesting' came out as the favourite and the pond, although a separate project, became included in the work. I kept a diary of my observations throughout the term.

Brainstorming

We started with a brainstorming session, in which the children gave their ideas and these, in turn, were written down without evaluative comments. Much of my course was about encouraging teachers to stand back and let the children do the thinking, with the teacher as facilitator. Whilst agreeing with this philosophy, I could see that it was not going to be easy.

There we were in the first session, me armed with my large bit of paper and felt tip, and the children bubbling with ideas. Could I do this neutral writing up of everyone's ideas and keep myself from commenting? No, I could not. The children kept on asking me what I thought, and I was just too ready to tell them!

It was easily solved though. Wendy could write rapidly, so she and Amie became scribe and group leader, and I sat at the back and watched them in admiration as they threw out their ideas. They wanted to plant trees and bushes, grow flowers for butterflies, make homes for animals and generally improve the area to help in the conservation of the countryside, and also to provide a place for study.

Getting under way

Most of the things I had predicted did actually get suggested (so my own preliminary planning had been helpful) and the next day, with Wendy as scribe again, the children sorted out the ideas into a topic web (see Figure 16.1). The seven groups were plants, animals, soils, equipment, people, money, and rules. I intervened to get a balance within the groups, allowing friends to work together but also putting them in groups that would, I hoped, function well.

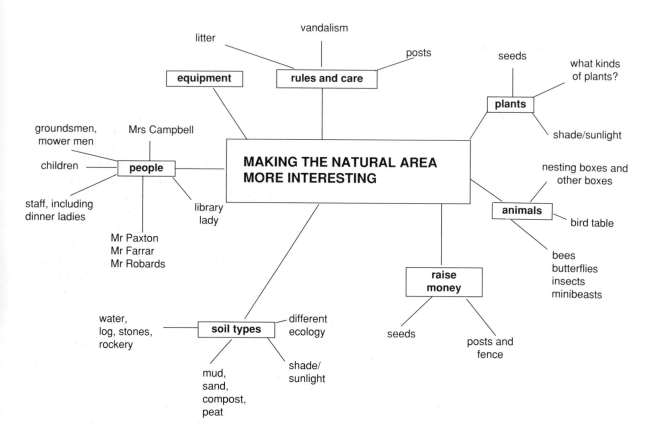

Figure 16.1 A topic web

By the end of the first week I was wishing that we had decided just to build a little garden instead of taking on an 80 metre strip of wild land! But the ecology books arrived from the library, gardening tools from homes, parents were offering help with plants and seeds, and there was no way I could stop the quite remarkable enthusiasm of the children.

The effects on the children

Some of the children were not too happy about the demands that the work made. Several needed a great deal of encouragement to work independently and to make their own decisions, then explain to the class group what they had done. I found story times and whole class times had to be more frequent than usual, and I had to do a lot of reassuring. On the other hand, Leigh and Jamie became incredibly bossy and tried to organise everybody's group. I realised that one sometimes has to discriminate positively in favour of girls in maths – or the boys might take over!

Going from whole class talking together, to small groups, then back to the whole class became the pattern for the work throughout the term. I thought that groups sharing their work in this way exposed the children to a very wide range of ideas.

How heavily should I intervene?

In trying to take more of a back seat I was watching my interventions very carefully, and realised that sometimes it is necessary to make heavy interventions. I had a problem getting the children to see that unless they actually did something quickly, they would never be able to implement one of their main ideas, which was to keep all the other children out of the area (it bordered the playground). They also needed to show the mower men the area which we wanted left to go wild. (The children had telephoned them.) Daniel had explained in a school assembly what the class's intentions were, but although the other children thought it a brilliant idea, it was hard for them to remember that this area was not for playing in. Christopher wanted a six foot wire fence around it, and I had quite a problem in scaling this down to something we could afford. I was perhaps more motivated to do this than the children were, having caught the mower man in mid-cut one day after school. My first wrangle with this tenacious and formidable man made me realise that speed and the odd heavy intervention might be called for to prevent the children's intense frustration.

A play-time raid into the depths of the games cupboard revealed a few assorted cricket stumps, so armed with these and a ball of string, a 'fence' was started. The effect was immediate. The five-year-olds stood in admiration as my class, rather bossily I thought, hammered in stumps, tied on string and announced that from now on, no one was to go in to the area without permission!

The 'rules' group came to realise the importance of politeness, and after a questionnaire was sent to each class, a very sensible list of rules was drawn up. My colleagues were incredibly understanding about the paramilitary way that this group patrolled the area and they brought their children out to the natural area for my class to explain what they were doing. This was very successful and I noticed how my class were functioning well as a whole group. They had a great sense of purpose, and those children whom I had worried about working out of my sight, were so absorbed in it all that, although fights did break out, they seemed to be about things like how big they could make the boggy area, so at least they were 'on task'!

Lack of money

The children decided that one of their biggest problems was lack of money to buy things like a buddleia to attract butterflies. They decided to hold a play-time sale of second-hand comics and toys. This was a major problem-solving event in itself and was very successful. The children then telephoned a local garden centre to see if they had a buddleia and one lunch time we went off to buy it. The staff at the garden centre seemed to find it amusing – me taking photos, the bags of coins to pay for it – and Christopher wanting to buy a gnome!

Once we returned with the buddleia (but not the gnome) things really started to happen. Parents said that they had never seen their children so excited about something at school, and I had never experienced such splendid parental support. One family brought in an enormous log from their garden, balancing it on a wheelbarrow.

The big log

The 'big log' became the favourite place for a group to retire to in order to 'sort something out', and it also provided us with shade. There were no large trees in the school grounds, so now with some shade available the children persuaded someone's grannie to part with some of her bluebells. But where should we put them in relation to the log so that they would be in shade? This led to some marvellous investigations and one group became so fascinated that they made a book about shadows, sun-dials and ways of measuring time.

I was astonished at the level of ecological understanding exhibited by the children. This was partly because of the good library books, but also because of very helpful parental input. One of the chief aims for the children seemed to be to get many different soil types represented. The children made good suggestions such as, 'If we have lots of different kinds of soil, then we will be able to have more kinds of plants.'

Someone gave us a huge piece of black plastic and the 'boggy area' was born. The soil mound left over from digging the pond was already colonised by certain plants so the fact that some plants liked specific conditions was easy to see. Someone donated two used 'gro-bags' of peat. A book about limestone plants led to the idea of trying to grow lime-loving plants.

The 'animals groups' planned a stony area for minibeasts, a bird bath, and a bird table (which Scott and his dad made one weekend). They also wanted to make a little house for animals in the snow.

110

The pond

My favourite time came when we began to concrete the base of the pond. 'The men' (some of the teachers' husbands) had decided that we needed 'two yards' of sand to do the job. This meant two 'cubic yards' and this was the signal for me to do some specific teaching on what a cubic yard was. We borrowed every metre rule we could find and a few rounders posts, and strung together two cubic yards. The children looked at them, and then they looked at the hole dug for the pond, a rather modest affair, and Alison, just seven-years-old said, '*Two* cubic yards seems an awful lot of sand.'

'Well, perhaps the men are wrong,' I said, 'I think they only estimated it.' There was a terrible silence at the thought that teachers' husbands could be wrong. Alison, a liberated child, was very quiet for awhile, then announced that her group would like to work out how much sand we really needed.

A question to one of 'the men' revealed that the concrete was to be four to five inches thick. It was no problem to find out how big the pond was, as groups had been drawing scale maps of it for the master plan of the whole area, but of course, these measurements did not give them the surface area of the bottom of the hole. It took a few days for them to solve that one.

All their efforts to try to represent the slope on squared paper failed. They were quite clear about their problem. 'When you draw a map of it, it will always be smaller,' said Amie. They then tried what I thought was a really remarkable idea. They made a cuboid out of centicubes about four to five inches thick, (all the transferring from metric to imperial measurements clearly worried me far more than it did them.) They explained to the rest of the class that this was as thick as the concrete and they were going to see how many times it would fit into the surface of the dug out pond. Listening to them explain why a scale drawing could not give them the information they needed because of the slope was almost the highlight of my teaching career.

They could see that their biggest problem would be the time that the measuring with their cuboid would take and how would they be able to mark the soil to show which bits they had already measured, 'String?' suggested Daniel.

So the next day they made a start on counting how many of their cuboids fitted onto the soil surface, marking where they were up to with string, but it was slow progress. When I was next aware of them they had moved from the pond and were working in the paved courtyard next to the classroom. When they explained their work I was forever converted to real problem solving as a way of teaching maths.

In the process of using the string to plot out the bits of the pond that they had already measured, they had realised that laying the string across the base of the pond would mean they could then stretch out the string into the size of the surface area. So they cut several lengths as informal measures and had taken these lengths of string into the courtyard, laid them down and drawn a large chalk oval that represented the surface area of the bottom of the pond. 'Our oval is bigger though because of the corners, so we will have to take a bit away,' said Amie. 'It's like when we did 3-D shapes at Christmas, you can't get the round bits, they get all scrunched up.'

They had remembered their abortive attempt to make a sphere six months previously and had been able to translate that experience into this work. They were quite confident that their method would work and I thought that despite its complexity, many of the other children were also following the thinking. This seemed to me to be the best maths I had ever done with children, but more was to come.

Using the courtyard

The group of girls waited behind as the other children left the room and begged to be allowed to stay in at lunch time. They wanted to change the size of their cuboid, 'because of the squares in the courtyard'. They wanted to make their cuboid into a cube that would fit a regular number of times into the paving stones in the courtyard. This involved an intriguing bit of division work, but when afternoon school started they were ready to get on with counting how many of their cubes would cover the pond base.

They needed 25 of their cubes for one paving stone, 'So we don't need to count all those middle ones,' said Wendy. They realised that they did not need to count all the whole paving stones in their oval, because each one would measure 25. They only needed to count up how many cubes fitted into the little odd bits at the edges of their chalked oval (see Figure 16.2), minus an estimate of 'the scrunched up bits'.

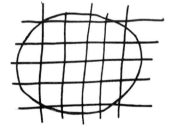

Figure 16.2

To cut a long story short, they worked out that one cubic yard of sand would be more than enough. They were a bit put out that two cubic yards were ordered! The smiles on their faces at the huge pile of left over sand after an evening of concreting was wonderful! Before nine o'clock in the morning they had got permission for the sand to be used to make a sandy area, and the theme of that day became how big the sandy area should be.

Money, again

Lack of money remained a perpetual problem – a good life skill to be learning – so for the summer fête the children decided to run their own games and use the money that they raised. Devising suitable games involved more maths in one week that I used to do in one term!

The most popular game involved throwing balls into a bucket propped up at just the right angle to make it difficult for the ball to stay in. If the ball did stay in, the prize was ten pence. Getting this game organised had involved hours of research into the most bouncy ball, the best distance

TB. 3.9   ~~SM 3p~~

~~AFB~~   BRB. 53.6

dropped from 1 metre

tennis	60cm	53cm	~~55cm~~	60cm	57cm	53cm	55cm	51cm	52cm	51cm	51cm
airflow	~~38~~ 40	35cm		47	40	34	33	31	35	40	42	40
~~lg sponge~~	40cm										
5m sponge	~~45cm~~	53 46	39	43	40	43	43	34	43	50	51
blue rubber	50cm		52	55	50	57	58	57	54	45	55	53

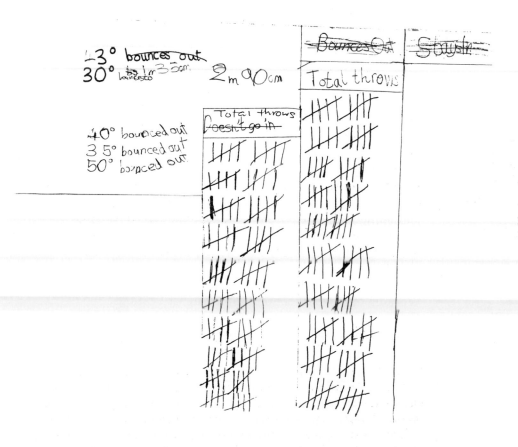

43° bounces out
30° bounces to 1m 35cm   2m 90cm

40° bounced out
35° bounced out
50° bounced out

Total throws / Doesn't go in

~~Bounces Out~~   ~~Stays in~~

Total throws

Figure 16.3 Children's recording of tests

for throwers, the best angle to prop up the bucket, and the probability of balls coming out. Similar maths was involved in the other games and the children recorded their results in their own way (see Figure 16.3 on previous page).

Scale maps

The scale maps the children worked on to plan out the different features of the natural area were criticised by other groups because they were 'too small to show the fence', so they had to re-draw them. The group that worked on the maps seemed to me to be using mathematical skills at a far higher level than I had been expecting. This seemed to be true for the whole term, for most of the children.

The following list shows the range of maths that one group encountered throughout the project.

Estimating the total money that could be raised.
Costing for each game in the fête – worked out from the probability of people winning.
Counting money, giving change.
Designing a rota of children available at certain times during the fête.
Finding the best angle for the bucket.
Making a rating scale of the best bucket angle.
Making a rating scale of the bounciest ball.
Measuring the height for the bounce of balls.
Finding averages of results.
Using a calculator.
Dealing with decimals.
Using a spirit level, clinometer, protractor, plumb-line.
Designing a 'fair' test.
Recording results on a table.
Working out percentages – for VAT purposes.
Comparing prices before buying.
Comparing discounts in percent.
Working out map directions and compass bearings.
Estimating the time in journeys.
Investigating shadows – movement of the sun – time.
Drawing up a balance sheet of expenditure.

This group also took on the organisation of the Grand Opening which included:

Planning the areas where classes were to stand.
Organising a length of ribbon for the ceremony.
Working out a timetable of events.
Calculating the mileage for the guest of honour's petrol money.
Calculating the cost of petrol per mile.

Other groups had similar wide experiences of maths, and in National Curriculum terms, these spanned most of the attainment targets, except algebra.

I had no idea that this work would have covered this range, or this depth of maths. It was obvious to me and the parents that the children were coping well with things like angles, averages and decimal points on the calculator. When the children needed to be taught a particular skill or concept, I did a straightforward exposition rooting what I taught within the 'real' problem that had arisen. Of course, there was a great deal of maths that they were only getting a glimpse of, and I would need to return to it at a later date to cover it in more detail. However, I was getting a clear picture of what each child understood, because they were having to think mathematically, and were not just manipulating numbers in a text book.

A profile of a slow learner

For my course, I had to write a profile of a 'slow' child, and Carol was my obvious choice. She had a 'thing' about maths – a maths block and was unable to count out reliably ten Unifix. She had severe orientation problems that showed up in 'mirror writing' and number reversals, and clearly somewhere along the line she had got lost in maths.

One of the biggest surprises of the natural area project was the amount of maths that Carol *could* cope with. In her 'diet' of maths for the term, Carol coped with large numbers (above 100), angles on a clinometer, division on a calculator, and adding up the 13 pounds from the playground sale. She could not manage any of this on her own – her problems were very deep – but I felt rather ashamed of the way that I had, up until then, confined her to such simple work.

Observing Carol carefully throughout the term, I detected considerable disinterest in the project at times. I decided that this was not so much that she found the project boring, or difficult, but that she was being successful and enjoying maths! Her disinterest was, I think, her way of retreating into 'I'm hopeless at maths and that is safe because you can expect nothing of me' which gave us a useful insight into her problems.

A profile of a bright child

Jamie would cope with most things. He was a confident and very able child. He could work out quite complex things, such as petrol money for visits to the garden centre etc., provided he had plenty of time. However, he sometimes surprised me. For example, he got incredibly bogged down adding up the fête money. I thought Jamie's recent experience in a very formal school became obvious, and at times he was at a disadvantage because of this. For example, he could do division on paper far better than the others, but in the 'real' situations that were arising, they could 'share' but Jamie was left confused, asking me 'what kind of sum is it?' This was a considerable shock to me. I regarded Jamie as one of the brightest children I had ever taught. That he was unable, many times, to see how to *apply* his knowledge was fascinating. It was so good to see his face light up on realising the significance of various things he 'knew' and it helped me to see that basing maths teaching on 'real' situations was a good way forward.

Conclusion

Writing this conclusion some years after doing the work, I know that I still feel, to some extent, insecure teaching maths in this way. However, I will not turn back from it, it has proved too beneficial for children and there are too many big issues at stake. The insecurity is partly due to the fact that it challenges me as a teacher. It isn't 'safe' to teach this way because it frequently surprises me and challenges my assumptions. It raises questions which I know I must try to answer if I am to go on growing professionally.

I recognised while doing this work what I intuitively believed, that this way of teaching gets the very best from children. Whenever I do this kind of problem solving, I get exactly the same reaction – enormous enthusiasm from children and parents and remarkable levels of achievement in maths from the children.

As my educational philosophy is founded on my respect for the child, to approach maths – and all the other areas of the curriculum – in this way, it is consistent with my belief. When the child learns, I learn too. It is by observing the child, by listening to her, by saying, 'What do you think, Amie?', that I am able to be co-learner, partner and explorer of our exciting world.

Implicit in this, is the much talked of belief that the child needs to be 'active' in her own learning. A great deal said about this in terms of 'child-centred' education seems to miss out the real corner-stone of this 'activity' – this co-learning and the importance of the relationship between the teacher and child. It is in my relationship with a child that I express my respect, my openness and my wish to try to stand in her shoes. By doing this I can draw out of her the intuitive 'home' learning that is shaping how she sees the world. This can then be built on, and her learning is secure and able to be applied in other situations.

This way of teaching is distinctively different from what many people seem to mean by 'child-centred'. I have an agenda, and make it quite explicit to the children. There is a curriculum to cover and a long-term aim in mind – the child as a confident mathematician and solver of problems. Sometimes I have to be very demanding of the children. Sometimes I have to intervene very heavily. I often have to give the children the language they need in order to express things in a mathematically accurate way.

It seems to me that this is the role that I play in the classroom in every area of the curriculum – it is not distinctive to maths. It is, I believe, a role that is part of true education – a drawing out. Not just drawing out of the child what she can do, but drawing out from the teacher too, within relationships in which, to some extent, all parties feel vulnerable. But that is the strength of working in this way. It is 'open' and 'real' in the sense that it mirrors good relationships within the 'real' world beyond school. That is why, demanding though it is, I choose to teach in this way.

−17− A young teacher starts off with maths with reason
Jenny, a primary teacher

Age	9–11
Situation	young teacher with whole class
Maths	fractions, division, 'activity' maths
Theme	text books leave huge gaps

Jenny works in a Primary School where all the teachers use the maths scheme in such a way that the children work on it individually. From the age of about eight, the children are encouraged to work without apparatus. What follows, is Jenny's own account.

I teach nine and ten-year-olds who come from a class where maths is taught entirely from a text book and examples on the board. This is nearly all what I call 'traditional' arithmetic, and my colleague in this class insists that by the age of eight the children should be working without any apparatus. We have lots of good discussions about our different approaches!

My colleague certainly can get children who are bright up to what she calls 'a good standard', and of course the parents really appreciate this.

Is is just a case of getting a 'good standard'?

I think that the 'good standard' hides some anomalies. Of course I want the children's work to be of a high standard too, but each year I find that the children I get from this class do not understand much of what they have been 'taught'. So each September, my intake – 34 children this year – is something of a challenge. There is, of course, a 'Cockroft seven-year difference' i.e. some children function like six-year-olds and some like thirteen-year-olds. I find that many of the children dislike maths and are extremely competitive about it. There is constant comment about who is on which book from both children and parents, and lots of parents buy their children the next book in the scheme to try to push them on.

I'm not against 'pushing' children. I expect the bright ones to do extra demanding tasks and I'm not at all against parents helping. I like to involve parents as much as possible. The trouble is that I find that children have 'done the book' but don't understand what they have done when asked to apply it, or even to explain what they have done.

Children do not sufficiently understand book-taught maths

The sort of thing that makes me feel that my thinking is on the right lines is an incident that happened the other day. Karen showed me that she could do long division. She could too! I gave her one to do and she got it right. She couldn't explain what she had done though, which I suppose didn't surprise me. Laura joined in and said she could do them too. She has special coaching to try to get her into a private girl's school when she is eleven.

But the odd thing was that I had been doing some mental maths with them that day and both girls, and several of the rest of the class, had real difficulty in multiplying numbers by 10! The other thing several children couldn't do was subtract 159 from 332 in their heads. They all wanted to write it down in the standard way! You would expect them to have more strategies than that for a relatively simple subtraction.

Laura and Karen are average ability nine-year-olds and should certainly have been able to cope with that level of computation mentally. They asked if they could write the subtraction down and I let them to see what they would do. All the children wrote it in the standard vertical form.

I asked a few children to tell me what they were doing. The said 'cross out the 3 and put a 1'. When I asked Laura and Karen why they had done that they did not know. Several others had the same problem. They could give no reason other than saying they were 'borrowing'.

Laura did this,
$$\begin{array}{r} 332 \\ -\ 159 \\ \hline 227 \end{array}$$
and Karen did this,
$$\begin{array}{r} 3\overset{1}{\cancel{3}}2 \\ 159 \\ \hline 253 \end{array}$$

and several other children made errors which indicated that they were not thinking about what the problem meant, and certainly not understanding it.

I get the general feeling that maths for them is more about learning *how to do something*, than about *understanding*.

'Laura isn't stretched enough'

Laura's mother often complains that her daughter 'isn't stretched enough', which worries me because Laura finds her work quite difficult! In the maths scheme she is clearly doing work that she does not really understand. Lots of the earlier stages seem to be missing. She lurches from page to page, constantly at my side asking 'How do I do this page?', 'Is it an add?', or 'Is it a sharing?'. It seems to me that despite all the 'pushing', many of these children actually achieve at a far lower level than I think they would if they were shown how to understand it first.

If I do the first few with Laura she is fine and goes away and repeats what I have shown her, but on a page of mixed problems she is all over the place. Today, Laura was trying to do some decimals. She was completely clueless about what 1.25 actually meant, so really I should take her back to earlier ideas. I can't take her off the scheme though because it is school policy that we do it in the junior department, and I do realise that with the National Curriculum, I need something as a structure, but as I'm such a young teacher I feel I have to keep quiet about my reservations about the scheme.

What can I do?

I am planning 'activity' maths twice a week and am integrating investigational things into that to try to build up confidence and understanding.

Sharing out the biscuits

I decided to start with sharing biscuits. It proved very successful. I made all the children wash their hands, and then got them to sit around tables in friendship groups. I said no group was to be smaller than 3 or larger than 6. I put a clean piece of paper on each table and put some biscuits on it so that each group had something that would take a while.

I said they had to divide out the biscuits fairly between everyone in the group and they were not to eat anything until they had done that and I had seen it and talked to them about it. I would then let them eat the biscuits, after which they were to draw a picture of what they had done in their group.

Some of the children who seemed from their book work to understand division and fractions got very confused. James said that 11 biscuits shared between 3 was 2 and 2 left over. The others wanted to share out the odd biscuits but he said it was 'a remainder' and they were to leave it. He can usually do maths really easily – he's on book 7 of the scheme, but he didn't want to admit that he was not sure what to do with those two biscuits!

It was fascinating how each group recorded what they had done differently. Figure 17.1 was typical of several children's work. They were quite unable to put down on paper what they had done. These two children had 9 biscuits between 2 of them. Figure 17.2 was also fairly typical of several children's work. This way of showing sharing is used in the text book. I thought it strange that this group of average-ability boys were unable to work out 21 biscuits shared between 5. They kept saying it was 5 each when I talked to them, but they had 5 pieces, not 5 whole ones.

Figure 17.1

each 5

Stewart

Figure 17.2

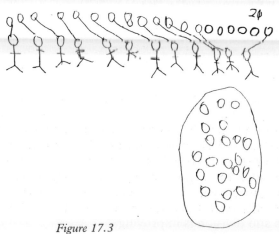

Figure 17.3

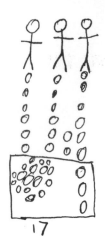

17

I started 17

Figure 17.4

Figure 17.3 on the previous was again an attempt to follow the methods of the text book. This child, and 12 others like him, could work it out with the biscuits, but he could not make sense of it on paper. I kept suggesting that he try a different method, but I noticed with lots of them that they thought they had to do it the 'right' way, the text book way.

Figure 17.4 shows how this group progressed. They first drew 17 biscuits, shared between 3 was 6 each. Then followed some fascinating discussion during which they worked out that it was 5 and two-thirds each.

Figure 17.5 shows 29 biscuits shared between 6 girls. They were fine on naming a half, but it broke down beyond this. The conversations of this group were remarkable as they tried to work it out to be totally fair. At one point they suggested that I could have some biscuit to have with my coffee as that would make the sharing easier! I thought this rather resourceful of them but politely declined.

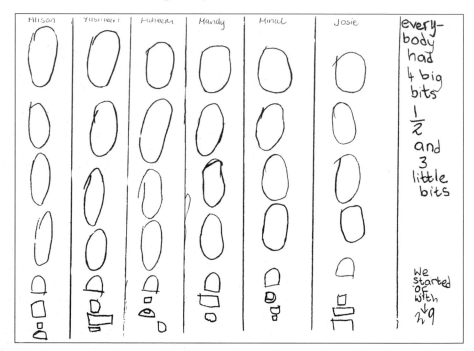

Figure 17.5

Conclusion

I think if I try to do this sort of maths about twice a week I will be giving the children some very good experiences which they wouldn't get just from the scheme. The discussions about the biscuits were the best bit. Just by looking at their recording you cannot see *the way* they arrived at what they did – the process of the thinking and all the talking. It was brilliant – the kids loved it and I definitely think that their work on fractions and division is improving.

$-18-$ Do they **really** know how to do it?
Shirley Clarke

Age	9–11
Situation	advisory teacher with a group
Maths	multiplication/problem solving
Theme	bright, text book taught children struggle with a task

In the previous chapter we saw how, although Jenny did not have much experience, she intuitively knew that, despite being well drilled in text book methods, the children seemed to have something missing from their understanding. In this chapter Shirley Clarke recounts a similar experience.

A teacher I was working with had spent half a term on multiplication working from a text book with his nine- and ten-year-olds. They could do long multiplication – the lot – and knew how to use all the four rules: division, subtraction etc. So where should he go from here? He asked me to take his two brightest children and to extend them. I set the two boys, Patrick and Andrew, a problem, to see how many 2p coins would cover the top of their table. I expected that they might use their multiplication knowledge in this situation. The fact that they did not seem to see that the problem involved multiplication flabbergasted their teacher. In the end, they proved to themselves that multiplication is repeated addition, but reading this account you will see why knowledge of text book multiplication seemed to leave these bright children with the inability to solve a simple problem.

I gave the boys three 2p coins, and asked how many would cover their table top (a standard half-metre table). Their agreed estimate was 175. Ten minutes later they had produced the work illustrated on the next page in Figure 18.1. By 'jumping' each 2p coin over, they had found how many fitted along each side. After some discussion Patrick asked for a calculator and put in 19×40, while Andrew did the sums shown overleaf in Figure 18.2.

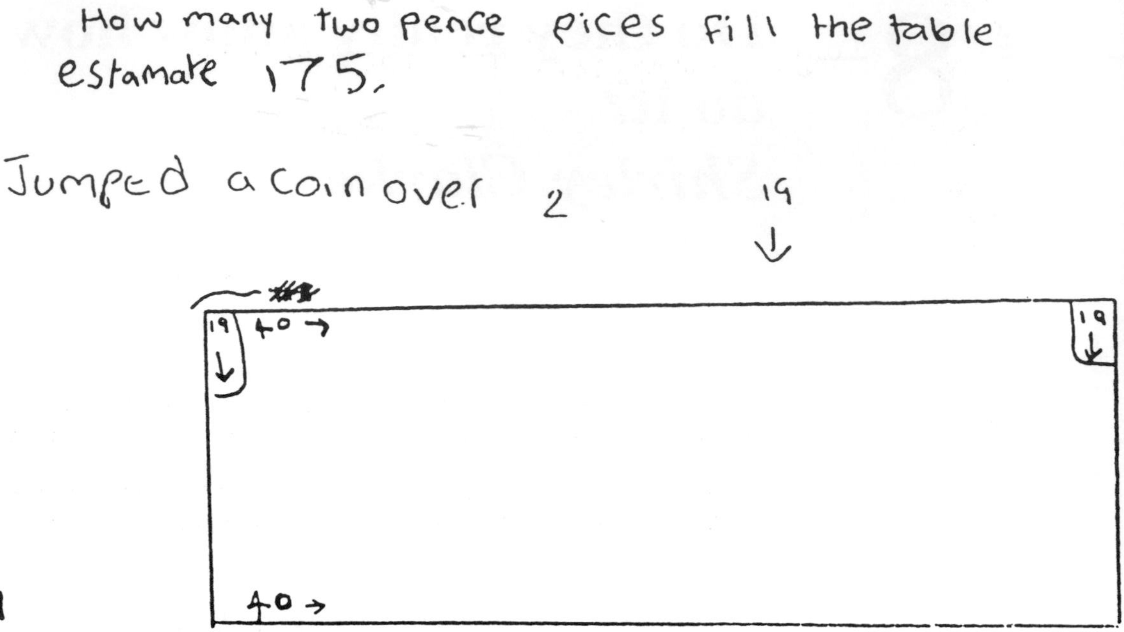
How many two pence pices fill the table
estamate 175.
Jumped a coin over 2
19
19
40 →
19
40 →

Figure 18.1

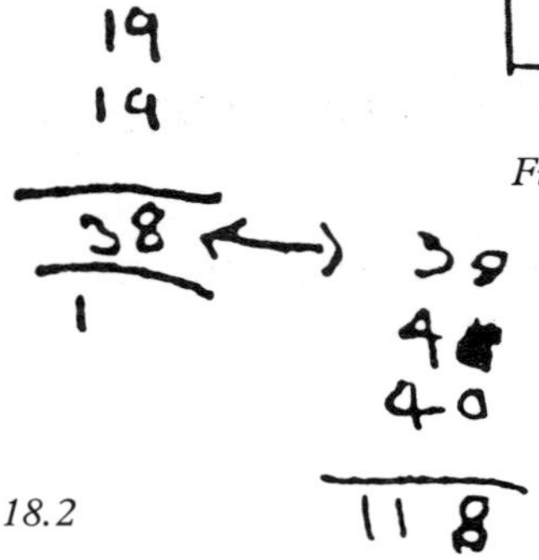
19
19
38
1
38
40
40
118

Figure 18.2

I asked how they were getting on. 'I thought 19 × 40 would be how many go all round the edge, but it's not. Andrew's made it 118.'

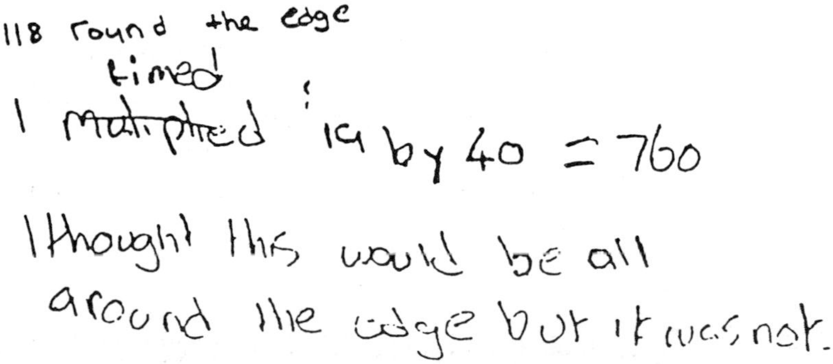
118 round the edge
I ~~multiplied~~ timed 19 by 40 = 760
I thought this would be all around the edge but it was not.

Figure 18.3

'We've got how many go round the edge, so now we're going to work out how many go all round inside that, then the line all round inside that and so on until we've covered the table.' (see Figure 18.3)

```
188
114
110
 96
 92
 88
 84
 80
 76
 72
 68

 64

 60
 56  ·5
 52
 48
 44
 40
 36
 32
─────
1304
```

I took 4 away from the last result.

Figure 18.4

They decided the next 'perimeter' would be 4 less than the first 'because there are 4 corners.' A long list of these was made, 4 subtracted from each number, then totalled on the calculator. See Figure 18.4.

The boys were not happy with this result. 'It can't be that many.' I suggested they find another way of solving the problem so they could check the answer (Figure 18.5).

we got a metre sticka mesuredthetable.

Figure 18.5

Having done this, they sat blankly staring at the table and the metre stick. More discussion together and they wrote (Figure 18.6):

we need to find a different method to make sure itisright.

Figure 18.6

Large sheets of paper were requested, which they taped to the table. They drew a line along the bottom of the table, the width of a coin. A second line was then drawn along the side of the table, also the width of a coin. I imagined this would be continued until they could count all the squares, but they seemed dissatisfied with this method. They wrote (Figure 18.7):

we coverd the desk with paper and drew squaes on it but it did not work because the lines would'nt go strait and the paper was not completly covering the table.

Figure 18.7

For the next five minutes the boys entered various sums into the calculator. (Figure 18.8)

$$19 \div 40 \qquad 40 \div 19 \qquad 40 \times 19$$

Figure 18.8

They seemed to have an instinct for the numbers they needed, but no clear idea of what they should do with them or why. They began to look distressed, then told me they were stuck. Their feelings were that they had lots of answers but didn't know which was right. I asked if they could tell me how they would place the coins on the table if they had lots. They said they would go all round the edge, then inside that, then inside that and so on, still obviously committed to this method of covering the table. I asked if there was a different way they could place the coins. After much thinking Patrick said, 'In rows' and then from both Patrick and Andrew a second later 'I think I've got it now'. Another list of numbers appeared. (Figure 18.9)

40
39
40
39
40
39
40
39
40
39

Figure 18.9

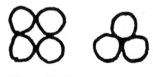

Figure 18.10

'The first row has 40, the next 39, then 40, then 39 etc.' they explained. 'If you put coins exactly on top of one another they leave a big gap, but if you put the coin above in between the two you cover more space.' See Figure 18.10. They then decided (Figure 18.11):

We aregoing to count rows andwe decided to use the most amount of paper as possible. The first row has 40 in it the next row has 39 in it. *Figure 18.11*

But how many rows of 40 and 39? This was the next dilemma. They decided it probably would be more than 19 because you may have space at the top of the table for another line. There seemed to be no way of finding this out without lots of coins, so a decision was made to go back to coins on top of one another. A list of 19–40s appeared. Andrew dictated the string of 40s while Patrick entered them in the calculator. This proved to be disastrous, as they keep losing one another, and had to restart. After three attempts they abandoned the calculator and combined pairs of 40s to make 80s, then pairs of 80s to make 160s, with an 80 and

Figure 18.12

a 40 left over. These numbers were successfully entered into the calculator with a total of 760. (Figure 18.12)

'That's what I did at the beginning', said Patrick. We looked back at what he had done. They were now confident that their answer was correct and told me they had added up 19 40s. 'And 19 × 40 is the same', said Patrick. They had proved to themselves that multiplication is repeated addition! (Figure 18.13)

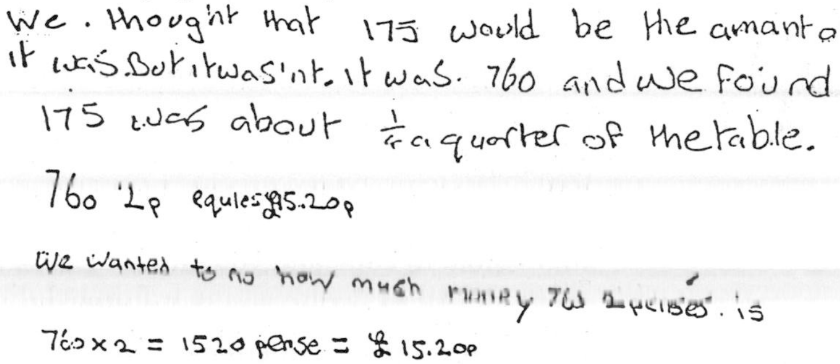

We . thought that 175 would be the amant of coins
it was But it was'nt. it was. 760 and we found that
175 was about ¼ a quarter of the table.

760 'Lp equles 85.20p

We wanted to no how much runiey 760 2ycises. is

760 × 2 = 1520 pense = £ 15.20p

Figure 18.13

'I wonder how much money that is' said Andrew. After asking them to write a comment about their work, I left them to it.

This article first appeared in *Investigator*, a newspaper devoted to promoting an investigative and problem solving approach to the teaching of mathematics. *Investigator* is published through SMILE, and this article is reproduced here with kind permission of the SMILE Centre. For more information about *Investigator* and other SMILE publications, contact the SMILE Centre, Isaac Newton Centre for Professional Development, Lancaster Road, London W11.

—19— Teachers talk about schemes

(a) Staffroom conversation – *Two middle school teachers*

(b) Teaching maths without relying on a scheme – *Moira Proudfoot*

A   Staffroom conversation

Age	all ages
Situation	two teachers talking
Maths	fractions; multiplication; division; written problems; investigations.
Themes	the advantages and disadvantages of working from a scheme; the need to keep maths active

Two teachers who work in a middle school, where maths is taught mainly from a scheme feel that the advantages of having some sort of scheme are often lost by teachers wanting to work the system where 'every child works at their own pace'. This is what they said:

- It sounds right – children working at their own pace, but it hides many problems.

- Children queue endlessly – so many are stuck that it is almost impossible to cope and you end up giving inadequate explanations so that you can deal with all the waiting children.

- Maths stops being something active and tends to become more passive with an emphasis on 'doing the page' rather than understanding the concept.

- The importance of language and the use of apparatus can tend to get lost using a scheme.

- Children ask questions that require in-depth explanations. I jotted down every question I was asked in a space of five minutes this morning. Six questions were about classroom administration, and five were about the content of the maths.

These five were:

1 Anna just did not understand her page of fractions. It was the third time she had been up to me. She could not see how to colour $\frac{3}{4}$ red and $\frac{1}{4}$ blue. Then she had to write $\frac{3}{4} + \frac{1}{4} = 1$.

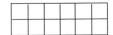

Colour $\frac{3}{4}$ red

and $\frac{1}{4}$ blue

Write $\frac{3}{4} + \frac{1}{4} = 1$

2 I could not answer Anna in any depth because I was working with David who could not see how to do a subtraction with Dienes, because he could not understand exchange. He thought the act of exchanging was part of what he was taking away.

3 Shakoar said 'I can't do these kind of sums. Are they times?'

$$4)\overline{0.96\ m}$$

$$5)\overline{6.80\ m}$$

4 Brian came up and asked 'What does this word say?' pointing to 'tessellate'. I explained quickly, then he went off and I could see that the was trying to do a tessellation with circles.

5 Elizabeth could not understand a 'problems' page. She had more or less successfully done four pages of subtractions but when it came to problems embedded in words she was totally unable to cope.

● That was all in five minutes. You can guess the sorts of replies that I was giving. I was saying how to do it, not explaining what it meant.

● I spent a lot of the rest of the lesson with Elizabeth trying to sort out what the questions meant. I sat by her. Of course there was a constant stream of questions from other children but at least I sorted Elizabeth out.

● Minal will be on that page soon. It would make much more sense to have these children in groups so that our efforts were being used more economically.

The two biggest weaknesses of this system

1 It is a waste of teacher time.

2 The children are not understanding in depth. (On a fractions section, you just about get a child understanding when the next page is shape. It would make much more sense to go on with fractions so that you obtained deep understanding.)

The advantages of a scheme

1 The children work on their own and free you to do other things (theoretically).

2 You have a structure to the maths which you need if you are not a maths specialist.

3 You hope that the bright children are catered for.

What can you do in a school where you must use a scheme?

The big question seems to be: How can you take the advantages of a scheme and make it work better in the classroom? Some teachers think it is better to see the scheme as back-up. Some would rather do some whole class work – there are lots of starting points that all abilities can cope with. Some think it is possible to link that to ability group work for some of the time.

Conclusion

- A scheme is a tool, not the master.
- Schemes can help to ensure that children follow a progression.
- They give practice in computation.
- Used *after* activities, they help to consolidate concepts.
- Used well they can build up confidence.
- Used badly they put the emphasis on 'doing the page' rather than the maths
- Used badly they can make maths into a solitary and silent activity when it should be a 'doing and talking' activity.

B   Teaching maths without relying on a scheme

Age	7–11
Situation	teaching head
Maths	investigations and setting tasks verbally
Themes	'real ' maths without using a scheme; helping children to develop their own methods

Moira is a head with a full teaching commitment. She writes here about her experiences during a year on secondment, and also of her work with seven- to eleven-year-olds in Primary Schools.

I have always enjoyed all forms of mathematics. During my schooling I was fortunate to have maths teachers who believed in allowing their pupils to work from first principles rather than by rote learning. We worked out tables for ourselves, saw the repetition, and then learned the significant numbers. Thus it was natural for me in my own teaching to consider presenting maths to children without using a scheme.

Not all teachers appreciate that this is 'real' maths. While on secondment, I spent many hours with a class of eight to nine-year-olds. I remember being delighted with the children's work. They had been thinking for themselves and I was pleased with their progress. When their teacher came back to take over her class, I heard her say 'Now it's time for *real* maths: get out your work cards and maths books.' I had a good laugh about this but I feel that this shows up a considerable problem. Many headteachers, teachers, governors, parents and even children see maths as something that comes out of a text book. This is a very false and narrow view of maths. Personally, I don't think you can do maths justice if you just work from a scheme because:

- it makes it boring;

- it can show only one aspect of maths – the content – but we must go for the processes too – the thinking; and

- children are held up if they cannot read the page in the scheme, but if you toss out ideas, it's all verbal and the child who is slow to read but mathematically able can do very well and develop a positive attitude to maths.

Using investigations and problem solving

In one school where I taught children aged between nine and eleven, the children came to me from a class where maths had been taught rigidly from a scheme. I found many of them had a very negative approach to maths. I tried to interest them by putting investigations in boxes around the edge of the room. When their other work had been finished, they could then choose an investigation. This element of choice helped to create a more positive feeling in the class. The children enjoyed the activities, and often became so involved that it led to class discussions. Gradually the children realised that often the maths problem/investigation had many answers – not only one right answer. For example, there are numerous ways of costing a residential visit, a class picnic, and a tuck shop for sports day. All would provide reinforcement of the four rules of number, and be much more exciting than a page of sums.

Gradually, as the children got used to this more open-ended way of working, and the idea that there often is no one right answer, I began to integrate investigations into the maths within the classroom. This formed a base for mathematical topics which did not rely on a scheme.

As a teaching head in a village school, I still use investigations as a start to a topic. I also have a couple of afternoons a week when I toss out ideas to the children. During a discussion, they are encouraged to voice their ideas before working practically on the problem. I try to get *them* thinking. So, for example, I might ask them what they think will happen when they throw two dice – will any numbers come up more than the others? When they have said what they think will happen they have to say *how much evidence they will need to prove their point.* So in this case the question would be how often would they need to throw the dice to prove their point?

If I was doing shape with seven-year-olds, I would ask them to tell me which of the shapes they think might tessellate. Which shapes would they use to cover a floor? If they think triangles, I would ask, 'Will any triangle tessellate?' 'What about circles?' If they say they will not tessellate, I ask, 'How could they adapt the circle? What could they add or take away from the circle?' I have used this way of working with children from about age seven, and I think that they enjoy maths enormously working in this way.

Why I use investigations

- Investigations tend to reinforce maths skills that the children have already learnt.

- They create situations in which you can clearly see what a child can do, and how far they understand it. They are good guides to a child's level of knowledge, and help the teacher with assessment and future plans.

- They provide starting points for a child to explore. It stops maths just being about right and wrong.

- It makes maths fun.

- It emphasises the child's own method. For example, James uses a rather slow process for multiplication (see Figure 19.1). Although I will help him to make his method quicker, at the moment he is secure with this method. It is *his* method, *his* thinking.

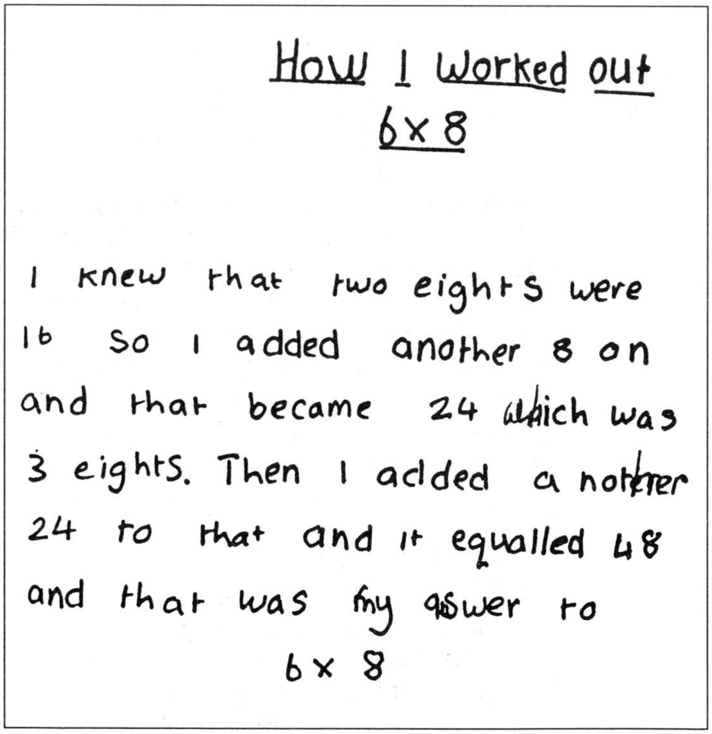

> ## How I Worked out
> ## 6 × 8
>
> I knew that two eights were 16 so I added another 8 on and that became 24 which was 3 eights. Then I added a nother 24 to that and it equalled 48 and that was my aswer to 6 × 8

Figure 19.1 James' method of multiplication

This emphasis on the relevance of maths and allowing children to develop their own methods is basic to my approach. By giving the thinking over to the children in this way, they become much more ready to use their own methods and become secure and confident with maths.

−20− I'll do it my way
Sue Atkinson

A Rachel explains her method

Age	9–11
Situation	individual in class
Maths	subtraction/place value
Theme	children's own methods

Rachel (aged eleven) was fed up being told by her teachers that she did her subtractions 'wrong'. She complained at home of being told off and told to 'start with the units'. When asked to explain her method for 372 take 187, Rachel said, 'I start with the hundreds. I wouldn't write this one down, it's too easy, I would just do it in my head. It's 372 take off 100 that's 272, take off 80 is 192, then take off 7 leaves 185.' (see Figure 20.1).

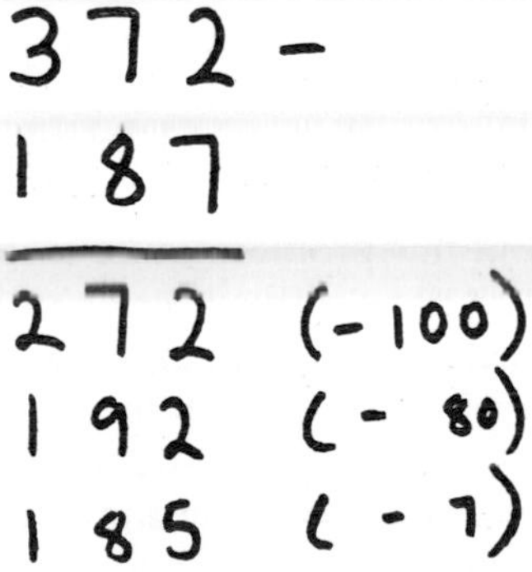

```
 372 −
 187
─────
 272  (−100)
 192  (− 80)
 185  (− 7)
```

Figure 20.1

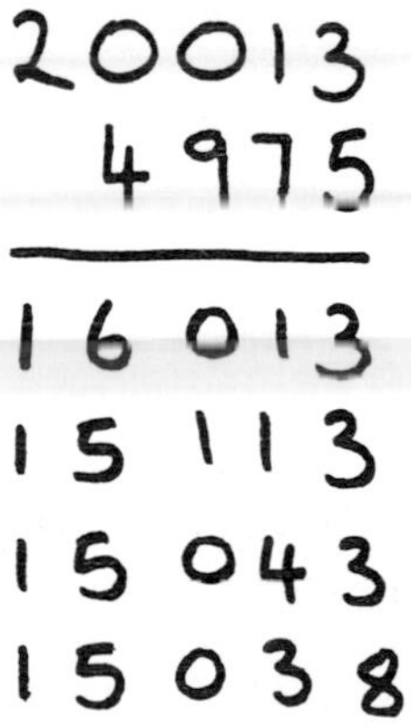

```
 20013
  4975
──────
 16013
 15113
 15043
 15038
```

Figure 20.2

When asked to explain a harder one she wrote the sum shown in Figure 20.2. It is the same as her mental method i.e. she first subtracts the 4000, then the 900 etc.

B   Alex explains what she does

Age   9–11
Situation   individual in class
Maths   subtraction/place value
Theme   children's own methods

Alex   I take a hundred, so that leaves 2, so that gives me 17, I have to take one of those and make this 12, then I take 7 from 12 is 5, 8 from 16 is 8 and 1 from 2 is 1.

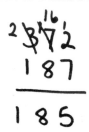

Figure 20.3

Adult   What were you really doing when you were crossing out the 17 and putting 16?

Alex   I was taking a ten from the 17 tens and exchanging it into 10 units so that I had enough units to take away the 7. (see Figure 20.3.)

C   Sabrena records in her own way

Age   7–9
Situation   individual in class
Maths   problem solving
Theme   children's own methods of recording

Sabrena (aged eight) was calculating how much milk we would need for our three-day residential visit. She was well below average in her maths attainment, but found this problem quite easy to solve, despite the fact that it used maths at quite a difficult level for her.

She brought a cereal bowl and a pint milk bottle in from home, and worked out that one pint was enough for five bowls of cereal. Her recording (Figure 20.4) shows how she worked out how much milk was needed for three days. Her recording shows a mixture of types of tallies; it was entirely her own invented method.

Another child worked out that six pints of milk would be needed over the three days for cups of tea. Then Sabrena set about finding out how much all the milk would cost at 21p per pint.

At first Sabrena was confused with her piles of plastic money, but then she put it out in sets of 21p, two 10p coins and one 1p coin. She then

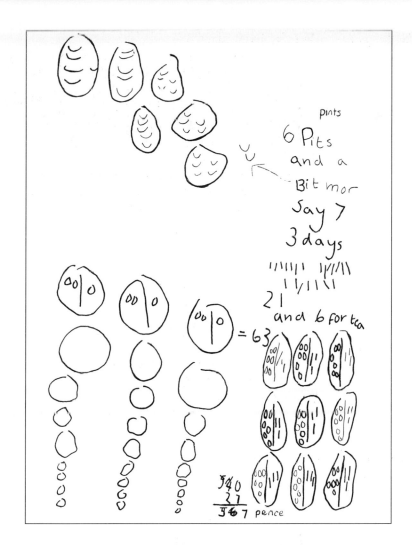

Figure 20.4

started to record her work (Figure 20.4) because, she said, 'I might forget what I have done'. She could see a real need to record. Then she said, 'This is too much drawing' and shorthanded her method by drawing sets of 63p. I was impressed at her place value understanding.

This use of sets became a strong feature of Sabrena's maths, and other children in the class adapted it whenever they needed to multiply. It was fairly easy, a few months after this, to develop Sabrena's multiplication skills using her own recording as a sound basis. She was soon able to multiply securely.

−21− Real 'real problem-solving'
Owen Tregaskis

Age	9–11
Situation	whole class
Maths	'real' problem solving
Theme	the effectiveness of maths teaching from real problems

In this chapter, Owen Tregaskis looks at real problem solving in school and describes a project undertaken by him in a junior classroom.

The term 'real problem solving' has been introduced to primary schools but has a wide range of meanings. To some teachers a 'word problem' is considered as being 'real' even though it has no relevance to the children (e.g. Tom has £2 to spend. How many 35p bars of chocolate can he buy?) It reflects the children's lives, but is not personal to them. To many other teachers questions like 'Where is the best site for a local airport' is considered real, but here again children are not personally concerned with the outcome. These types of problems or simulations are a vital part of our maths teaching but I want to argue that they need to be seen as additional to real problem solving which involves children's *real* lives and actually brings some change to those lives.

I want to describe a real problem which was solved by a group of children, and then outline some ideas about real problem solving in our classrooms. (This problem-solving work owes much to the Open University course 'Mathematics Across the Curriculum'.)

Sports day

I asked my class of 32 nine- to eleven-year-olds for ideas to improve the school. The ideas ranged from 'Burn it down' to 'Longer playtimes' and 'Swimming every day'. Many children suggested a sports day and this seemed the most popular suggestion, so our real problem solving project was born. Over the next month the children worked on this problem using some of the maths lessons, but mainly playtimes and odd moments during the day. The children had the satisfaction of solving a problem and seeing how maths could help to produce a more satisfactory solution. The main differences in this real problem solving and those outlined above are in the ownership of the problem and the role of the teacher. This was a problem which was about the children's own lives and, when solved, one which would change their lives.

Role of the teacher

The traditional role of the teacher is to set children problems, dictate the method of solution and then tell the children if they got the right answer. In real problem solving the teacher's role is one of helper or facilitator. The teacher helps children to clarify what the problem is and supports children's efforts at finding solutions. The answer is correct if the children agree that it works in practice

In this instance, the children organised and ran a very successful sports day, which therefore means that they came up with the right answers. Right from the initial brianstorming sessions, the teacher had to take a role which helped the children to solve the problem but not input any ideas. Most importantly I felt that I must not veto such ideas as 'motor-bike scrambling', or 'horse racing', because such a veto would take the problem away from the children. On the day of the sports I gave myself the role of photographer and was far too busy to solve any problems for the children.

The teacher, therefore, is vital in order to give the children the necessary mathematical skills and to help them develop social skills.

Mathematical skills

The children had used the skills of brainstorming and sorting ideas by creating a topic web before this particular project, but they were now given a real situation in which to practise these skills. After about one week of working in sub-groups, each sub-group working on one branch of our topic web, I felt that the children were getting frustrated because of lack of experience in organising a sports day. I then stepped in and proposed a 'mini-sports day' which would last for ten minutes one playtime and have very simple refreshments. This is really the mathematical process of simplification used in a practical situation.

The group working on refreshments were given plenty of practice in the traditional arithmetic and graph-making skills. A survey of local shops had been made and it was established that the cheapest way to buy crisps was to buy a box of 48 packets. The problem was to decide which flavour to buy. Catherine made a graph of the children's favourite flavours (Figure 21.1). From this graph Catherine found that the favourite was 'sausage and tomato'. Unfortunately, Catherine did not like sausage and tomato and what is more, she suspected that other children did not like them as well. She tried another survey: 'Do you like sausage and tomato crisps?' She found out that eight children did not like sausage and tomato. Try again. 'Which crisps do you not like?' Here, Catherine gives everyone two chances to name flavours that they do not like (Figure 21.2). The result is a graph to show that sausage and tomato flavour is the favourite, but also the most disliked. Bacon flavoured crisps are the least disliked and so this is the flavour to buy. Catherine, and the rest of the class have learnt that the most important thing about carrying out a survey and making a graph is to ask the right questions.

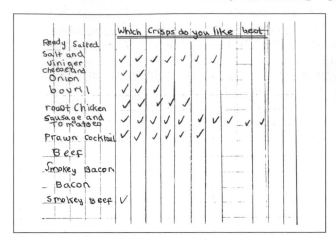

Figure 21.1

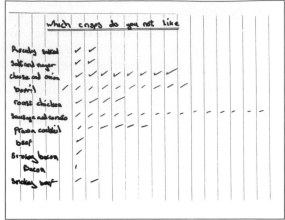

Figure 21.2

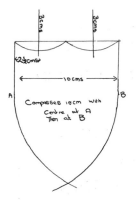

Figure 21.3

The group concerned with the prizes decided to make a shield for the winning team. The problem came when they wanted to draw the curves at the bottom. I suggested that a book on heraldry might help. They found out how to use a pair of compasses to draw the curves (Figure 21.3). Later on, when the group working on drawing out the course for the races wanted to make a staggered start, I sent them to see how the prizes group had solved the problem of drawing a shield. Both groups began to realise the usefulness of drawing arcs to produce a line or series of points at a constant distance from a given point. Imagine the delight of the children, when the groundsmen came to mark out the course, to see adults using the same method that they had invented for themselves (Figure 21.4).

When the men marked out the football pitches they used a piece of string to make circles. one man held the string the end was tied to the marking machine.

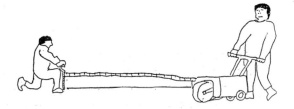

Figure 21.4

The groundmen, on the other hand, were a little put out by the children's request for a running track of 37 metres. Twenty-five or 50 metres made sense, but why 37? The children had been concerned that everyone should have a fair chance in the race so the slowest runner had been asked to run as fast as possible for as long as possible. This distance was 37 metres and so, to be fair to everyone, this had to be the distance of the race. Once again, the important thing about maths is the question you ask in the first place.

The pricing of the refreshments caused a few problems in arithmetic. Much experiment and long division was required to prove that more profit could be made if sweets were bought in large packets and repackaged for sale than if the children made their own sweets. Frances (a good mathematician) produced a very elegant long division sum to

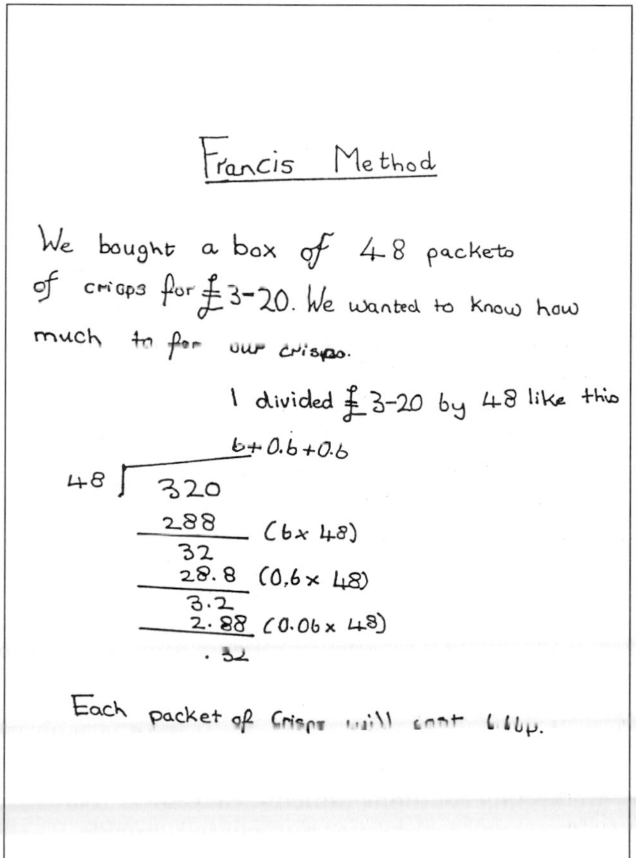

Figure 21.5

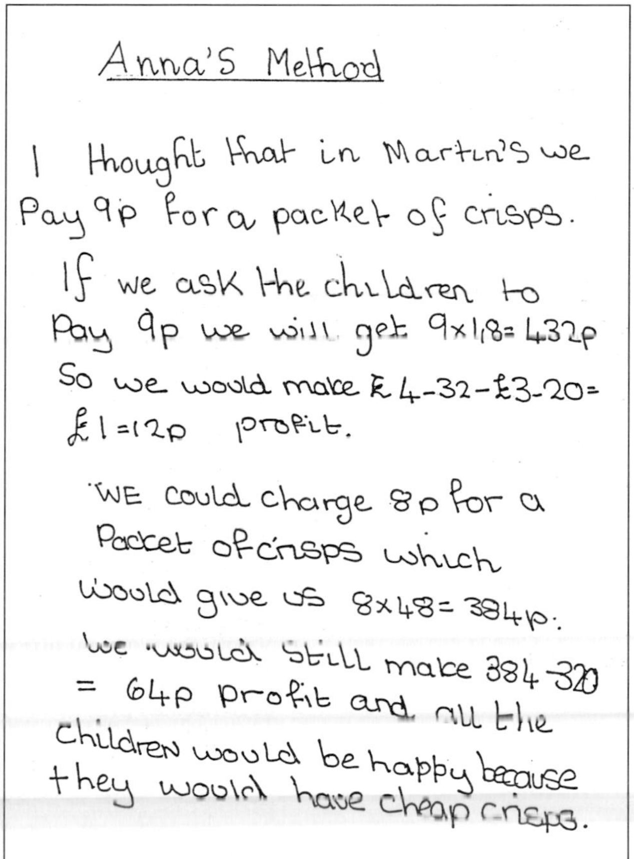

Francis Method

We bought a box of 48 packets of crisps for £3-20. We wanted to know how much to for our crisps.

I divided £3-20 by 48 like this

$$6 + 0.6 + 0.6$$

$$48 \sqrt{320}$$
$$\underline{288} \quad (6 \times 48)$$
$$32$$
$$\underline{28.8} \quad (0.6 \times 48)$$
$$3.2$$
$$\underline{2.88} \quad (0.06 \times 48)$$
$$.32$$

Each packet of crisps will cost 6.66p.

Figure 21.6

Anna's Method

1 thought that in Martin's we Pay 9p for a packet of crisps.

If we ask the children to Pay 9p we will get 9 × 48 = 432p So we would make £4-32 - £3-20 = £1 = 12p profit.

WE could charge 8p for a Packet of crisps which would give us 8 × 48 = 384p.
We would still make 384 - 320 = 64p profit and all the Children would be happy because they would have cheap crisps.

find what we must charge for a packet of crisps (Figure 21.5). She came up with the answer of 6.666p and did not know what to do with the answer. Anna, not such a sophisticated mathematician used trial and error to produce a much more understandable answer (see Figure 21.6).

Language and social skills

Although the children were working in groups to solve parts of the problem, I brought the class together to enable each decision to be

139

agreed by the whole class. This gave the children plenty of practice in putting forward arguments and in voting. Many of the debates became heated and we became involved in looking at various methods of voting (multiple votes, transferable votes and especially when a vote became really important, secret voting). The writing of rules for some of the games stretched the children's writing skills, especially as the rules had to be written for the parents (who were invited to act as starters, judges etc.). Cooks and dinner ladies were pressed into acting as readers, to make sure that the rules could be understood before they were printed and sent out to parents.

Real problem solving and the National Curriculum

The National Curriculum states that pupils should use maths in real life problems. The Non-statutory Guidance, which has been written to provide a reference for teachers in planning and implementing the National Curriculum, tells us how important employers see the need to teach children how to use their maths effectively. The Guidance continues to suggest that applying maths does not come easily to many pupils and, 'For this reason, pupils, at all stages, need to have experience of tackling "real life" problems as an integral part of their experience of mathematics.' (Non-statutory Guidance, National Curriculum Council, 1989 D4, Section 2.2.)

Finally

This was a major project spread over many weeks, but real problem solving need not be on such a large scale. There are many classroom tasks involved with storage, tidiness, ease of access etc. which can be tackled in a single afternoon. I have found it important to involve the whole class as this ensures that more mathematical skills are introduced. Last year, while working with a class of ten-year-old children, we worked on the scissor problem. Each group of children discussed and produced a list of uses of the scissors and problems of storage, care etc. The whole class voted on the order of importance of the problems. Back in groups, solutions were suggested and these voted on by the whole class.

Larger problems can involve parties, educational visits, assemblies or activities at playtime. The most important aspect to create in the classroom is an atmosphere of awareness of the problems around us and confidence on the part of the children so that they can solve the problems. If the children are finding solutions difficult, they know that the teacher is there to help them with techniques but will not provide suggestions as to possible solutions.

−22− Does maths with reason work?
Nick James

Age	9–11
Situation	advisory teacher with a class
Maths	fractions
Theme	attainment in maths, maths with reason tested over time

Throughout this book we have shown how children can achieve at high levels when they are taught in a way that makes maths have a reason, and where doing *and* talking *comes before* recording.

Here, Nick James tells the story of two girls he worked with when making the Video for the Open University Course 'Developing Mathematical Thinking'. The story now has a fascinating sequel because Kelly became the first woman engineer to graduate from her college – a real success story for a child who was failing in her education.

The girls, Kelly and Samantha, both then aged nine, were in a classroom where do, talk *and* record *was the basic framework for their learning of maths. The class was doing a topic on fractions, and had worked on several specific examples of activities that embodied the concepts involved in the naming and equivalence of fractions. This was done so that they would gradually develop a growing awareness of the underlying sameness of the concepts.*

One morning, Kelly came to school really mad.

'We had sausages last night for tea! There are five of us in the family and there were eight sausages in the packet. Do you know what Dad did?! He gave us one sausage each, then he cut the remaining three into halves, gave us one half each and… then he ate the remaining half!'

Clearly she had another view of how to share out the sausages! This was the problem we watched Kelly and Samantha solve on the video extract.

Figure 22.1 shows Kelly's record of her solution; an operation which Samantha performed on eight sausages on a plate nearby.

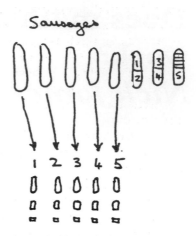

*Figure 22.1 Kelly's record of how she would share out
eight sausages between five people*

There is nothing particularly remarkable about this drawing until you listen to the discussion which followed between the two girls and their teacher, Geoff Adams.

> 'One of these little pieces is one fifth of half a sausage.'
> 'That's a tenth of a whole sausage, because the other half could be cut into ten as well!'
> 'Yeah!... so one-fifth of half a sausage is the same as one-tenth of a whole one!'

This was particularly interesting because nobody had ever spoken to these girls about multiplication of fractions, but they seemed so secure about the naming of fractions that the above truth was self-evident. And what about this next conversation? ... all the more surprising since addition of fractions, improper fractions and the notion of lowest common denominator had, likewise, never been explicitly mentioned!

> 'So each person gets one whole sausage, a half of a sausage and a tenth.'
> 'That's one whole and six tenths... so each person gets sixteen tenths!... of one sausage.'

As if that's not enough, Samantha suddenly announces:

> 'This (a fifth of half a sausage) is a sixtieth of the whole packet because there are six sausages in the packet. Oh no... it's one-eightieth because there are eight sausages and each one is cut into ten pieces.'

Nobody in the class has ever looked at fractions like 'eightieths'. Their concept of naming fractions is being transferred to a novel situation. Later the girls go on to explain that...

> '... each person gets one whole, five-eightieths and one-eightieth of the whole packet of sausages... that's sixteen-eightieths each!'

And this is all the more remarkable when I tell you that the head teacher was just about to have Kelly and Samantha referred to special schools because they had 'learning difficulties!' He had to go immediately and withdraw all the paperwork he had done!

Two years later, I was in the same classroom as Kelly. We were, for some reason which escapes me now, trying to find a fifth of ninety-five. Said one pupil, 'Oh you need to split ninety-five into fives!' 'No you don't,' said Kelly, 'You have to split it into five!' The teacher and I then stood at the side of the class for the next thirty minutes whilst Kelly proceeded to convince the class why it was splitting ninety-five into five and not fives.

Only the letter 's' separates the two statements. The answer is the same in both cases, but there is a world of difference in the actual processes being used ... only Kelly's process is correct in this context. Setting the mathematical niceties aside for the moment, the significant thing about this anecdote is Kelly's retention of the concept. How often have you found yourself saying, only a few weeks after spending considerable time in class on a particular concept, 'But we've just done the naming of fractions! Can't you remember?' or, at the start of a new academic year, saying, 'Didn't last year's teacher do fractions with you?' Well, here is Kelly, two years down the line, and she still has all the confidence and clarity of understanding on the matter, not just to remember but also to convince all her peers.

The suggestion in the National Curriculum Proposals is (DES 1988) that the most able ten per cent of pupils might be expected to attain Level 6 or higher at age eleven. Yet these girls, thought by some at one stage to be low attainers and at the very opposite end of the ability spectrum, were achieving these levels at the age of nine plus. It's my experience that most fifteen-year-olds cannot operate with fractions like these nine-year-olds and certainly most pupils seem to need constant revision because retention is so low.

I therefore leave you with the wonderfully exciting possibility ... taught to work investigatively, as we've described it, and then encouraged to transfer these thinking strategies to the formation of concepts conventionally listed in syllabuses using programmes of study exemplified by do, talk and record activities, might not these below-average pupils in fact achieve Grade 1 in their exams? Will those low attainers not become high achievers? And what of any set of national criteria in the subject – given the teaching approaches explored here, might not the achievement of any attainment targets become purely academic?

This chapter is based on an extract from *Investigative Approaches to the Learning and Teaching of Mathematics*, an unpublished paper by Nick James.

-23- Whole-school approaches to maths with reason
Sue Atkinson

Age	3–11
Situation	whole school working together
Maths	aspects of the entire curriculum
Theme	maths with reason as a whole school policy; working with parents; discussion starters

Here we look at how teachers have tried to work together to develop a whole-school approach to the teaching of maths. By 'whole -school approach' we mean a policy agreed by all the teachers, so that the approach to maths is consistent throughout the school. This policy is not static but in a continual state of revision and reformulation.

One of the many ways that schools can start to review their maths policy is to have some sort of maths event such as an evening meeting with parents, or a workshop session to make some games with both children and parents. One school had a teachers' meeting in which they brought every bit of maths apparatus out and looked at it to see what was there. It was found to be a source of renewed enthusiasm for practical maths. Other schools have other approaches and we will outline a few of them.

A small-scale maths activity afternoon

One school planned a maths afternoon before an evening meeting at which they were going to talk about their maths policy to the parents. Every teacher put out maths activities tables and every child did maths in some form or other throughout the afternoon.

For the younger children, aged between five and seven, the different apparatus that was available included:

- polydrons;
- interlocking cubes and other small construction apparatus and puzzles;
- Lego, including technical Lego and motors;
- bricks and other large construction toys;
- a table of playhouse material, designed to help children count, match and sort;
- games which involved shape, counting, logic, place value, money etc. and a variety of strategy games;
- water and sand trays for capacity work;
- sewing, cooking, woodwork; and
- role play within the playhouse, such as shopping (with paper and pencil for writing, and a calculator).

The older children, aged between seven and eleven, were split into three main groups. One group worked with the headteacher in the hall, using two computers, exploring number patterns, and working with LOGO. The two other groups had a variety of mathematical activities that the children were currently using as part of their on-going topic and maths work. These included:

- each child doing a detailed plan of a picture as the basis for a tapestry;
- sewing patchwork cushions using a variety of templates, squares, hexgons, etc.;
- scale drawings and maps;
- strategy games and other mathematical games;
- maths puzzles and investigations;
- working on a time-line as part of the historical aspects of the class topic; and
- various aspects of practical maths which were a part of the on-going work in the class, like finding the volume of 3-D shapes and gathering data for a database to be put into the computer.

Organisation for this maths afternoon was simple and the parents expressed how much it helped them to be able to observe and join in, then to talk about it in the evening discussions.

A large-scale maths afternoon

Another school planned a large-scale maths event to take place all afternoon throughout the whole school. Each class teacher planned with her children a few mathematical activities, and parents and ancillary staff were each allocated a group. Other advisory support teachers and students from a nearby training college, were brought in to help. Some of the activities involved the children all afternoon, while for others they took turns in groups.

1. One group made a chequerboard garden.

2. All the water trays were taken outside and different aspects of capacity and volume work, floating and sinking, and other science ideas were explored.

3. Several groups were engaged in cooking for the 'cafe'.

4. Others, helped by some parents, ran the cafe, providing refreshments throughout the afternoon taking and counting the money.

5. A local college lent computers and a turtle, and several groups worked on LOGO.

6. Children took it in turns to play calculator games.

7. In the hall, the PE apparatus was set out for groups of children to act out *Bears in the Night* (Berenstain and Berenstain, 1972). In this story words like 'under', 'around', 'over', 'through' and 'down' are explored in story form, thus making the mathematical words clearly understood.

8. Some children ran stalls, as in a fête, taking money in payment for games they had devised.

9. Some children had planned large-scale drawings and games on the playground drawn in chalk. During the afternoon, parents supervised them painting these in various colours.

10. In another room, a large selection of maths games were available for parents and children to play (many made by the children).

11. Some of the older children had puzzles and investigations to show to, and often dumbfound, parents.

12. In one room typical workcards and worksheets were laid out, along with appropriate apparatus.

Parents were invited to walk around the school, looking at the variety of maths activities going on, and to join in where appropriate. Each teacher had put up a small notice by each activity, explaining its mathematical content and value. Everyone enjoyed the afternoon, and it led to very interesting parent–teacher discussions about the maths curriculum.

Parents work with teachers

Making games for a 'maths library'

In several schools, parents have worked with teachers to produce mathematical games and activities which their children can borrow and take home. These games are kept in a library at school with a card-index system.

Schools which have operated this system find that children enjoy maths, and parents appreciate the amount of involvement it gives them with their child's learning. For the children, it helps to integrate school maths with home maths.

Maths gardens

Schools with space have found it very beneficial to build a 'garden' in which mathematical ideas can be explored in lesson time or at playtime. This might include concrete shapes, a small raised pond (for water investigations rather than fish), gutters set in concrete for testing speeds of boats, a pendulum, and various slopes and inclines for testing speeds of toy cars. This can be built in several stages (see Figure 23.1)

Maths trails

Trails can be as simple as sending children around the school to look for, say, rectangles, squares and triangles, or can be much more complex involving the local environment beyond the school grounds – the streets, shops, fields, houses, in fact anything that will involve the children in searching and observing. Some of the sorts of questions might include:

1 Name the shapes on the nursery climbing frame or in the structure of the school roof. Try to build this shape with a construction kit.

2 What is the height of the big tree? How could we find out?

3 Why does the shadow of the netball post move around? Does it move in the same way every day?

4 Which shops in the high street are used the most frequently?

5 Could we fit everyone in the whole school into the big yellow circle on the school playground? If not, could we draw a circle big enough?

School maths policies

School maths policies are often thought of as a written document, whereas often the real policy is what actually goes on in the classroom – often less to do with anything written, and more to do with *attitude*. It is

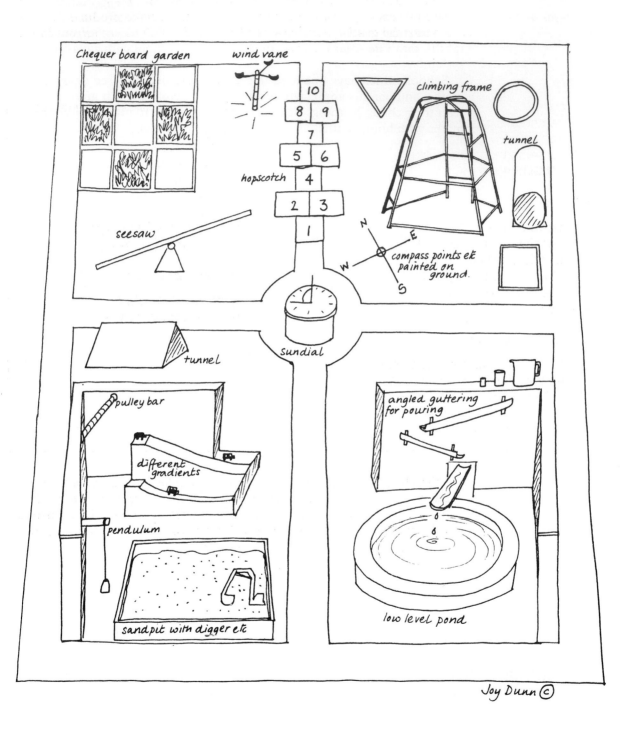

Figure 23.1 A maths garden

not so much *what* you teach, although of course this is important, it is *how* you teach it.

Headteachers and maths co-ordinators work with their colleagues and parents to set up a way of approaching maths within the school that will develop the crucial 'positive attitudes' (see Figure 23.2) as set out in the DES publication *Maths from 5–16*.

A   FACTS

1. remembering terms
2. remembering notation
3. remembering conventions
4. remembering results

B   SKILLS

5. performing basic operations
6. sensible use of calculator
7. simple practical skills in maths
8. ability to communicate maths
9. use of microcomputers in maths activity

C   CONCEPTUAL STRUCTURES

10. understanding basic concepts
11. relationship between concepts
12. selecting appropriate data
13. using maths in context
14. interpreting results

D   GENERAL MATHEMATICAL STRATEGIES

15. ability to estimate
16. ability to approximate
17. trial and error methods
18. simplifying difficult tasks
19. looking for pattern
20. reasoning
21. making and testing hypotheses
22. proving and disproving

E   PERSONAL QUALITIES

23. good working habits
24. positive attitude to maths

Figure 23.2

One helpful way to review the policy is to take an area of maths, say shape or number, and for everyone to work at this aspect of maths. One school took six different maths topics and worked on them for a fortnight each throughout the term, with regular discussions that were therefore focused on the real issues in maths education.

Section C   Practicalities and ways forward

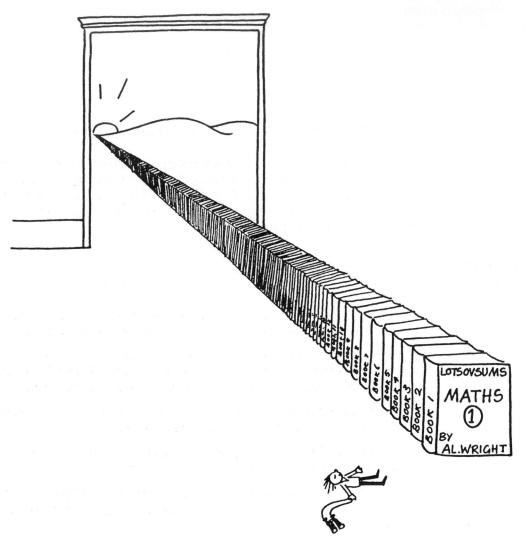

Joy Dunn ©

$-24-$ Starting off
Sue Atkinson

I THEMES: starting points; adult role; discussion starters

In the previous section we have suggested some starting points for maths with reason. For instance, you might like to try 'planning a picnic', p.75; 'building a natural area', p.107; or 'explode a number', p.91. If you work this way, you may have some surprises. This section explores some of the things that might happen.

What can I expect?

- You will not necessarily feel total success first time! You may find it particularly hard learning to stand back and let the children do it.

- Bright children who have been used to getting pages of ticks rather easily, find this more demanding way of working difficult. They are not always the first to 'see' a way to do it and this is hard for them.

- You will need to take care that your interventions are not so heavy that you are telling the children how to do an activity.

- You may well enjoy this approach more and get more from it if you have a parent or a colleague in the room with you.

- Learn to work *with* the children, and try the investigation yourself too. You are the role model for the children; they may be very unsure what you mean by 'investigate it'.

Useful pointers

1 The aim is more to get children to explore possibilities than just to 'get a right answer'.
2 Teachers should try to make the mathematical thinking processes of

maths *explicit to the child*. The different processes are shown in Figure 24.1.

Specialising Manipulating specific examples to see the underlying pattern and to gain confidence.

Generalising Once the pattern has been seen, attempts are made to explain it. What is it that is the same about each of the specific examples?

Conjecturing Verbalising your generalisations. Posing a possible explanation for the pattern.

Verifying Explaining *why* your conjecture is valid, not just for your special examples, but also in general.

Figure 24.1 Mathematical thinking process

3 Teachers often find some sort of 'rubic' helps them to give some structure to this investigative work (see Figure 24.2). Some teachers put this rubic up on the classroom wall and get the children to refer to it.

STUCK! It's OK to be stuck – use it as a time to gather your thoughts together.
I KNOW... What is it that you know?
I WANT... Where are you trying to go?
TRY... I've got an idea.
CHECK Always check everything you do.
REFLECT What were the 'key moments' in solving the problem?

Figure 24.2 Rubric to help mathematical thinking

- The word 'stuck' is particularly useful. It is much better than saying 'I can't do it.' 'Stuck' is a temporary state and children are encouraged to unstick themselves without the intervention of the teacher. This gives them considerable independence and improves their confidence and self-esteem.
- Children are encouraged when stuck to say what they want and what they already know. Usually it makes the situation clearer to think it through in that framework.
- It makes being 'stuck' part of the normal experience of mathematicians. In classes where this is made a part of the ethos of the class, children do not laugh when a child makes an error. Everyone gets stuck. It's important to show that the teacher gets stuck too!

4 The children should be encouraged to:
  - look for pattern;
  - say 'What if I... ; 'Would it be the same if ...';
  - explore – to 'play with it'; and
  - see the 'human sense' in maths – it can be used to solve real problems

5 The children should learn to put their own meanings into their work. Because there isn't a 'right' way, they will more readily apply their intuitive knowledge of maths to the situation.

Investigations and the National Curriculum

It is assumed in the National Curriculum that children will be working on investigations. More than that, though, the whole approach of the National Curriculum is *investigative*.

There is often some confusion between the terms 'investigation' and 'problem solving'. Figure 24.3 illustrates the distinction.

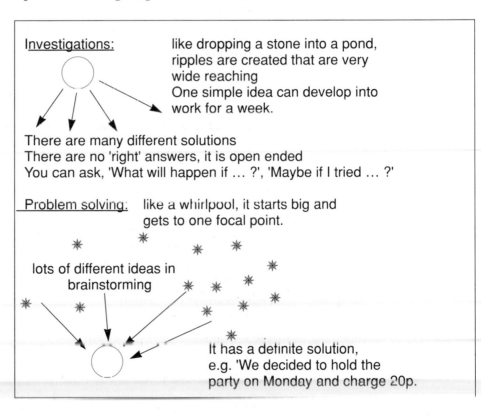

Figure 24.3 Two types of good maths

But the mathematical thinking processes and strategies are the same for both types of maths.

Hints for successful investigations

- Give a choice of investigations whenever possible.

- Give investigations *verbally*, as this tends to help children. The discussion is particularly important when children are new to this way of working.

- It is often a good idea to set aside a whole afternoon for maths activities.

- If you want to start with your whole class, it works well to choose a 'real' problem that everyone will be interested in, e.g. planning a party. If you want to start with an investigation, choose about six investigations of varying types, i.e. spatial, number, puzzles, etc., and read these out to the children as well as having copies that they can come back to later. They can then get into groups, choose an investigation and try it out.

- In the early stages it is important to let children change their minds about what they want to do.

- If you have been used to working in a way where you tell the children exactly what to do, or if you have children who are rather unwilling to think for themselves, be ready for some insecurity to show itself. They *don't know what you are expecting of them* – be patient!

- Investigations where a pattern can be built on the table with Unifix or interlocking cubes can be helpful, as in the making of the patterns you can encourage the children to talk about what they are doing. You can also see who can build the next pattern and who is having difficulty.

- Try to have activities for children to fall back on if interest flags, or you get very involved with one group. I use strategy games 'Ways to win' (p.172), polydrons, interlocking cubes etc. The shape investigations in 'Shape Workshop' (p.173 – one of the Manchester Polytechnic books) fascinate children of any age.

The adult role

- You have an important role to play as *encourager*.
  'That's really good, Jasmin.'
  'What a good idea!'
  'Did you see what Sarah was trying?'

- Keep the atmosphere positive.

- Try not to be 'Big Boss', but silly behaviour needs to be jumped on! Working in this way requires a thoughtful working atmosphere.

- End lessons by sharing ideas. Have a class discussion and let groups explain their work *if they want to*. Do not pressurise. At this early stage – this talking is *a vital parts of maths with reason*.

–25– How can I organise myself?
Sue Atkinson

THEMES classroom organisation; record-keeping; children evaluating

General organisation

- After just a few investigation sessions you will have a great deal of paper! Keeping an investigation folder for each child for loose work is one way that teachers deal with the variety of sizes and types of paper in use. It can go on to the next class and a progression in work can be seen.

- Children can design their own folders. Give them the dimensions of the finished article – to fit into the cupboard, box or tray – discuss what it *must* have, like a clear name, and flaps to keep the work in. They are then challenged to design an envelope by folding. They can use rough paper for a trial design. The finished product could be covered with mathematical designs.

- I use a box to store the folders. This makes it easy for children to put their own work away.

- Put out a choice of investigative work for children to choose from that will move the focus of maths away from a scheme and make it enjoyable and less competitive. This selection of work can also include language tasks like cloze and crosswords, etc.

- Gather together all the maths resources that you can find and split them up into files of the different areas of maths. So, if a child needs more work on, say, area, it is readily available.

- Make maths apparatus easily accessible in the classroom. Label shelves or drawers so that everyone know where everything is kept.

- End lessons with *everyone* tidying *everything* up!

- Reserve a special place to keep any 3-D work. Small classrooms may need to have extra shelves.

- Make a maths investigation board and encourage children to put up their own work, or to use it to pose problems for the rest of the class. This board can include the 'rubric' (shown on p. 152) to help maths thinking.

- Make specific maths displays so that maths is seen as a vitally important part of classroom life.

Planning

TOPIC DATE			
Exposition			
Discussion child/child child/teacher			
Practice and consolidation			
Investigations			
Problem solving			
Games			
Relevant practical			
Maths across curriculum topic			
Technology and information technology			
Mental maths			
Cooperative group work			
Aesthetic pattern design			
Evaluation			

Figure 25.1 Planning chart

- You may find it helpful to use the chart shown in Figure 25.1 to plan work. This shows the elements of a 'balanced diet' in maths, (developed from the Cockroft Report and *Mathematics 5–16*). The chart helps to check that over the term, the children are receiving a balance of teaching.
- The chart can be used for long-term plans, perhaps half a term, and also for weekly/fortnightly plans.

Children evaluate

- Gathering all the children together sitting on the carpet is an important aspect of my maths teaching. These are times to evaluate, to look at the next stage and times when everyone's ideas go into the melting pot – often a time when children will get their own ideas for future work.

- This will only work if there is an ethos in the class of mutual support, where everyone respects everyone else. Saying that you do not understand must provoke the reaction, 'Can I help you?' It must never provoke a laugh or a put-down – a frighteningly common feature of children in the more competitive environment.

- Planning and working on a balanced maths diet in this way, children are very naturally involved in their own evaluations of their work. Using a maths diary is one effective way to do this.

A maths diary

This is simply a notebook, that can replace the traditional squared maths exercise book, in which an entry is put most days by either the child, teacher or parent. I use a diary in combination with a loose-leaf folder as this gives me maximum flexibility. I also make special little books that may reflect class project work or a specific maths topic, for example 'My book of sharing', 'Colour maths', or 'Roman maths'.

Some pages from Alex's maths diary are reproduced here (see Figure 25.2 overleaf). Everyone becomes involved in the maths diary, part-time support teachers, classroom assistants, parents, and the headteacher. Children as well as adults can be encouraged to write evaluative comments, so that the diary has a much wider purpose than just a straightforward maths exercise book.

Record-keeping

Basic day-to-day record-keeping can be focused in a maths diary. In addition to this, your own notes can include jottings of interesting things, gaps in children's understanding, areas covered, and observations etc. I put these notes on a class list on a clipboard, then each half-term or full term, the child's diary and my own notes can be used to write a half-page 'maths profile' of a child for their record folder. These are my comments about Alexander (aged eight):

Alexander has made good progress this half-term. For a few weeks he found it hard to see that '3 groups of 4' did not mean 'a group of 3 and

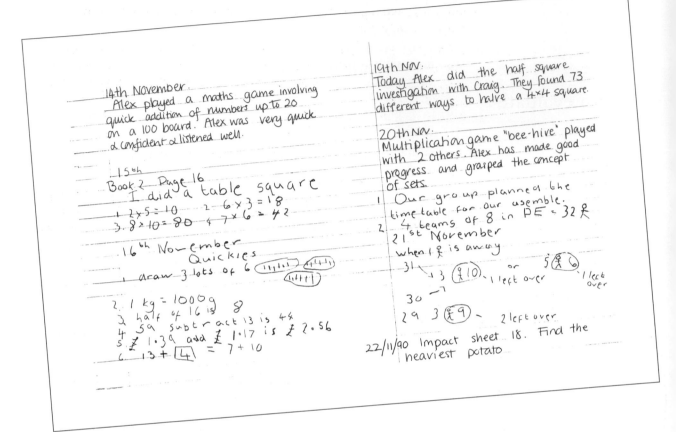

Figure 25.2 Extract from Alex's maths diary

a group of 4', but he has grasped this concept now. He has covered work on multiplication and money, and in IMPACT he has worked on shopping and weighing. He is much more confident these days and willing to discuss his work openly in class. He continues to work well in a group, and understands problems clearly and enjoys solving them.

Alexander's recording of his work is clearer, and he is now more prepared to try things in his own way. He enjoyed the challenge of finding ways to shorthand '3 sets of 4 makes 12 altogether'. He is becoming more systematic in investigative work.

Alexander likes learning tables and his mother is helping him. They have a tables chart for his bedroom wall.

He is becoming increasingly confident with the calculator, and seems to be clear about the '+' and '-' signs. He has learnt the multiplication sign, and calls it 'sets of', or 'times', and uses it well in calculator activities, but this needs consolidating.

Alexander is enjoying his IMPACT sheets, and most have been returned this term. He has a great deal of home support.

The key issues for any record-keeping system are:

- it must be simple and concise;

- you must like the system and develop it for your school or your cluster of schools;

- it must show not only work covered and the level of attainment in National Curriculum terms, such as a simple tick list would show, but it should also show the child's attitude to maths, their confidence etc., as we have discussed throughout this book. (This latter point relates closely to New Attainment Target 1, and to the issues of confidence etc. addressed in this book.)

- it must be clear to parents, readily available to them and include their comments.

Some schools are developing this aspect of maths record-keeping along the lines of Liz Waterland's (1985) circles used for reading (see Figure 25.3a). Other schools are developing similar ideas, but using a brick wall (see Figure 25.3b).

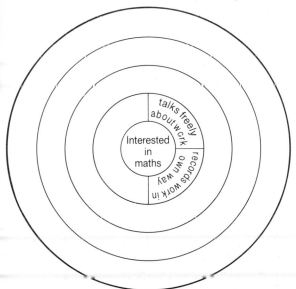

Figure 25.3a Concentric circle record

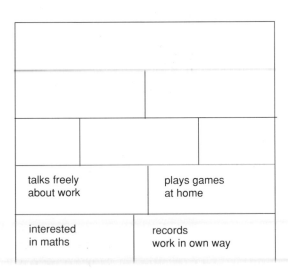

Figure 25.3b Brick wall record

Examples of some of the sections of the circle, or 'bricks' of the wall for reception children might be:

- interested in maths;

- talks freely about work;

- able to record work using own 'writing' and pictures;

- approaches tasks confidently;

- relates 'home' and 'school' maths;

- engages in maths activities at home;
- able to 'see' and describe a simple sequential pattern;
- uses own symbols for words;
- uses own symbols for numbers;
- uses standard symbols for numbers;
- uses a calculator;
- understands addition with small numbers;
- understands subtraction with small numbers.

Many of these would clearly be appropriate at later stages also.

—26— How do I develop my confidence?

| THEMES maths panic: maths from picture books; parents and teachers working together; discussion starters

Parents and teachers working together

1 Talk about the 'blob tree' (see Figure 26.1 overleaf). Who can you identify with when it comes to maths? Sometimes this helps people to identify their feelings about maths.

Do feel you are falling off! Do you just need someone alongside you? (Not everyone may want to share their feelings in a group, of course.)

2 Discuss Figure 26.2 – 'Panic about maths'.

3 Have a special maths games/activity time once a week – perhaps Friday afternoon while all the tidying up is going on.

4 Look at your needs together and decide on priorities. Is the class so big that help is needed in small groups? Does the water play need an adult there to do some language development? Do the bright ones need some special help? Do you need more storage space?

5 Think of starting some simple home/school maths games or worksheets, see p. 147. Start small, then review it.

6 Could the PTA raise money for some special maths or technology/construction equipment?

7 Many schools have invested time and money in making maths games and this has proved an excellent source of confidence boosting for both children and adults.

Figure 26.1 The 'blob tree'
(Reproduced from Games Without Frontiers *with the kind permission of Pip Wilson, this book, published by Marshall Pickering, contains other group ice-breakers and ideas from getting groups thinking. The book is available by post from Romford YMCA, Rush Green Road, Romford RM7 0PH.)*

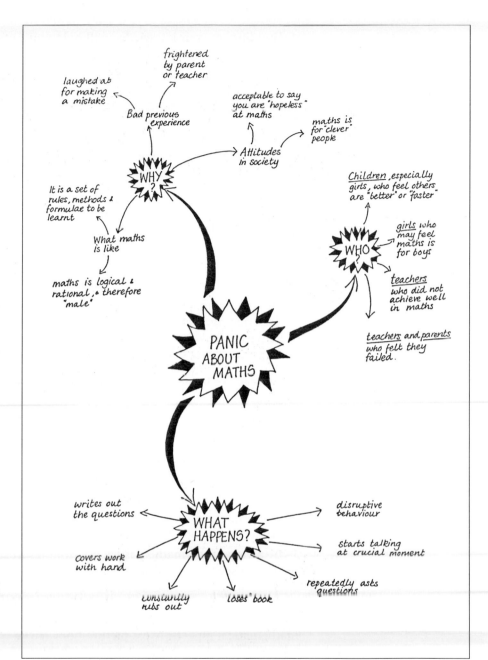

Figure 26.2 Panic about maths
© Sue Atkinson and
Joy Dunn
(developed from
'Genderwatch'
SCDC)

For teachers

1 Try out one of the ideas from the teachers' stories in Section B.

2 Observe what is already going on. Where are your real needs?

3 If you find it too threatening to have parents in the room while you do maths (and for lots of teachers this is the case) then think how you could involve parents to benefit the children.

4 Building up your knowledge will help you to feel more confident. There are two aspects to this:

(a) Good classroom resources for ideas and starting points.

(b) In the long-term you will need to build up your 'craft knowledge' of what you are doing in maths and about the processes of mathematical thinking.

There are some very good and easy to understand packs and courses available and these are listed on p. 173.

5 Ask someone to work with you. It does not have to be someone confident with maths, just someone who is willing to work alongside you and support you as you try to improve your practice.

For parents

1 Do a mathematical activity with your child where you feel confident like cooking, gardening or DIY. Think how you could develop this activity. Does she need more help with reading weighing scales, or with measuring distances? Could you find recipes, or some gardening that he could do entirely on his own?

2 Build up a collection of mathematical games. Plan to play them two or three times a week – rather like the way you help with reading.

3 Don't focus on 'sums'! Try to broaden your child's view of maths and boost his confidence.

4 Give out a positive aura. Don't say 'I was no good at maths so I don't suppose you will be either'!

5 Get a good book to help you.

6 Ask your child's teachers what you can do to help. Tell them you do not feel very confident! They probably don't either!

7 Be aware of the mathematical possibilities in story books. Once you start to see them, you will be hooked!

Of course, the child entering into the magic of the book is the crucial thing, but at the end, as well as discussing the story, try to think of the mathematical aspects. Most picture books have considerable mathematical content. Don't just count things, but think of all the position, measuring and quantity words that your child needs for maths, for example, 'between', 'through', 'under', 'around', 'heavy', 'more than', in', 'out of', 'grew', 'enough', 'became smaller', 'late', as well as words for probability, such as 'probably', 'might happen', 'chance', and 'impossible'.

Here are a few examples of questions you could use after reading *Dogger* by Shirley Hughes.

Where do you think Dogger was when he was lost?

Do you think Dave thought he had a good chance of finding Dogger again?

How much are the hats at the fête?

Many familiar stories are good for sequencing events – a vital skill for secure maths understanding: *The House That Jack Built*, *The Enormous Turnip*, and *Jack And The Beanstalk*.

Some quotes from parents

'I panic about maths. As I am talking to you now my heart is pounding. I had to learn lots of the formulae for exams just when I was going through adolescent traumas, and I just couldn't cope. Now, if maths is mentioned, I go all hot and cold. I cannot help my own children, because I panic as soon as they tell me the problem. I want them to understand, not just be told to learn it by rote... Most of all, I don't want them to panic like I did.'

'I coped with maths quite well until I was eleven and went to Grammar School, and then it was all xs and ys, and I didn't know what they were talking about.'

'I wasn't any good at maths, so I don't suppose my child will be either.'

'They do things like cooking at school, and lots of practical maths, but now she is seven, I want her to get on with some real maths.'

'I don't want my child to suffer what I went through. I want her to enjoy it and understand it.'

'You're failing my child. She is four, in the nursery, and she doesn't know her tables yet.'

'My child needs *more* arithmetic, *more* straight computation. That's what I failed on. I just couldn't do it and I am conscious that I failed at it. I don't want that to happen to my child... I don't approve of all this messing about with shapes and cubes.'

(*To a teacher doing home/school maths project*) 'We loved it, we all did it together, it was great fun. My husband and I agreed that the maths we had done as children was boring. This was great fun and Mark learnt a lot. Please could we have some more tonight?'

(*Mother of a six-year-old child*) '... but they ought to be learning their tables. I go into help some days, and they ask me to play maths games. I quite enjoy doing that and the children love it, but it is not real maths, is it?'

'I couldn't believe it. Daren, aged five, said to me, "Mum, twenty point five is half of forty-one, so we get twenty and a half sweets each." He worked it out on a calculator... he brings it to the supermarket and adds up the shopping. And he gets it right, which is more than I can do – I keep pressing the wrong buttons.'

(*Mother of children aged eight, six and four*) 'We love the maths games that we borrowed from school. We get one each week and the kids are really keen on maths now. I hope they never hate it like I did.'

−27− Asking ourselves questions
Marion Bird

THEMES questions for teachers; professional development;
discussion starters

In this section, Marion Bird asks some questions that we will always need to go on asking ourselves. There is always more for us to learn when we are dealing with young children – that's what makes it so exciting! By keeping these questions in our mind we make maths a time of exploration for us, as well as for the children.

Through these questions I am trying to capture the essence of some of the thinking which I feel lies behind my on-going actions and reactions when working with children.

- How can the children be encouraged to carry out mathematical activities themselves rather than merely to learn the results of someone else's mathematical thinking? By 'mathematical activities' here, I mean such activities as searching for patterns, setting patterns, making conjectures, testing conjectures, generalising, asking 'why?', trying to be systematic, classifying, transforming, searching for methods, deciding on rules, defining, agreeing on equivalences, reasoning, demonstrating, proving.

- How can the children also be encouraged to ask their own questions, make their own suggestions and choose which ideas to pursue? What possibilities for development are embedded in what the children are doing/observing? How can I involve the children in seeing these for themselves?

- Is the starting point accessible to all the children? Is it something which is likely to throw up other ideas? How can I phrase the initial invitation-to-explore so that it is meaningful to the children and something with which they can immediately engage?

- How can I avoid becoming involved in explaining?
  How can I seek to stop myself intervening when such interventions are likely to end up disturbing unconstructively or taking away potential for initiatives from the children?
  How can I stop myself from exhausting a situation in front of the children?

- How can I slot in terms and notations so that meaning can readily be ascribed to them? ... so that they can be seen as helpful? ... necessary?
  How might the pupils be encouraged to find their own ways of expressing their findings and questions?
  How might the pupils be encouraged to decide on their own terms and notations?
  How can I stop myself simply asking children to 'write it down'? How might they be encouraged to feel a need to write or talk?
  How can I seek to make fruitful use of any scope for pupils to be involved in interpreting what others say and record?
  Can any comments about the importance of being careful how thoughts and calculations are recorded come up as a result of children actually experiencing the importance themselves? (For example, because they have misread something they wrote earlier.)

- If pupils find that something they thought would continue to work actually breaks down, how might I focus on this constructively?
  How can I stop myself indicating to them that something will not work before they have perceived that that is the case?

- How can I try to ensure that their convictions have come about through their own thinking and actions and not just through believing me?

- How can I stop myself passing on any idea that a particular method is to be used? If a variety of methods/strategies are being used, how might I draw attention constructively to these?

- If discrepancies or difficulties arise, can the children be encouraged to work at these and sort them out themselves?
  How might the children be encouraged to check what they are doing for themselves?

- How can I encourage the children to seek connections?

- Suppose I want to make a point about something. Can I use what a child has done to help make the point so that it does not appear as merely my idea?

- Is there scope to draw attention to the distinction between 'It is impossible because I have not found a way' and 'It is impossible because there is no way to be found'?

- If a child comes up with something which appears to me as off the track for the moment, can I stop myself from immediately implying that that is so and ask myself whether in fact it is so? What about the possibility of it being kept as a 'further idea' for later?

- Is working at the arithmetic itself getting in the way? Might using calculators help?

- Are any children perceiving constraints which I did not intend? How might I try to involve them in relaxing these?

–28– Conclusions

We have seen how children need maths to be set in meaningful situations, with experience rooted in the manipulation of appropriate apparatus, and the opportunity to talk to each other and to adults.

Where these conditions for mathematical learning are not given, the children will tend to develop their own meanings and 'tricks' for mathematical work, which are often based on misunderstandings. At its worst, maths can become meaningless gibberish.

There is probably no one right way to teach maths, but one of the central features in the craft of teaching seems to be creating real-life situations in which children can apply their own intuitive meanings and learn to self-correct and check their own meanings against what they have learnt in the new situation.

In this learning, language and activity play vital roles. We have seen the importance of demystifying maths, and making it accessible to children by encouraging the use of their own symbols and recording, and focusing on the language and contexts that they already understand. Within these meaningful contexts, panic is much less likely to arise. Maths does not become an area of fear and mystery but is seen as a useful and relevant part of life.

As Martin Hughes points out, children come to school with far more mathematical ability than we often recognise, and we have seen how parents and teachers can build on this intuitive 'home' learning and language.

When we set maths in contexts that make 'human sense', and we allow children to use their own symbols, and to develop their own meanings, we are respecting their view of the world: 'This is what I think, Amy. What do you think?'

It is exploration together – co-working – that holds the essence of good educational practice. The minute we treat children as empty vessels with buckets of knowledge to be poured into them, we lose that excitement of exploration. Of course, there needs to be a curriculum. We cannot wander aimlessly around in human knowledge. And as the child gets older, there is an increasing need to learn facts and for exposition from the teacher.

Effective teaching unleashes the power of the children's own thinking, their use of symbols, language, and ideas. Creative teaching harnesses all that into the constructed curriculum and, as we show in this book, teaching 'maths with reason' also means that children can function exceptionally well in National Curriculum terms.

Ideally, adults try to give children experiences which make the skills of maths secure, where children have to apply their knowledge in depth until they develop a firm 'brick wall' of knowledge, with a foundation based on confidence and understanding. They come to school as potential mathematicians, and 'maths with reason' helps this potential to emerge.

Repeatedly, teachers are finding that they can give children these types of experiences with maths with reason. Children seem to perform well in complex and unfamiliar mathematical settings, provided, as in any task, they are given the time and space to see the meaning in what they are doing. These teachers view with alarm a 'back to basics' approach to maths, simply returning to the old method of repeated practice. They believe that this will not necessarily reduce the deficiencies that show up at present in maths attainment. Repeated practice of basic skills does not lead to the highest standards. Maths set in meaningful contexts does.

Reflection sheet

This sheet can be used in a variety of settings and is intended for individuals to think through on their own. It works well at the end of a discussion, so that issues are not just talked about, but acted on! As the information is personal, it may be best not to try to share it. Allow five minutes for the activity.

Take a sheet of paper and divide it into three horizontal sections. The sections represent the three lights of a traffic light.

In the **red** section (*stop*) enter things that will be hard for you to do. They might include things that require:
- cooperation, perhaps a whole school activity;
- further discussion; or
- time – maybe a whole year;

In the **amber** section (*get ready*) enter things that are reasonably simple to do but need further thought and planning. These may include things you could organise in half a term, e.g. starting a maths diary.

In the **green** section (*go*) enter things that are straightforward for you to do on your own tomorrow, or this week, e.g. observing your children, asking a parent to help, tidying your maths resources.

Resources

Books for parents and teachers

How Children Learn Mathematics by P. Liebeck (1984). Harmondsworth: Penguin.
Maths through Play by R. Griffiths (1988). London: Macdonald.
A Parent's Guide to Your Child's Maths by R. Merttens (1988): London Octopus. (There are many books in the Parent and Child Programme, published by Octopus books and available in high street shops.)
Help Your Child with Maths by A. Walsh (1988). London: BBC.

Resources for games

Angela Walsh's book, as above.
Make games resource book, from NARE, 2, Lichfield Road, Stafford ST17 4JX. (An economical starter).
Design a Board Game. Longman. (Great for age 7 and above.)
Count me in. HBJ Maths, Foots Cray High Street, Sidcup, Kent DA14 5HP. (A set of games – send for the brochure.)
Song books:
This Little Puffin compiled by E. Matterson (1969). Harmondsworth, Penguin
Count Me In (1984) A & C Black.
Ways to Win, Strategy games. Manchester Polytechnic books. See opposite page. (A brilliant and economical book of strategy games.)

Home–school maths

Any of the other resources mentioned.

Ruth Merttens book as stated previously, or send for the IMPACT starter pack, Polytechnic of North London, Holloway Road, London, N7 8DB.

Resources for maths in the classroom

Tarquin and Dime Publications, Stradbroke, Diss, Norfolk IP21 5JP. (Lots of creative ideas, games, posters, activities etc. In a class of its own)

Many useful resources e.g. *Sharing Mathematics with Parents* by S. Thornes, and various books by Marion Bird can be obtained from the Mathematical Association, 259 London Road, Leicester, LE2 3BE.

ATM, 7 Shaftsbury Street, Derby, DE3 8YB. (Mostly books for teachers.)

The Mathematics Centre, West Sussex Institute of Higher Education, Upper Bognor Road, Bognor Regis, West Sussex, PO21 1HR.

Claire Publications, York House, Bacons Lane, Chappel, Colchester, Essex, CO6 2EB. (Good quality photocopiable resources produced by teachers.)

Triad Publications, 15 St. Peter's Court, Hospital Road, Bury St. Edmunds, Suffolk, IP33 3LY. (Produced by teachers for teachers; some unusual starting points and photocopiable.)

Books by Sue Atkinson on photocopiable classroom activities, e.g., probability, place value etc. can be obtained from Philip and Tacey Ltd., North Way, Andover, Hants SO10 5BA.

Manchester Polytechnic books. Gillian Hatch, Manchester Polytechnic, Didsbury Site, 799 Wilmslow Road, Didsbury, Manchester M20 8RR. (Don't be without these resources. Produced by teachers. The cheapest books of their kind. *Bounce to It* is an outstanding collection of investigations for 5–7 year olds.)

Resources for Learning and Development Unit, Bishop Road, Bishopston, Bristol BS7 8LS. List of products and prices on request. Particularly recommended: *Piers is Lost*.

Maths on Display: creative ideas for the teaching of infant maths by B. Hume and K. Barrs, Belair.

Nuffield Maths Teacher's Handbooks. Longman. (Get the book that relates to the age of the child you are teaching. It is full of activities for teaching particular concepts.)

Primary Mathematics Today by E. Williams and H. Shuard (3rd edition). Longman.

Maths in-service

Supporting Primary Mathematics – A pack to support maths and the National Curriculum. Open University.

Maths in the National Curriculum. A course unit in the modular Primary Profile, Open University. For details of both of these, and other Open University materials, write to: The Centre for Maths Education, Open University, Walton Hall, Milton Keynes MK7 6AA.

Children, Mathematics and Learning, produced by the PrIME team, Hilary Shuard *et al.*, Simon and Schuster.

Games without Frontiers by Pip Wilson. Starters for groups of adults or young people. Available from: Romford YMCA, Rush Green Road., Romford RM7 0PH.

Resources in North America

Didax, 1 Centennial Drive, Centennial Industrial Park, Peabody, MA 01960 (Comprehensive general resources, manipulatives etc. including the wonderful Unifix cube.)

Zephyr Press, 3316 N. Chapel Ave., PO Box 13448-C, Dept., Tucson, Arizona 85732 – 3448. (Mostly good quality books for teachers.)

Good Apple, 1204 Buchanan St., PO Box 299, Carthage IL. 62321 – 0299. (Produced by teachers for teachers.)

Creative Publications, 5040 West 111th Street, Oak Lawn, IL 60453. (As its name suggests, these are creative ideas for teaching maths; books, manipulatives etc. These are distributed in Britain by Jonathan Press, York House, Bacons Lane, Chappel, Colchester, Essex. CO6 2EB.)

References

ASSESSMENT OF PERFORMANCE UNIT (1980) Mathematical Development. Primary Survey Report No. 1. London: HMSO.

BERENSTAIN, S. and BERENSTAIN, J. (1972) *Bears in the Night*. Glasgow: Collins.

BIRD, M. (1991) *Mathematics for Young Children*. London: Routledge.

BRISSENDEN, T. (1988) *Talking about Mathematics: Mathematical Discussion in Primary Classrooms*. Oxford: Basil Blackwell.

BRUCE, T. *Early Childhood Education* (1987). London: Hodder and Stoughton.

BRUNER, J.S. (1984) *Beyond the Information Given*. London: Allen and Unwin.

BUXTON, L.G. (1981) *Do You Panic about Maths? Coping with Maths Anxiety*. London: Heinemann.

BUXTON, L.G. (1982) Emotional Response to Symbolism, *Visible Language*, **xvi**, 3, 215–20.

CAN (Calculator Aware Numbers) Project. Part of the PrIME project, Shuard, H. (ed.) 1991. London. Simon and Schuster.

CLAY, M. (1975) *What did I write?* London: Heinemann.

DEPARTMENT OF EDUCATION AND SCIENCE (1967) *Children and their Primary Schools* (Plowden Report). London: HMSO.

DEPARTMENT OF EDUCATION AND SCIENCE (1978) *Primary Education in England* (HMI Report). London: HMSO.

DEPARTMENT OF EDUCATION AND SCIENCE (1982) *Mathematics Counts.* (Cockroft Report). HMSO.

DEPARTMENT OF EDUCATION AND SCIENCE (1985) *Mathematics from 5–16, Curriculum Matters 3.* London: HMSO.

DONALDSON, M. (1978) *Children's Minds.* London: Fontana.

DONALDSON, M., GRIEVE, R. and PRATT, C. (eds.), (1983) *Early Childhood Education.* Oxford: Basil Blackwell.

DUFOUR-JANVIER, B. et al. (1987) Pedagogical considerations concerning the problem of representation, in JANVIER, C. (ed.), *Problems of representation in the teaching and learning of Mathematics.* New Jersey, USA.

FLETCHER, H. (1979) *Mathematics in Schools.* London: Addison Wesley.

FLOYD, A. (ed.) (1981) *Developing Mathematical Thinking.* London: Open University/Addison Wesley.

GELMAN, R. and GALLISTEL, C.R. (1978) *The Child's Understanding of Number.* Cambridge, Mass: Harvard University Press.

GINSBURG, H.P. (1977) *Children's Arithmetic: the Learning Process.* New York: Van Nostrand.

GRAVES, D. (1983) *Writing: Teachers and children at work.* London: Heinemann.

GROEN, G. and RESNICK, L.B. (1977) Can pre-school children invent addition algorithms? *Journal of Educational Psychology,* **69**, 645–52.

HALL, N. (1989) *Writing with Reason.* London: Hodder and Stoughton.

HART, K.M. (ed.) (1981) *Children's Understanding of Mathematics: 11–16.* London: John Murray.

HUGHES, M. (1986a) Bridge that Gap, *Child Education.* **63**, 2 p. 13–15 and **63**, 3 p. 13–15. London: Scholastic.

HUGHES, M. (1986b) *Children and Number: Difficulties in Learning Mathematics.* Oxford: Basil Blackwell.

HUGHES, S. (1977) *Dogger.* London: The Bodley Head.

JAMES, N. and MCCARTNEY, R. (1987) *E802 Applied Studies in Mathematical Education.* Milton Keynes: Open University Press.

JAMES, N. and MASON, J. (1982) Towards Recording, *Visible Language*, XVI, 249–58.

MCGARRIGLE, J., GRIEVE, R. and HUGHES, M. (1978) Interpreting inclusion: a contribution to the study of the child's cognitive and linguistic development. *Journal of Experimental Child Psychology.* **26**, 528–550.

MASON, J. et al. (1982) *Thinking Mathematically*. London: Addison Wesley.

NATIONAL ASSESSMENT OF EDUCATIONAL PROGRESS (1983) *The Third National Mathematics Assessment: Results, trends and issues* . Denver: Education Commission of the States.

NATIONAL CURRICULUM COUNCIL (1989) *Mathematics in the National Curriculum*. London: HMSO.

OPEN UNIVERSITY (1980) Course PME 233; *Mathematics Across the Curriculum*. Milton Keynes: Open University Press.

OPEN UNIVERSITY (1982) Course EM 235. *Developing Mathematical thinking*. Milton Keynes: Open University Press.

PIAGET, J. (1953) *The Child's Conception of Number*. London: Routledge and Kegan Paul.

SCDC (1989) *Becoming a Writer* (National Writing Project). Thomas Nelson & Son Ltd. London.

SHUARD, H. and ROTHERAY, A. (eds.) (1984) *Children Reading Mathematics*. London: Murray.

SHUARD, H. (1986) *Primary Mathematics Today and Tomorrow*. York: Longman.

SKEMP. R.R. (1976) Relational Understanding and Instrumental Understanding, *Mathematics Teaching 77*, 20–6.

SKEMP, R.R. (1982) Communicating Mathematics: Surface Structures and Deep Structures, *Visible Language XVI 3*, 281–288.

SKEMP, R.R. (1986) *Primary Mathematics Project for the Intelligent Learning of Mathematics*. Department of Education, University of Warwick.

TIZARD, B. and HUGHES, M. (1984) *Young Children Learning*. London: Fontana.

VYGOTSKI, L. (1978) *Mind in Society*. Cambridge, Mass: Harvard University Press.

VYGOTSKI, L. (1983) School instruction and mental development, in DONALDSON, M., GRIEVE, R., and PRATT, C. (eds.) *Early Childhood Development and Education*. Oxford: Basil Blackwell.

WATERLAND, L. (1985) *Read with Me. An Apprenticeship Approach to Reading*. South Woodchester, Stroud: Thimble Press.

WATERLAND, L. (ed.) (1989) *Apprenticeship in Action: Teachers Write about Read with Me*. South Woodchester, Stroud: Thimble Press.

WELLS, G. and NICHOLLS, J. (eds.) (1985) *Language and Learning: An Interactional Perspective*. London: Falmer Press.

WINNICOTT, D.W. (1971) *Playing and Reality*. London: Tavistock Publications. Also (1984) Harmondsworth: Penguin Books.